The Mind of Watergate

The Mind
of Watergate

An Exploration of the
Compromise of Integrity

LEO RANGELL, M.D.

W · W · NORTON & COMPANY · NEW YORK · LONDON

Published simultaneously in Canada by George J. McLeod Limited,
Toronto. Printed in the United States of America.
All Rights Reserved
First Edition

Library of Congress Cataloging in Publication Data

Rangell, Leo, M.D.
  The Mind of Watergate.

  Bibliography: p.
  Includes index.
  1. Watergate Affair, 1972–2. Corruption (in
politics)—United States. Psychoanalysis. I. Title.
E860.R36 1980   364.1'32'0973   79–22408
ISBN 0–393–01308–1

1 2 3 4 5 6 7 8 9 0

From the beginning, this book has been for Anita.
Now it is also in memory of our eldest son, Richard.

Contents

Author's Note

This is the story of the Watergate years as observed, reflected upon, and recorded by a psychoanalyst.

It has been a six-year study. Everytime I tried to close the book events began to happen fast again, and there never was an easy point of cleavage. That is how it is with a patient as well. Analysis typically continues long after symptoms have disappeared. Termination is spoken of and a rush of new material emerges from which the analysis can then continue.

My interest in the Watergate phenomenon began at the time of the break-in in June of 1972, and quickly became steady and sustained. In addition to what was dishonest, the irrational was apparent at once, and because of this I felt at home with the subject and felt that my experience applied. As events unfolded, I came to feel that the dishonest and neurotic belong together in a psychoanalyst's total field of observation. What we were seeing was a combination of the corrupt and irrational, a syndrome blending the two.

In July of 1973, with my eye on events at home, I delivered the presidential address to the International Psychoanalytic Congress in Paris on what I called the "compromise of integrity." From a growing conviction that what was appearing at the top level of government was a reflection of what was latent and widespread in the entire population, I stressed how this problem was interwoven with neurosis and how integrity was increasingly the central problem of human character. At the time of this writing, after it is all over, I would add the trait of courage, the courage to live by integrity and one's principles. It is generally easier in the short run not to.

Upon my return home that summer, the faces of the Senate committee and the witnesses were being seen on television daily—the first such event since the McCarthy hearings of twenty years back. I now began to attend to the Watergate phenomenon in a serious and committed way. What took place from that time on became my extra "patient" for the next few years.

The subject matter I was observing was never Richard Nixon alone, but always three-tiered: Nixon, the forty or so men under him, and the people's ways of reacting or not reacting to what was happening. In place of the free associations I listen to from my patients, I absorbed all the information I possibly could from news media, from observing faces and listening to speeches on television, from the talk around me of friends, colleagues, patients, the public. My aim was to be as uncensoring as I am in my work, as complete and objective in putting the data into a more coherent organization than was apparent on the surface. My vantage point as a participant-observer was not an impediment but an advantage; it was not dissimilar to the way an analyst samples and feels the output of each patient, to place it in perspective and uncover its meaning. The theory through which I filtered my "data" was the same one I live by as an analyst: the theory of human behavior in depth, which serves as my map and guide in understanding what I hear each day.

What took form was not the psychobiography of a man, nor was it the usual psychohistory of a country or era. The latter is typically a retrospective operation with motivations and meanings inserted retroactively; I have come to believe that these are of questionable accuracy. What was emerging seemed to me a new form of the recording of history. One of my colleagues who heard me present segments of this book at a seminar at the Langley-Porter Neuropsychiatric Institute in San Francisco suggested that it was a "psychochronicle." I like that name.

To my knowledge, this is the first time that the emotional aspects of a piece of national history have been chronicled and interpreted in statu nascendi. The reactions and emotions accompanying events were

experienced and sampled as they went along: sifted, caught, and fixed
—like a slide in a laboratory—before they could vanish or, as emotions
do, be defended against and later denied, or substituted for by other
affects, even opposite ones. A running documentary of national emotions, given the infinite complexity of collective as compared to individual reactions, is perhaps the only way such a psychochronicle can be set
down with a sense of validity. Even then it will be questioned in retrospect.

It was as if I had been sitting on a seat in an empty Madison Square
Garden having lunch, with a camera and tape recorder in my pockets,
and happened to look up and see the heavyweight title battle of all time
going on. The titanic "illness" which I found myself describing was
given a name by the press. It was referred to as "the sick society," and
was obviously more than the problem of Nixon. The symptoms were not
caused by but exposed by the Watergate trauma. Overt during this
Watergate period but otherwise latent, the pathology exists in a state
of suspension with acute breakdowns at periodic intervals.

One aspect of the "sickness" had been seen repetitively in this country before Watergate, during the years of Vietnam, and before that
during the McCarthy era. Numerous examples may be cited throughout
the world, wherever and whenever people passively endure or—as I
came to amend it—give permission to or even encourage the tyrants,
the corrupt, and the self-seeking leaders to whom they periodically
voluntarily submit. This led me to the subject of the leader and the led.
A mutual arrangement exists between the two which derives its stability only from the strength of the mass. A common pathology, running
from tip to base of the population pyramid, results periodically in collusion between the two levels.

A central aspect of the basic pathology is the relationship of man to
the group and the influence of the group on the individual mind.
Whether in the psychology of cults or in the political climate just described, the subjugation of individual judgment to the will of the leader
and the group is the psychological atmosphere in which choices are
made. Here is where the issue of individual courage becomes important, not in the sense of heroism but in the ability to retain one's integrity against the pressures of the surrounding group. The group at whose
behest the individual forms his conscience is, under certain conditions,

a force which influences him to compromise it. Each of the men directly under Nixon faced this challenge and failed. In a less visible sense, this was also the conflict faced by individuals in each of the crises our country has gone through.

I gave the disease a new name, the syndrome of the compromise of integrity, and described the psychological underpinnings upon which it stands. I was not talking about conscious lying, which Nixon did, and his men too, or about the behavior of the psychopath or the more overt criminal. I was concerned with the chronic everyday erosions of integrity. Besides being conscious and accountable, they are as automatic and unconscious, as much an outcome of internal conflicts—and as camouflaged into everyday life—as any other emotional symptoms or traits.

I would like to tell you a bit about myself. I have long been a Nixon watcher. We both came to Southern California in 1946 following service in World War II, he returning to where he had been born, and I, previously from the East Coast, to settle in California. I first became aware of Richard Nixon when he ran for Congress the following year, and was galvanized immediately to the Nixon phenomenon. What I was impressed with most—as a psychiatrist I had already been inoculated and sensitized to this interest from different directions and previous experiences—was the union, almost the immediate marriage, between Nixon and the people, between Nixon and his future constituents. What I saw made me wonder and reflect and shake my head from the start. It always made me think about people and groups as much as it did about Richard Nixon.

I was struck with a feeling of something awesome and uncanny, even, if you will believe it now, ominous and frightening, in the public's willing acceptance of the style and tone of his words; the uncritical and compliant acceptance of the artificiality, the obvious opportunism, the insincerity, and the questionable credibility which came across in his every utterance. Nixon at once polarized people into those who felt this way about him and those who did not, those who felt the inconsistencies between phrases, the illogical and mutually exclusive sequences within the very structure of his sentences, and others who regarded those who felt this way as prejudiced.

From the beginning I watched the sure-footed seedling grow into a spreading tree. Sometimes I saw directly and sometimes with subliminal perception, but Nixon was always there. Watergate, a quarter of a century later, came to me, as it did to many others of the same vintage and sociopolitical-temporal background, as no surprise. It was a natural sequence.

There were two other points of contact and identification during the years which followed which, besides a contiguity of geography, must have caused my observations of Richard Nixon to linger a bit more than my scientific interest would have caused. We were both born in the same year. Whenever I saw Nixon moving along, I saw how old, or how young, I was. During the late fifties and the sixties, as Nixon was aspiring to, approaching, and finally reaching the presidency, I had also been made the president of a succession of my own professional groups, first of local and regional societies, then of my national association, and in 1969, a year after Nixon reached his major goal, of our International Psychoanalytic Association. This made me know, in a miniscule way, what it was like to be entrusted with a position of leadership. I could see the dangers which go with the heady privileges, the transferences which can reach grotesque proportions on either the positive or negative side, the temptations and hurts, and the need at all times for constructive, if difficult, solutions. The special problems which accrue when one has power, or even if people think one has power—whether to use it, or not to, or how to—can result in outcomes across the spectrum from lofty to disastrous, to oneself or others.

In his work with patients, an analyst's empathy stems from filtering the patient's thoughts and feelings through his own cognitive and emotional processes as these have derived from his life experiences. These distantly shared challenges over the years, during my quarter century of peripheral observation of Nixon's progress and rise, led, I believe, to my being especially alerted to Nixon data, and perhaps unconsciously sensing the emerging drama several years before events came to a head.

The syndrome of the compromise of integrity has become normal again; it has gone back into hiding where it usually resides. As with a detailed clinical case report, this study could never be repeated from memory. The sequences and timing, the relationships between events, and the subtle fleeting moods which accompanied them could not be reconstructed at a future time. They do not in fact want to be remembered. At a meeting of a professional scientific society, when the importance of integrity was being mentioned as a prerequisite for training, one member voiced the opinion of many when he said, "I'm tired of integrity. I would like us to look for friendliness instead."

The tendency to repression is part of the data that analysts work with in assessing the whole. This is balanced, however, by a drive to know, both of which were operative at all levels during the entire sequence of Watergate events. Perhaps only now are we in a position to gain a total perspective, not too close to the conflicts involved to be threatened by their force and not too distant to have repressed or distorted them out of hand.

The story moves in irregular sequences in tune with the rhythm of the unfolding of Watergate. Early into the "case" my hope was to close before the decision about Nixon, to let the book stand on its predictive value. But the rapidity of events would not permit this, and history caught up. With a sudden rush the end came, and it all could be checked one against the other, the present against the past, the actual against the theoretical, the reality against the speculations.

More than half of this book was written when no one, including Nixon, knew which way it would go—when, if one can conceive of it now, it could have gone either way. It is now like a mystery story after the solution is known, or a mathematics text in which the answers can be read in advance. But nothing can replace the problem-solving process itself. The waverings and oscillations, the ambiguities, uncertainties, and mixtures of reactions, the narrowness of outcomes, what could have been as well as what did become history are all part of the field. Expectations which came true and hunches which did not can be equally informative.

At times, the material of this book accumulated before segments could be written, so that the time sequences are not an absolute straight line. However, no opinions or predictions were changed as a result of subsequent facts. A patient's hospital chart is not rewritten after the outcome is known.

This book was made possible by the life surround provided by my wife, Anita. Neither this nor any other works which may be regarded as accomplishments could have been carried through without the nutriment which comes from her.

The project would not have resulted in a final product without the loyal and dedicated assistance of several other special people.

It was my good fortune to follow up on a meeting some years ago with Carol Houck Smith, who became my editor. Her skill, perseverance, and firmness made the manuscript a book. The interaction between an editor who has to cut and round out and an author who has not only to allow this but to like it would be an interesting subject for another book. I am also grateful to George Brockway, chairman of W. W. Norton & Company, for his interest and enthusiasm.

Ann Brooks has been an indispensable member of my support system for over eleven years. She kept up the day-by-day typing which became the original, long manuscript. She contributed not only her efficiency and utter dependability, but her reverberation to the material nurtured and furthered it.

At the end, when deadlines suddenly pressed and brought a near state of emergency, Carol J. Wolff came into the picture. Working all hours as needed, she added ingenuity to her intense efforts. Again, it was her personal interest and involvement which sustained the work and enabled us to meet publication requirements.

I thank all these people.

Now I invite you to transport yourselves back to when things were happening, to recreate the mood of anticipation, and to join the adventure of prediction.

Leo Rangell

Los Angeles and Carmel, California
June 1979

I

Background
and Beginnings

Convulsive times turn up new views into inner man. I sat up with special interest when I heard Sen. Howard Baker ask a witness early in the Senate committee hearings, "Sir, did you not feel at any time that what you were doing was wrong? What happened to your basic instincts?" Which prompted a commentator later that evening to remark, "Perhaps this question came closest to the heart of Watergate."

Aside from a slight technical error—it was not instinct but the human conscience that was at fault—I wondered where we psychoanalysts were. We are the ones who spend our working days at man's inner core where, I agree, the heart of Watergate resides. So far, nothing from us. As silent as McGovern and the Democrats. The mental state of the nation has been probed and dissected by the media and the entire range of behavioral and social scientists—by every discipline, that is, but psychoanalysis.

Psychoanalysis has always had a reciprocal relationship with its culture. On the one hand, it confronts the latter with what ails it and attempts to offer guidelines. Some good may be claimed that the twentieth century has been called "the century of Freud." On the other hand, psychoanalysis takes its cue from the environment with regard to the problems to be studied and understood.

Thus, the theory of sexuality and its role in neurosis emerged from repressive Victorian Vienna. An understanding of the role of aggression in human affairs followed the experience of World War I. The nature

of psychosomatic illness and of the effects of the psyche on the soma
came to the surface in the thirties in the competitive Chicago of Franz
Alexander and the New York of Flanders Dunbar.

Today a different problem confronts us. We are concerned not with
the hysterical Viennese female of the turn of the century, but with the
corrupt American male of the seventies. What our current scene presents for examination is, unfortunately but no less important, the problem of integrity.

Violence or sex assures an audience on TV or film. Add corruption.
In the summer of 1973, people sat glued to the Watergate drama as they
do to programs dealing with aggression or sex, to an orgy of either. Rapt
observers, they were in and of the performance, not separated from it.
The cast of characters could have been any of us—if, that is, he had
reached the "in" group, had achieved his ego ideal, had been the frater-
nity leader, "the man most likely to succeed" (the stereotype in this
drama was that of a decade ago; styles have changed, to be sure, but not
the principle). The parade of witnesses before the Senate committee
were life's bright young men, not the scholars, not first in the class or
editors of a law review, but shrewd, ambitious, and clever-bright, so-
cially poised, high on the ladder and moving up fast. They were models
of what many of us wanted to be. And—we had to wonder—what any
one of us might have become had we reached so near the top.

The spotlight today is on the prosecutors of yesterday: an attorney
general, John Mitchell, the chief watchdog of the Justice Department;
the president, Richard Nixon, the main potential defendant, a vigorous
investigator in years past at the side of Joseph McCarthy. Analysts have
always maintained that policemen too—or especially?—need to be
studied so as to gain understanding of the vicissitudes of aggression. And
let us not forget that the leading apostle of law and order, Spiro Agnew,
left the second highest office of the land in quiet disgrace.

The quality of integrity is a rare commodity, to be prized when found.
Sometimes in an obituary a man's integrity is especially stressed. This
is not occupationally bound. In a memorial service for a prominent
psychoanalyst, each speaker repeatedly pointed to his integrity. The
man was, incidentally, unpopular in life. None of these facts is new.
Diogenes went around with a lamp looking for an honest man twenty-

four hundred years ago. And the story, which makes a point about the unconscious of man, survives.

The role of values, thrust so forcibly upon us by recent events, is ripe for examination by psychoanalysis itself. The first third of this psychoanalytic century was occupied with studies on the id; the second with the so-called ego activities; and now the third important psychic agency, the superego, is coming up for fuller attention and understanding. For the purpose of shorthand communication, the *id* can be defined as the reservoir of man's primitive instincts, his drives and urges. The *ego* is the sum of his efforts at mastery, his means toward solutions, adaptation, success. The *superego* is comprised of his ethics, values, the group of principles which guide him. *Reality,* to add a fourth element, is the external world in which he lives, which is constantly exerting its influence from without.

It is no accident that the superego and its functions are the last of the psychic agencies to be studied in depth. Analysts, in their zeal not to be judgmental or to impose their own values, may appear at times to separate themselves unduly from the ethical aspects of psychic life. The truth is that morals must also be understood objectively, and their roles in conflict squarely dealt with. "What is this? Are you talking about right and wrong or about what is fair?" a patient complained to me recently as we were analyzing some of her inconsiderate behavior. "That's not supposed to come into it here." Actually, the analyst sits equidistant from all three psychic agencies and includes them all within his purview. The patient has the freedom of choice, always vital in analysis, but the task of the analyst is to point out all the factors at work.

Analysis has always moved from the tip of the iceberg to the larger and more important bulk below the surface. The discovery of the Oedipus complex was matched by the recognition of its universality. The conflicts which lead to severe illness also provide insights into the lesser anxieties and depressions of life. It is the same with problems of integrity. While breakdowns at the top wreak public havoc and receive the most dramatic attention, similar pressures weigh on every individual and affect the aspirations and actions of everyday life. The current drama of the Nixon White House is to the superego what Sophocles' Oedipus was to the libido—even if the drama is not as classic.

"The Watergate complex" is more than a group of apartment buildings in Washington. It is a complex, I suggest, in the mind of man. "The Watergate" with its ramifications is as much a complex as "the Oedipus." From each complex, mechanisms can be seen undiluted which can then be understood in more attenuated and disguised forms. It is no coincidence that in the wake of Watergate not one or a few men, but our entire country and our times are being called sick. What is meant by "sick" is obscure and disturbing. The word "sick" is not used here in a conventional sense. It refers to a problem of living with accepted values, of maintaining integrity, not in a lofty but in a common sense.

Syndromes resulting from compromises of integrity are endogenous to humankind. A form of "cheating," pejorative in name only, has been absorbed into the practical realities of life. One need only think of attitudes toward income tax preparation or marital fidelity, two examples where double standards are accepted norms. But there are many other mini-Watergates in everyday living. The ingredients which bring these about are as ubiquitous in unconscious mentation as are the unconscious backgrounds which result in neuroses.

These compromises are acceptable, to the self and others, compatible with and, we must admit, often accompaniments of success. They no more connote criminality than neuroses connote psychoses, nor are any of them incompatible with normal behavior. Such compromises, slipping into daily conversations, or into smaller or larger actions, are as common as headaches, toothaches, or the common cold. But before we get carried away, let us realize that we need not have any of these— a headache, a cold, neuroses, or deception.

Conflicts of interest exist in all of us. Neuroses result from conflicts between the ego and the id, between man's deepest instinctual urges and forces within his ego which oppose their satisfaction. The resulting behaviors are the stuff that analysts have dealt with in their three-quarters of a century of existence.

There is another equally important internal conflict, between the ego and the superego, the aggregate of man's values; his efforts to adapt are guided but also limited by the sense of right and wrong with which he lives. The results of this struggle are the stuff the country has been dealing with for the past few years. The present syndrome of the compromise of integrity is new in emphasis, but as old as man. Analysts

merely uncover what has always been there. Just as Michelangelo felt
that he did not create but liberated the statue within the marble slab,
so Freud did not discover but uncovered the Oedipus complex. The
same is true with every psychoanalytic "discovery" since.

The ego strives for mastery, for solutions, for achievement. Mastery
brings power. The satisfaction of these ends produces the ambition for
more. With these two words, "ambition" and "power," we sense that
we are getting close to our subject. Power and ambition, like politics,
have become bad words; they make us feel that we are speaking of
dictators or tyrants. A third such word is "opportunism." Ambition,
power, and opportunism: these could be called the three horsemen of
the syndrome of the compromise of integrity.

But all three are good things in themselves (so is politics!). Ambition
leads to mastery. Mastery conveys power. Both spur an individual to
seek and to make opportunities. All of these are accompaniments of
competence, skill, even creativity. We should not fall into the trap of
misusing these words to discredit people who achieve. We want our
children to have ambition and to take advantage of opportunities. How
sad we are if they do not. After all, an adult without power is im-potent!

But any or all of these elements can get out of hand. Cell growth and
multiplication are normal processes which can advance to the point of
malignancy. Ambition and power can similarly grow wild and proliferate, as much out of control as a malignant tumor into the body or a
mushroom cloud into a placid atmosphere. Mastery and control can
range from benign to oppressive, from a good master to an evil dictator.
Power can be transformed from something we all seek to a danger
which hovers over a people.

Narcissism, self-love (from the Greek myth in which the young man
Narcissus saw his reflection in the water and fell in love with it), has
suffered a fate similar to the above three traits in today's world of
misinterpretation and misuse. Narcissism is an important mechanism of
self-preservation, as normal within the human psyche as sex, aggression,
or anxiety. It is not only desirable, but necessary for survival. But as with
the other traits, it is subject to frustration, expansion, and lack of containment. Narcissism unbridled is the enemy of integrity. A major problem in psychiatric patients— who love only themselves and not others
—it is also a crucial character problem in life. Some of the defendants

who justified their actions as a protection of the president were concerned not for him but for their own "selves," their interests and lives
through him. For the one or two individuals who knew that what they
did was wrong, there were others who protected their actions as right
in one way or another. The White House staff was acting in the name
of national security, the "Committee to Re-Elect" acted under the
imperative need to elect the president, the Cubans who broke in did
so for the good of the country. "The election of the president," said John
Mitchell, or "national security," said John Ehrlichman, "were of such
overriding importance as to make the break-ins justified."

There was a hierarchy of values; the highest reasons were chosen;
integrity, even loftiness was achieved. Other, thinner rationalizations
were also employed. To Fat Jack Buckley, who picked up documents
against Muskie from a spy, copied them, and conveyed them to others,
"What I did was not dishonest, it was deception; not a crime but political espionage. I didn't break in, steal anything, wear rubber gloves or
anything like that." Donald Segretti knew what he was doing but
viewed the dirty tricks as "college pranks." The same type of distortions
served the citizenry. Under various guises their collusion has been
rationalized. They were not guilty of overlooking or accepting behavior
they should have opposed; they had judged it and decided "nothing is
proven," or "everyone does it," or "they did it, so what?"

Man's value system, originally born when the child takes in the values
of the parent, remains forever bound to the culture of which he is part.
When a Palestinian terrorist, standing before his captors next to a group
of corpses, raises his fingers joyfully in a "V for Victory" sign, whether
he is sick, criminal, or a hero depends on where you live. The superego
is the least structured and the most fluid of the three psychic agencies,
which is both a blessing and a curse. Continued accessibility of the
superego to outside influences leaves an individual open to social progress, but it also makes him prey to the fickle whims of a crowd—from
a mild suspension of critical judgment to a sudden and complete regression to barbarism.

Every human being continues to need love throughout life, not only
from his own superego but from others around him. When Senator
Baker, still pursuing his questions of motivation, asked young Herbert
L. Porter, "Did you ever have any qualms about what you were doing?

... I am probing into your state of mind, Mr. Porter," the answer came back uncomfortably, "I was not the one to stand up in a meeting and say that this should be stopped . . . I mean. . . . I kind of drifted along." The questioning continued.

Q.: At any time did you ever think of saying, "I do not think this is quite right, this is not quite the way it ought to be." Did you ever think of that?

A.: Yes, I did.

Q.: What did you do about it?

A.: I did not do anything.

Q.: Why didn't you?

A.: [After evidence of much inner thought on his face] In all honesty, probably because of the fear of group pressure that would ensue, of not being a team player.

The need to belong—to be a member of the team—is another primary human motivation. And what a special team this was; it was hard to leave it. Only one man did, Hugh W. Sloan, Jr.; only he, of all of them, felt he had had enough and walked out. The others stayed, for many reasons, including loyalty, ambition, fear.

The Soil Was Cultivated

Analysts always look behind the symptom to the soil from which it springs; to the background as well as the figure. Watergate occurred on a prepared soil. The phenomenon came about in steps, hardly as a surprise. Credibility and sincerity were at a low ebb. The *Pentagon Papers,* released a year before, in 1971, had already shaken trust at the highest levels. But both events pointed to conditions that had existed long before.

The Vietnam War provided the moral climate. Terms like "protective bombing," "defensive aggression," or "the clean bomb" conspired

to remove trust in the very language spoken. Such contradictory semantic linkages were coupled with the daily logistic reports of dead and
wounded, which critical readers learned to ignore—it came out later,
for example, that we were secretly bombing Cambodia and reporting
the dead in Vietnam. The pattern had been set for a dull disbelief
combined pragmatically with a numb acceptance.

There was an overriding mechanism more specific to the White
House which antedated Watergate and gave this period its psychological stamp, personified in the phenomenon of the two, or more, faces of
Nixon. Consider, for example, that only a president whose entire political life had been based on a virulent anticommunism could attempt to
claim his place in history as achiever of détente with Moscow and
China! His defeated opponents, who espoused these policies all along,
would never have been allowed to do so—by him. Or the fact that only
a hawk could be entrusted to end the interminable war—and incidentally then continue to push to bomb. And when Congress and public
opinion forced him to stop—both in North Vietnam and Cambodia—
this was the man to take credit for the peace. A hawk turned dove is
the stuff a hero is made of. Always having been a dove was no good.
Daniel Ellsberg, by the way, was also once a hawk.

A premature anti-Vietnam stand was a detriment to a record. When
a candidate—George Romney is an example—returned from Vietnam
with an antiwar statement, his political career was over. This mechanism is a sequel to a syndrome of the thirties, of those who were
"premature antifascists." Subsequent history did not make them right.
They were right too soon, therefore wrong.

This sequence and method of judgment—that right before the times
is wrong; and that wrong all along, but right when it was ripe, is right
—is not limited to a political party, a nation, or even to a particular time.
It is a widespread cognitive mode of living. Dip into the history of any
country, past or present, East or West; no group or population can point
a finger or take solace.

But with Richard Nixon this was seen in a concentrated dose within
a time span that could be embodied in one man. Flexibility, the ability
to change one's mind, to admit one was wrong, to learn from experience, are signs of ego strength, a positive set of character attributes. But
the flip-flops seen here, the relentless sequence that one was always

right, that it is never the mind but the times which have changed, is a complex distorting mechanism combining denial, repression, and rationalization, a deception of the self as well as others. What is it when the Chinese are permitted into the United Nations by the one person who has vehemently opposed them for decades—and then claims credit for softness and one-worldedness? Did anything happen other than Nixon's change of mind or tactic? Now that the step must be taken (it is wanted and the time has come), have it come from you. It is like the patient who rejects the analyst's interpretation but accepts the same idea when it can come from himself.

Is this a piece of neurosis, a character trait, a compromise of integrity, or the norm for the day? Or perhaps even a special capacity to adapt? A case can be made for all. And this internal psychic process, of elevating one's motives to the loftiest levels and denying more personal or self-serving aims, bridges across states of consciousness. The unconscious makes the changes nimbly, retaining righteousness and self-esteem along the way. In his travail, Nixon identifies with Abraham Lincoln. "He stood tall and strong despite vilification," the president declares in a speech on this Lincoln's birthday, 1974. I believe that in the deep layers of his mind Nixon made this connection with himself and believes it.

To any rational critic Nixon would seem to have painted himself into a corner. Everything he did which was good was what his opponents had been for all along and what he had always opposed, not only on the international scene but in domestic affairs as well. Increases in social welfare benefits, a national health plan, the institution of price controls when the economic spiral started its upward rise—policies which had previously been anathema to his personal and political philosophies were executed as though they had always been exactly what he had stood for.

But there is much in universal mental life which has always met this behavior of Nixon's halfway. Nixon's easy change of face turned a small minority into what became known as "Nixon haters," but also drew to him the majority he always needed. People did not vote for Nixon in spite of this but largely, in my opinion, *because* of it. (When I use the word "people," I do not mean all people in a nation of over two hundred million. There are poles at each end. I do, however, mean that significant number in the center of the bell curve which determines the outcome of every election.) There was a deep identification with "the two faces" which attracted Nixon's audience from the very start and which grew into national proportions as he reached up to the presidency of the United States. In our last national shame comparable to Watergate, the McCarthy drama of twenty years back, Nixon was second lead. Although the name of McCarthy had already become a source of deep embarrassment, Nixon, who actually was McCarthy's model during those years, was lifted to the top by an electorate which forgot and remembered what it wished. Nixon's training and credentials were never held against him. McCarthy had only one face and rose and fell on it. Nixon, however, could rise on one, change it near the top, and continue upward on the other. For McCarthy to have gone on to a détente with communism was unimaginable.

The ambivalent attraction felt toward Nixon mirrored the ambivalent look of an individual into himself. The ability to change faces as the weather changed, to come out with contradictory behavior without apparent conflict, is a wish but not a capacity generally attained. People, those in the middle that is, watched with increasing awe and fascination, as though they were witnessing a juggler or a trickster. Who would not like to be able to do the right thing for the wrong reasons, to do the wrong thing and be cheered, to say one thing and do another, to get credit for what others have proved is right and you have always opposed? It is an intrapsychic dream come true.

Two faces of Nixon—in fact two Nixons, an old and a new—had become fact, not a political jibe. Even a third would have been accepted. There is talk every now and then of a third Nixon, the moral Nixon. A cartoon depicts two men at a bar, one of them saying, "Look, Nixon's no dope. If the people *really* wanted moral leadership, he'd give them moral leadership."

In the public sector, there is a ping-pong effect between a leader and a group in which the superego floats suspended between them and needs to be claimed by none. On the basis of this, an uneasy liaison is established in which behavior is acceptable in the leader but also permitted in the group. In this case, Nixon, and therefore the people as well, are allowed to change their minds and actions, and motives remain unquestioned. It is interesting to note that during this period the most popular and commercially successful motion picture was one with the advertising theme: "Being in love means never having to say you're sorry." This need not be restricted to love; Nixon permitted it to apply to all behavior.

Having two Nixons serves the people well, better than either one alone. Because they are able to support opposite sides in the same person, the peaceful and aggressive, the passive and active halves of each individual can be kept in a state of sufficient satisfaction. And each assuages the guilt of the other. In addition to never having to feel sorry, this mechanism counters the need for consistency, which is a superego requirement, and even counters the superego principle of having to live up to superego principles. The alternative offered, of the permissible switch, is accepted to condone and protect the "trickiness" in all of us. There is a saying, which I have heard attributed both to Harry Truman and Lyndon Johnson, that it is not so hard to know what is right to do as to do what you know is right. People unconsciously long for permission to do what they feel is wrong as easily as what they feel is right. Unfortunately, or fortunately, guilt is apt to intervene.

In an interesting variation of this psychic defense, Spiro Agnew, while still vice-president of the United States, demanded that draft dodgers stranded in Canada first say they were "sorry" before amnesty would be granted. In truth, they felt *he* should say he was sorry. All along they had been against a war which he only later realized must end. Later, when Agnew himself was confronted with criminal evidence, he pleaded neither "guilty" nor "not guilty," but "nolo contendere," meaning he simply did not deign to contend. Nixon, too, who expected praise and admiration for having been the one to end the war, was against amnesty for those who had opposed it before he did. This attitude is part of a larger inconsistency in two men who have come to personify "law and order." It is a curious example of the mechanism of projection. In the type of projection usually seen, one attributes to others impulses and wishes which one denies in oneself. In this current version, one demands of others a form of superego behavior which one refuses to live by oneself. Both mechanisms project outward what is denied within.

If the leader/group relationship between Nixon and the people had remained at the level described, perhaps there would have been no problem. But things were not to stay the same, or, more accurately, Nixon was not one to permit things to stay the same. On June 17, 1972, the Democratic National Headquarters at the Watergate was burglarized by a group of five men, four Cuban residents of Miami and James W. McCord, Jr., chief security officer of the Republican National Committee and of the Committee to Re-Elect the President. Interrupted in the act by Washington police, the five were captured at 2:30 A.M. with gloves, lockpicking devices, cameras, electronic wiretapping and surveillance equipment in their possession, and were charged with second-degree burglary. An angry outcry came from John Mitchell, chairman of the Committee to Re-Elect the President, who promptly disowned the actions of McCord, fired him from his position, and declared his "apparent actions . . . wholly inconsistent with the principles upon which we are conducting our campaign." Another response came from Ronald Ziegler, Nixon's press secretary, who said that he would not comment on "a third-rate burglary attempt" and predicted that "certain elements may try to stretch this beyond what it is." From the public there was no demonstrable reaction. From the press there was gentle and cautious reporting.

On October 10, 1972, one full month before the national presidential election in November, the *Washington Post* reported that the break-in was a result of a massive conspiracy and campaign of sabotage directed by the White House and the Committee to Re-Elect the President. The only reaction of anger came from the White House, which now suspended rules barring criticism of the press. No reaction from the public could as yet be measured. From the press, there was still restrained and gentlemanly reporting.

Here is a clinical vignette of interest mainly because it is solitary; as a stark exception, it said much about the atmosphere which prevailed. On October 10, 1972, a patient of mine, having read on page 17 of the *Los Angeles Times* the story which appeared that day in the *Washington Post,* developed on the spot and in the weeks which followed what could clinically be called an obsession about Watergate! She was not a small and elderly lady from Pasadena who wore tennis shoes, but a young, attractive, heretofore apolitical, suburban housewife-mother.

She became incensed at what she read, could not believe it, could not let go of it, and began at once a one-woman campaign to find out more and "to do something about it."

She telephoned reporters around the country to ask why the story was receiving so little attention, wrote to senators and congressmen, started chain letters, and implored her friends to do likewise. She wrote to Rep. Wright Patman whose House Banking and Currency Committee had started an investigation of the Watergate break-in in connection with laundered money, and thanked and encouraged him in his efforts. In return, she was generally given a wide berth or met with skepticism and irritation (we do not know whether with guilt as well). When she called up Democratic headquarters in Los Angeles to give them "her material," the workers there were appreciative but condescending, told her not to get so excited, and said that this was "done all the time."

As an analyst, I concentrated first on what there was in this woman's background to account for her intense and singular reaction. There was a good deal, centered around a superpatriotism and a passionate love of this, her adopted country, which had rescued her small family and given it a haven when she was two, after her father had been released from a concentration camp. When she read the October 10 article, she was broken-hearted and reacted with panic. This could not be; how could it be happening here? "Why were people not upset?" was the main thrust of her fear, anger, and concern. Why are they not asking, doing, finding out? It was too reminiscent of the past, too acutely reviving of personally sensitive and tender spots—not necessarily of memories but of thoughts, fantasies, and preoccupations of her early inner mental life.

But while this helped explain the intensity and obsessiveness of her reaction, retrospectively and to my future relief, I did not thereby discount her concerns. Instead, while giving due place to the relevant past, I concurred in the reality and appropriateness of her concerns and commented on how difficult I thought her task to be. Many months later, when the country caught up with her, she handed her obsession over to the people!

Nevertheless, for those months she was alone. And she definitely met a resistance, the usual public syndrome to a darkening cloud, political

or otherwise. If one can generalize from the empirical fact that only one
of the forty or so men around the president had the wish or the courage
to act as an individual, perhaps there is a similar lesson to be derived
from this lone clinical experience. It was the only spontaneous verbali-
zation I heard about this news from other patients, who were also
free-associating to all their thoughts, or from friends, colleagues, or the
public as I could see them. Instead, as on other occasions of history,
there was, if anything, a collusion of silence.

On November 7, 1972, Nixon was resoundingly reelected president
with 97 percent of the electoral vote, perhaps the most challenging
piece of empirical data in this psychopolitical history. He was inaugu-
rated on January 20, 1973, with the sequestered Watergate jury watching the inaugural parade. The Watergate break-in criminal trial had
opened in Washington two weeks before. And on January 18, the second
Ellsberg-Russo *Pentagon Papers* trial had opened in Los Angeles. Nixon
could hardly have returned to the White House after the inaugural
ceremony in a mood to celebrate and enjoy the evening.

Danger lurked in a ring around him. A week earlier, at the overlook
on the George Washington Parkway a few miles away, John J. Caulfield,
of the Committee to Re-Elect the President, pressing James McCord to
accept executive clemency "from the highest level at the White
House," had said to McCord, "The president's ability to govern is at
stake. Another Teapot Dome scandal is possible. . . . Everybody else is
on track but you." McCord, rejecting for the second time the offer of
executive clemency, determined to pursue his independent path. Two
weeks before that meeting, McCord had sent an anonymous letter to
Caulfield. Objecting to maneuvers going on at the top to lay the Watergate operation at the feet of the CIA, McCord wrote, "every tree in the
forest will fall. . . . If they want it to blow, they are on the right course."

While the Miamians involved in the break-in had pleaded guilty and
played their parts, it was McCord who was showing the greatest strain.
As chief security officer of the Committee to Re-Elect the President and
of the Republican National Committee, he was the potential weak link
in the chain of security surrounding the president.

The central theme of Richard Nixon's second inaugural message—I
remember distinctly how it impressed me—related, dictu mirabile, to

personal and individual responsibility, that people should decide and do things for themselves!

Here are some excerpts from President Nixon's Second Inaugural Address:

> Abroad and at home, the key . . . lies in the placing and the division of responsibility.
>
> A person can be expected to act responsibly only if he has responsibility. This is human nature. So let us encourage individuals . . . to do more for themselves, to decide more for themselves . . .
>
> Let us remember that America was built . . . not by shirking responsibility, but by seeking responsibility.
>
> In our own lives let each of us ask . . . what can I do for myself? . . .
>
> From this day forward let each of us make a solemn commitment in his own heart: to bear his responsibility, to do his part, to live his ideals—so that together, we can see the dawn of a new age of progress for America . . . as we celebrate our 200th anniversary as a nation.

Could Nixon have been unaware of how exquisitely these words suited the activities going on around him? Whatever repose he may have felt during this inaugural address was soon to be disturbed, for the year 1973 contained an incremental series of revelations and accusations.

The first of these was the letter of James McCord, written March 19, 1973, to Judge John Sirica, Jr., and read in open court, basically confirming the news report of the *Washington Post* of the previous October. The White House was indeed involved in the break-in, perjury was committed at the Watergate trial, and McCord and other defendants were under "political pressure" to plead guilty and remain silent. On June 25, 1973, came the dry staccato recital of John W. Dean III, counsel to the president, to the Senate Select Committee on Presidential Campaign Activities. Observed live on television, with his cameo-like wife seated behind him, the country watched Dean with fascination as he laid out in unflinching detail a much wider area of dirty tricks engaged in by Nixon and the extended White House staff, and stated that he personally knew that President Nixon was involved in the cover-up since September 15, 1972. The third piece of information to add a new dimension to the investigation came on July 16, when Alexander P. Butterfield, former appointments secretary to the president, in a spontaneous answer to a casual question put by the same Senate select committee, told of the existence of a White House taping system. A new sense of responsibility accrued to the judges of the country, the committees, the courts, and behind them the public. Concrete potential evidence was now known to exist which could hardly be overlooked and which had to be acquired and investigated.

The quantity as well as quality of mental life is regulated and controlled. When psychic perception reaches a critical level of intensity, either in the quantity or quality of incoming stimuli, repression can no longer be initiated or maintained and other methods of retaining equilibrium must be forthcoming. In the absence of these, the conditions of psychic trauma have been reached. What had been revealed about Nixon had exceeded that limit. His actions could no longer be permitted to be elusive, to produce their momentary effects, and then be allowed to disappear.

The Oedipus complex is tolerated, is even normal, but not the oedipal crime. The same applied to the Watergate. The complex, the chronic cumulative compromises of integrity, yes; crime, no. There would no longer be only an occasional solitary critic, like my patient, or an eager reporter. The entire country would be troubled and on the alert. It was like awakening a sleeping giant. His sleep had been fitful and uneven for a year. But he was now roused. Nixon could no longer count on passive compliance.

The Cancer on/in the Presidency

On June 25, 1973, when John Dean testified before the Senate committee, he said that on March 21 he had told the president "that there was a cancer growing on the Presidency and that if the cancer was not removed that the President himself would be killed by it." An interesting slip or ambiguity appeared in the printed versions of this statement. While some articles reported Dean as having said "on," others repeated it as "in" the presidency. Was it "on the presidency" or "in the presidency"? Was it within the president himself?

The source or origin of a malignant lesion may exist in a dormant state for many years, conceivably even from birth, and not become a full-blown or active mass until later favorable conditions of the host bring it about. The same principle holds with regard to a malignant mental process. While a disposition may exist for many years, a certain external situation is needed to stimulate growth. Speaking of the cancer on this presidency, while John Dean was referring only to the increasing pressure of the cover-up, its malignant character was established long before.

Specific traits which became as characteristic of Richard Nixon as his fingerprints could be identified twenty-five or thirty years earlier. Nixon brought Watergate with him from Whittier to Washington. A young navy lieutenant with the proclivity for a specific type of behavior arrived home from the war in 1945—and conceived the idea that he could unseat a competent and previously popular young congressman in his hometown. The mental processes he displayed immediately could not have been implanted upon him; they came forth as if by instinct. In his very first political speech, made spontaneously to the "Committee of 100" Republicans which was interviewing him, Richard M. Nixon revealed the characteristic which was to be his from then on: the palatable untruth wrapped in the banal cliché. His answer to a question about his political philosophy was spontaneous: "I believe the returning veterans—and I have talked to many of them in the foxholes—will not be satisfied with a dole or a government handout." The fact is that Nixon was never near a foxhole but held a comfortable administrative position in the rear echelons. He had not talked to veterans there or elsewhere about their political philosophies. And they had never supplied him with a poll on their opinions about governmental subsidies. But the words came out smoothly and automatically, without the friction of guilt. What he said was close enough to the possible not to be challenged. Above all, it was emotionally tinged and timed with perfection. It took the committee of Republican businessmen ten minutes to choose Nixon as their candidate.

Nixon's method, the stamp which was to emerge as "Nixon politics," took shape rapidly. His motto was to attack, to smear, accuse, kill, and not to stop at overkill. Any statement which would have an effect was permissible. Congressman Jerry Voorhis, who had an outstanding record for independent honesty and who had therefore incurred many vested institutional enemies, was a stunned sitting duck. His loyalty, his patriotism, his very manhood were mercilessly attacked. Never head-on but with innuendoes and half truths; always with apologies and noble-sounding preludes. "I have been advised not to talk about Communism," Nixon said, "but I am going to tell the people of California. . . ." This was the zinger in those days. "Voorhis sat safely behind a desk in Washington," disclosed Nixon, "while he [Nixon] was defending the country in the stinking mud and jungles of the Solomons. . . . I do not question the motives of my opponent," he said by way of qualification, but, he went on, Voorhis was backed by the Political Action Committee (PAC) of the CIO, which of course was left-wing, Communist. This was false but effective. This group had not only not supported, but had actually opposed Voorhis. At a strategic moment in a debate at which proof of this repeated assertion was demanded, Nixon waved an ambiguous document in the face of his opponent, which could never be checked or countered. Voorhis was flustered and thrown off. Every honest statement he gave in reply made things worse. Nixon pressed on, lied, claimed Voorhis had admitted his guilt.

The same tactic was used four years later by the rapidly moving Nixon in his senatorial race against Helen Gahagan Douglas. "The pink lady" was associated with "the left wing Congressman Vito Marcantonio of New York," voted with him 354 times—"We stopped when the total reached 354"—and always voted "against the security of this country." The charges were repetitive, the same dose of poison in many different forms, always stopping short of the possibility of being checked. Pink leaflets were distributed in the campaign against Douglas. Against Voorhis, the day before the election, anonymous phone calls had been made to Democratic voters with the question, "Did you know Jerry Voorhis was a Communist?" And against Douglas, "Why has she followed the Communist line so many times?" Another future portent appeared in 1946: Nixon ads against Voorhis on huge commercial billboards, which were tax deductible for corporations. In a prelude to the

Watergate, tax deductions contributed to the defeat of his political opponents. The spice of fraud was added to the brew of slander and dirty tricks. Another characteristic of young Nixon was articulated at that time: Nixon, he told an interviewer, "had to win."

The Nixon face we know today, which has endured through all of his masks and changes, was etched and took form many years ago. Jerry Voorhis was not defeated; he was killed. He refused to return to the scene and run again in 1948. There have been other aggressive political figures throughout history, but Nixon was a unique phenomenon in this political generation. The combination of aggression with his manner of delivery became typically Nixon's. While delivering the killing blow, he can smile, gesture, pull back, divert attention; he can become humble, modest, one of us, kind. "I hate to do this but it is for you, for our country. . . ." And it is always especially for him.

But this package of traits was only half of the organism, the male half of genes and chromosomes, which had to meet its mate before it could be complete. It could not grow or flourish by itself. For an embryo to take root and develop, a receptor is necessary, a female half to provide the nourishing host environment. This was provided by the people of the Twelfth Congressional District of California, who accepted Nixon's "proposition" in 1946. The marriage was consummated, the significant union made. The people, for their part, agreed to be seduced. A colloquialism might better express the emotional tone of subsequent events: the people were willingly "screwed" by Nixon. The word has a double meaning: to be serviced and to be betrayed. Both were to come.

The family grew from the 1940s to the 1970s, from the Twelfth District in large increments to the entire country, as Nixon's affairs kept getting larger and more successful. With two exceptions in his rising career—and on one of these he narrowly missed becoming president against the popular John F. Kennedy—the people gave him their support to do whatever he wished to his rivals and competitors. What the people expected to get out of this marriage was a share in Nixon's fascinating capacity to discharge aggression without guilt. Guilt is a widespread internal oppressor. People are intrigued by one who shows them that their self-torments are not necessary. Nixon does not have other ingredients of charisma, but this aid in winning votes was distinctly his. Most people live with their egos constantly checked by their superegos. Nixon's has free reign, allowing it to satisfy ambition at will. In that respect this president was the opposite of our first one; George Washington, they say, could not tell a lie.

It was over a quarter of a century later that the growth which had been nourished so long became overtly malignant. Ironically, but perhaps by poetic justice, the areas it invaded, and which are now hurt by its spread, belong to both Nixon and the American people. Both suffered from the breakdown of the moral tissue and the rampant effects of the wild growth. In the somatic sphere, it is said that potentially malignant cells exist at all times but are kept within normal limits by chemical and immunologic controlling forces. It is the same in the mental apparatus. Here it is the superego values which keep instinctual impulses and ego interests within normal bounds. Organically, when the controlling forces fail, cells multiply and cancer results. In the psychic system, when the superego fails, it is behavior over which control is lost and which goes wild.

This analogy between power uncontrolled and a tumor, brought to the fore by John Dean's statement about a cancer on the presidency, has an unexpected precedent. Henry Adams, in his autobiography at the turn of the century, wrote:

> The effect of power and publicity on all men is the aggravation of self, a sort of tumor that ends by killing the victim's sympathies; a diseased appetite, like a passion for drink and perverted tastes; one can scarcely use expressions too strong to describe the violence of egotism it stimulates.

A "tumor" caused by "power," which aggravates the "self," causes "violence" of "egotism" and kills the victim's sympathies for others!

How Many Years of Watergate?

"One year of Watergate is enough," the president said in his State of the Union address in January 1974, and several times since. But it is two years! A year had already passed before we started counting. It is startling how automatically this is accepted and never questioned. The

measuring starts, with our permission, not when the crime was committed, not when it was discovered, but when it was widely publicized.
Nixon is measuring from March back to March, when McCord told us
all and when the president says he first knew about the cover-up from
Dean.

Why do we only speak of March and thereafter? What about the
previous October? Or even the June before that? Watergate began on
June 17, 1972, almost two years, not one year ago. Was the president not
interested in "the original" Watergate, even if only the amount of it
which the public, and therefore he also, knew each time something was
made known? Was it nothing to him that the chief security officer of his
Committee to Re-Elect the President and of the Republican National
Committee was caught and arrested as a common thief—not in a bank
or store, but in a political office—not in any political office, but in the
offices of the opposition party, and of his opponent for the presidency?
Was it still little or nothing to him that four months later the newspapers throughout the country carried the charge that this event had
been part of a large conspiracy reaching up to the White House?

How are these two glaring events reconciled with the announcement
made by Nixon on April 17, 1973, that "serious charges" had been
brought to his attention on March 21 for the first time—not before then?
Furthermore, lest anyone recall the vigorous denials of all charges
which had been repeatedly made by the White House before that time,
it was announced by Ronald Ziegler on that same day that all past
denials were now "inoperative." This was the pattern set at the top
following each unfolding event: the absorption of charges, denials and
countercharges, retractions later when further exposures occurred, and
notices given in one form or another to pay no attention to previous
denials.

For such actions to have any success there of course needs to be a
reciprocal compliance on the part of the audience, which over the long
range has been consistently forthcoming. After two years of such continued behavior, it has been gradually eroded and is wearing thin, but
is still visible. While inner feelings to this ploy of Ziegler's may have
reached the point of revulsion, outcry was mostly internalized.

One does not easily acknowledge that his "father" is a crook and lend
efforts to his demise. Sadness, upset, and hesitation result—a mixture of

fear, depression, and guilt. Just as the fear of the father originally does not occur in a vacuum, when the child is literally at the mercy of the father, so is the anxiety on the present scene not necessarily without a practical base. It was only when "the enemies list" became so exposed to shame and ridicule that such actual fear abated a bit and some were even proud to have made it. But deeper underlying guilt and depression and the reasons for them are not that easily acknowledged or dissolved. On the basis of a deep aversion and guilt over patricide, universal in the heart of man, from Oedipus to Hamlet to the possibility of impeachment now, leaders under appropriate suspicion are allowed to get off the hook of accountability.

Such a collective reaction permitted the first year of Watergate to pass almost unnoticed. The emphasis even since then has been almost entirely on what the president did after March 21, 1973. With regard to the nine months before March, interest was directed at first only to those who were caught, then to those who could have put them to it. No matter how much the latter group enlarged, it remained always a ring around the president, who was allowed, by widespread agreement, to be kept insulated and protected.

There are two lines of questioning about this first year of Watergate which have never been sufficiently followed. One is what did Nixon do or not do to "know more" after each new revelation was presented? If he did investigate with honest intent and found out nothing, what does this say about his efficiency, about the workings of the central machinery and staff of the president of the United States? If upon investigation he did find out the true facts, he would be in even greater trouble, caught in a web of moral questions. If, on the other hand, the president did little or nothing to investigate, what would this say about his judgment as well as his motives?

Second, one must question whether Nixon's lack of closeness to the situation, which he claims, fits the character of the president as we have come to know him. The test here is of a psychological fit, whether the explanations given are synchronous with the psychological profile of Nixon as he has carved this out during his political history. There is no doubt that the day of greatest personal threat to Richard Nixon was not June 17, 1972, when the event occurred, but could still be contained and go undetected; and not March 1973, when it all came out much more openly—but when the election and the mandate were already safely his. To Nixon, the pragmatist, not idealist, the most acute alarm signal must have come on October 10 when the searchlight of Watergate lit on the White House, when the big prize, weeks before it was to be his, could have been snatched out of his hands. If the president ignored the danger in June, would he still have done so in October?

Was this Richard Nixon? Was he one, in his previous career, to be passive and unconcerned about his elections? When Nixon explained in one of his later speeches that if people really knew him they would understand that he was engaged in foreign policy of the highest and most sensitive nature and therefore left his campaign entirely to others, he was asking them to overlook the Richard Nixon who scratched and clawed and gouged his way up from congressman to president. Had he changed so much that, at this moment of decision marred by unexpected crisis, he did not care, not investigate, not know? Not likely. Hardly a psychological fit. If one had to guess from past performance, he would have been not outside but very much in the center of it all, gesticulating, directing, and taking command. It would be unusual for such a crisis not to galvanize into action any candidate so much threatened and with so much at stake.

It is strange that there is not more emphasis on this dark and supposedly inactive period. The people wonder and do not believe. Not because they do not want to, but because they know they no longer can. While the president should not be hounded or harassed, and should be considered innocent until proven guilty, he should also be held as accountable where reasonable questions exist as would anyone else.

"Let us not have an obsession about Watergate," the president says as questions and criticisms mount. Actually, the opposite is the case. An obsession is a compulsive remembering characterized by an inability to forget. What we see here instead is a chronic repression or denial, i.e., a compulsive blanking out of the event or its significance dedicated centrally to the aim of forgetting. The one case of obsession I described earlier was a lonely island of normalcy in a sea of apathy. Since then, however, such reactions are more frequent.

"The people gave me a mandate, and I will carry it out," says Nixon, referring to the landslide victory they gave him in November 1972. It is true that they did. Let us look next into that.

The Mandate—and the Ending of the Vietnam War

The crucial month between October 10 and November 7, 1972, election eve in a broad sense, was in retrospect one of the most decisive periods in recent American history. Perhaps the present distance can give us a new look at the facts, especially in view of what has become further known since then about credibility.

The push to end the Vietnam War began in earnest precisely at the moment that Watergate was first reported in the *Washington Post* as a conspiracy which reached up to the White House. Henry Kissinger's nonstop travels from Paris to Saigon to Washington, a marathon of trips by a diplomatic virtuoso unprecedented in modern times, received a sharp increment in the intensity and seriousness of the negotiations virtually on the day the news story appeared.

There was Kissinger's trip to Paris from October 8 to 11. A spurt in activities, in secret conferences, and in news hints, surfaced during that period and continued to occupy center stage through the rest of October on to Election Day. (A first and less intense phase of the negotiations described by Kissinger as having taken place from July to October 8 had, by a similar temporal coincidence, followed by a short time the actual Watergate break-in in June.) These "accelerated negotiations," Kissinger explained, resulted from a "breakthrough" and were wholly responsive to a softening of attitude shown in a proposal made by Hanoi on October 8.

After more than a decade of war, and four years of an administration elected on the promise to end it (Lyndon Johnson had been pressured out of running again because he failed to keep his promise to end the war), action toward ending the war was started at such a time, and acceleration of the action pushed at such a point, that the culmination of these efforts rushed toward Election Eve with just enough time left for the people to absorb the impact of this stunning news. "As for the point that this is by a so-called coincidence," Kissinger was to say later at the news conference announcing these developments, "I can only repeat that the deadline was established by Hanoi and not by us, and that we were prepared to keep this whole agreement secret until it was consummated, and we would not have revealed it if it had not been consummated before the election."

What was even more striking, however, than this extraordinary timing was the manner in which this was accepted by the American people —automatically and almost unquestioned. A series of events not only led to the end of the long and paralyzing war but, concomitantly, by resulting in the almost automatic election of our next president, dictated the course and direction of our immediate future history. And it was initiated and therefore made possible, we were told, by a decision of the government of North Vietnam.

Twelve and ten and eight years earlier, the Vietnam War had been initiated and had been stepped up by gradual but definite increments on a number of occasions. Each time, we were similarly told in official announcements, this was as a result of actions or intentions on the part of North Vietnam. In August 1964, the Tonkin Gulf Resolution, authorizing reprisal air strikes against North Vietnam, severely escalated the war which had had its quiet origins during the Eisenhower and Kennedy years. This act also, it is striking to note in retrospect, was passed through Congress with "virtually no domestic criticism." The ostensible reason for this sharply stepped-up war was that two American destroyers, the *Maddox* and the *G. Turner Joy*, had been unlawfully attacked in the Gulf of Tonkin by North Vietnamese P.T. and torpedo boats. Seven years later, in 1971, the *Pentagon Papers* revealed that these claims had been false—that the attacks had been preceded by six months of clandestine military operations against North Vietnam by the United States which had provoked and set the stage for the attacks on our ships.

Dr. Karl Menninger, in his book *Whatever Happened to Sin?* writes, "Lying is a sin in large letters. And lying by leaders is unforgivable." Should the explanations of these events, as given by the participants in whom a severe conflict of interest existed, be written into the history books? Automatically? Especially when, a few months later, the credibility of these same informants evaporated? Credibility has never been one of Nixon's strong points. And Kissinger must regretfully be included here. Although he has managed to remain relatively clean of Watergate, at least of its central features, he has not emerged untouched. He was not beyond secret bombing and false reporting, wire-tapping, dirty tricks, the long continuation and prolongation of the war before ending it, and the twists and turns and hypocrisies of foreign policy, many of which certainly came about with his knowledge and participation, even if not under his stewardship. Even as the war was coming to an end with every evidence of our shame, Kissinger was proclaiming its moral base and the "admirable restraint" shown throughout its long course by the United States.

There must come a time when history can be judged currently, on the basis of the past, with greater reliability than is usually the case. If history cannot be read prospectively, at least it should not depend solely on a much later retrospective view. While it is happening would be much better. Otherwise the gloomy insight of Santayana, that those who fail to remember history are condemned to repeat it, will continue to exact its heavy toll.

A psychological and motivational view of history rather than a mere chronology of events supplies the cement which binds them together. History is, in the last analysis, the product of individuals. This is particularly so with leaders in decision-making and policy-setting roles and applies especially at historical moments of crisis and crossroads. Whether the kaiser or Churchill, Napoleon or Hitler, Franklin D. Roosevelt or now Nixon, to know the psychic makeup of each is to amplify the history of their times.

By now we must seriously consider that temporal contiguity, i.e., the coincidence of events in time, the existence of psychological motives to connect them, and the human and commonsense aspects of historical events, are more reliable indicators of the reasons for political acts and should supersede the official explanations proffered at the time by the political figures themselves. Analysts have long learned to make this distinction in the analysis of individuals, subjecting explanations offered even with the best conscious intentions to more meaningful and critical interpretation. Although in analyses unconscious motives are substituted for conscious ones, while in these reconstructions of historical events one conscious explanation may be replaced by a more compelling one, the same principle holds. The distortions in both cases are in the interests of self.

Many political observers today do not feel that the fine print of this period bears out the official explanations given. It is the opinion of many people, and the accusations of some, that the same results with regard to the ending of the Vietnam War could have been achieved at any time during the previous four years. Or that the terms achieved, as Senator McGovern pointed out on the one occasion that he would comment, were no different from those given to the French in Geneva in 1954 when they pulled out of Vietnam. A qualitative change of the degree claimed, significant enough to explain the sudden change of pace, has not been unequivocally or convincingly demonstrated.

Might it be that with this longest and most demoralizing war in our history, our official descriptions of its ending contain the same quality and degree of distortion as have been shown later to exist in our past official statements of its beginning? And in the same direction—although for different reasons each time—projecting to Hanoi what we in each case wanted to and did bring about? The *Pentagon Papers* revealed the falsity of our official history of the start and early development, although many had suspected and said it before. It might take another *Pentagon Papers,* this time a White House Papers, ten, twenty, or fifty years from now (perhaps this time, never!), to answer the questions which exist now and to document what actually did take place at the end.

The explanation could either be confirmed or corrected. But should we not acknowledge this time that we were told, but that from past experience we cannot say that we know? L. Patrick Gray, former acting director of the FBI, in his testimony before the Watergate committee in August 1973, declared, "I had a responsibility . . . not to permit myself to be used, not to permit myself to be deceived, and I failed in that responsibility. . . . And it hurts." Do we not all have that same responsibility?

To be fair and complete, the DRVN (Democratic Republic of Vietnam) in a statement of late October did give some credence to Kissinger's assertions of their own stepped-up pace for peace, whatever the motivations for either their initiation or compliance in supplying this. In fact the motives for their actions are difficult to fathom. The reasons which have been suggested, that they were sure Nixon was going to be elected and thought they could do better negotiating with him before rather than after his election, do not seem to make much sense. If it was they who were going to "give in" anyway, they could have done that after as well as before the election. They knew they could count on the American people to keep up their pressure for peace. It seems difficult to imagine that the North Vietnamese were motivated to hand Richard Nixon his reelection in addition to his terms for the peace. From whichever side one approaches it, the motivation seems clearly to have been ours. Even a target date of October 31 was attributed to them. Asked "Why did Hanoi want that deadline?" Kissinger replied, "You will have to ask Hanoi"!

After secret negotiations the agreement had been that two "simultaneous" announcements would be made. Our side accused the other of breaking their pledge in releasing news of the agreement unilaterally in advance. Xuan Thuy stated that a precedent had been set for this long before by Nixon when he had revealed, against their agreement, that there were secret talks going on. So while "agreement" and "peace" were being announced by both sides, each was calling the other a liar. These were the two informants recording current history.

To a few mild questions put to him at his crucial news conference on October 26, Kissinger went further than his questioners and volunteered, "I would like to suggest to you, ladies and gentlemen, that while it is possible to disagree with provisions of an agreement, the implications that this is all a gigantic maneuver which we will revoke as soon as this period is over is unworthy of what we have gone through." Nobody had said it was "a gigantic maneuver"; the thought may have been there but was obviously considered inappropriate to pursue. The "gigantic maneuver," however, which Kissinger volunteered was slightly off target. It would not have been that either side would revoke its agreement after the election. That was not what was on people's minds. The question which was not asked would have been about the timing of such a maneuver just before the election.

Certainly there were long preparations for what seemed to take place suddenly. News such as this is not built on one confrontation, especially when a stubborn other side must cooperate. The plan which ensued could only have been long in the making, carefully prepared and meticulously timed. The creative contacts with China and the Soviet Union, made long previously, were not without linkage to these coming events. There were many small news items in the months before October 1972 of contacts by China and the Soviet Union with North Vietnam on our behalf. There is no reason to believe that this month of activities was not scheduled to take place long before October. Or that the basic plan would have been any different had the Watergate problem not intervened. The day of the election was a set one and was sufficient to explain it all. The timing was fixed and had not changed. And in the long preludes leading to it, in addition to the major performances in China and Moscow, Kissinger had made eight flights to Paris and one other to Saigon earlier that year, as well as six to Paris in 1971 and six in 1970 for then totally secret talks with Le Duc Tho. There are enough hidden records to explain another whole history than what we have. And our own "acceleration" had begun long before that initiated by North Vietnam.

Multiple motivations are not the exception but the rule in human functioning. Most acts operate under what is known as "the principle of multiple functions." And an act started for one psychic reason can acquire a "change in function." Is it indeed conceivable that the new revelations just weeks before Election Day were of no concern to the White House—could have produced no added motive to cover or divert? No matter how little or how much Nixon himself knew about the truth, would not these stories have impelled him to "cover" even false reports?

Not to consider the multiple motives involved, or to ignore Nixon's past as possibly relevant to the present, would be like studying a full-blown illness, psychic or physical, without being interested in its antecedents. The past may illuminate the present, and in this instance the present the past, and both help to point the way to the future. If we failed to observe causative events as they were happening, it may be helpful to see them at least in retrospect. It could be, from a closer and more intensive look, that this most unpopular of all our wars had an ending, although welcome beyond words, as dubious as its dishonorable beginning—even though the peace was announced as being "with honor." Maybe that is why it had to be. Was there ever really a danger of a peace without it?

Speaking at ceremonies commemorating the first Vietnam Veterans' Day, on March 29, 1974, President Nixon declared, "History will record that the American effort in Vietnam was a good cause honorably undertaken and honorably ended. . . . The verdict of history, I am sure, will be quite different from the instant analysis that we presently see and sometimes hear." Actually it is Nixon who oversimplifies, at least in his dealings with the American public. Ignoring all exposures and established facts, his statement is to be taken on trust against all that is known. It only increases the distrust. It is interesting that he had to add "honorably ended."

To return to what happened during that eventful month, Nixon now began to move with atypical speed, atypical, that is, for him in this direction. On that same October 10, Kissinger explained later in the month, the president still raised some complex objections to the proposal by Hanoi. But on October 22, with a dispatch unknown in the preceding four years, Nixon was convinced and gave his complete agreement. The stage was set for the well-timed piece of news. Returning to Washington before the deadline, Kissinger made the momentous announcement in a historic news briefing on October 26: peace was at hand, a treaty was imminent. To a question put to him about dates, Kissinger explained, "We did agree that we would make a major effort to conclude the negotiations by October 31." But unfortunately, Kissinger went on, "six or seven very concrete issues" were still to be resolved. For this, one more negotiating session of three or four days was needed. This could come "in weeks or less"!

Speaking the same night in Ashland, Kentucky, President Nixon told a fired-up political audience that the "significant breakthrough . . . [assures] peace with honor."

Three birds were about to be killed with one stone. More accurately, two hawks were using one dove as a decoy. The ending of the war, so long wanted, was being granted now, carrying along with it two attached riders which would bypass all opposition—the submersion of Watergate and the re-election of Nixon—all in one brilliant fused finish. Twelve days remained until the election. The story of sixteen days earlier in the *Washington Post* was invisible. The country sat glued to the new news. One thing stands out as striking. Whatever was authentic and unmanipulated during those crucial days, it is surprising how little —really nothing—was ever made of this timing by the press, on the campuses, or by the people. Occasionally an observer who looks back at that period asks how the American people gave Nixon their mandate so easily after the *Washington Post* article of a month before. One might say, in the simplest and most direct way, that there was no time for a reaction, or that the people believed what they were told, that nothing else occurred to them. Neither of these do justice to the complexity of the human mind.

A state of passive expectancy was again multidetermined. First there was the reward being dangled to a war-weary people. There were other ways of being prisoners of war susceptible to bribes than being in an enemy camp. There was the well-known mechanism of identification with the aggressor; a person wielding and displaying power, especially to one in a weakened state, is one to be identified with. There was also inhibition based on fear and guilt. When the leader is known to be particularly aggressive, he is treated with inhibition, as a bully by children, up to a point. To be a member of the team, the winning team, is a powerful incentive. Ionescu's *Rhinoceros* does not carry an isolated message; its theme is universal and is made for times like this.

But there was another process taking place, as strong as all the others. Nixon trained his voting public to feel that not to support him was disloyal—disloyal to the United States of America and the republic for which it stands. Honor, they were led to believe, was always very much on his side. Against him, when he sought his first public office over thirty years ago, and in almost every campaign since, was dishonor.

Early in Nixon's career such a stance against his opponents was conscious and deliberate, brought about by dirty tricks. Today it is more subtle and refined, even unconscious, but just as much there. "America" and "American" appear in his speeches repetitively, whether appropriate or not, but with special force during conflict or crisis. That is when this stance works the best, under pressure or in areas which are gray. In troubled times, especially in conflicts of conscience, whenever Nixon is involved the people are not left to make their delicate decisions, each in accordance with his own conscience and values.

Nixon stood for and claimed the group superego. In the fifties you were either for communism or for America and therefore for Nixon. In 1972, "peace with honor" was his and his alone. This policing of the superego involves an invasion of privacy which has always gone along with Nixon's political presence. For the freedom which is given up, something is gained in return—protection and license; by escaping from one's conscience, even temporarily, one need no longer use it against one's self. When an individual permits such processes to take over, he expends psychic energy to keep himself from consciously knowing the primitive rather than rational processes at work.

The people prepared themselves to grant the authority which was being asked. If any chose to believe, as Kissinger suggested, that this was "simply some trick," they chose not to say it, perhaps not even to know it. Senator McGovern, who was reported to feel like a man who had just heard the other shoe drop, declined to characterize this latest development as "an election eve settlement." On the other hand, Sargent Shriver declared the timing "an election maneuver" and revealed that McGovern, Humphrey, and other political leaders had predicted that the Nixon administration would negotiate a peace between October 15 and Election Day. His own prediction, Shriver said, missed by six days.

Twelve days after Kissinger's announcement, on November 7, 1972, Nixon got his "mandate." This is the mandate to which he constantly returns and which he vows to carry out. This mandate does indeed need to be returned to but as a phenomenon to be explained, not as a guide to action in the present. As one commentator observed, Nixon had won the people's votes but never their affection, and not even in this land-slide did he win their trust. This second greatest election victory in our history did not prove something positive about the man who won it but something to be questioned about the masses who gave it.

In the earlier days of our republic, individuals, perhaps less informed, were left more to their own inner decisions. I wonder how much more independent is the "registered" voter of today, newspaper clippings and instructions in his pocket, as he faces the electronic voting machine in his politically carved-out precinct. Do the media and the professions of advertising and public relations bring greater information or undue influence? How much do the increased facilities for dissemination of information bring increased possibilities of suggestion as well? How much have the techniques of behavior modification already been instituted, with effects which can lead by insidious steps to the state of "mind control"? In any study of the meaning of voting in our "advanced" society, this mandate of 1972 will be an important chapter. It is not a lifeline for Nixon out of his present difficulties nor does it vindicate him in 1974.

Dan Rather, attempting to explain the astonishingly poor performance of the media in reporting the Watergate story from June 17, 1972, until McCord broke the case to the public on March 23, 1973, attributed this, among other reasons, to "the deadly daily diet of deceit sent us from the White House" during that period. "They lied, schemed, threatened, and cajoled to prevent network correspondents from getting a handle on the story. And they succeeded." His conclusion as to what there was to be learned, both inside and outside of journalism, was "that more skepticism should be encouraged in every reporter on the payroll . . . not cynicism but skepticism, especially when dealing with people in power."

Was the widespread lack of reaction from October 10 to November 7 due to suppression or repression? There is a difference, which is not academic but of importance in savoring the depth of the problem. Suppression is a conscious submerging of facts or impulses while repression is unconscious and takes place outside of conscious awareness. I feel that the distortions which took place on such a global scale, the denial of perceptions, the suspension of the critical faculties, the repression of anxiety, and the exaggerated position of innocent receptivity, were part of an unconscious process, born out of wish and fear and hope, a widespread regression which spread by contagion and shared need.

The month described was a crucial period in American history in which the past, the present, and the future converged. It can well stand a thorough reevaluation with the necessary skepticism inserted and the benefit of retrospective events. Such reassessments of history frequently reveal unexpected findings even under normal subsequent conditions. How much more is this indicated when the period which immediately followed reveals a collapse of trust of unprecedented degree during the worst moral crisis in our nation's history?

No coach, to use a favorite metaphor of the president, ever blew a game so in the bag. No athlete ever jeopardized a victory so decisive by such an unnecessary foul. What nervous insecurity, what a gap between ferocious desire and shaky expectation must have been present to permit such a lapse, or total collapse, of judgment. A landslide was assured, the victory was his if he had just performed his job, with no risk taking, no push, no maneuvers; and no "tricks" for good measure.

Senseless and desperate acts must be viewed as symptomatic, as stemming from unconscious processes. To have had to enter and burglarize two offices, not one—one on each coast. Here I am speaking of Nixon and his staff as one, and of psychological, not of legal guilt—the latter has yet to be determined on specific points. Since the history of Nixon's earlier career is compatible with what followed, and the "dirty tricks" in which the president has been unambiguously involved were preludes to the final crimes, I am taking the president at his word: in an address broadcast by Nixon on April 30, 1973, he stated, "I will not place the blame on subordinates. . . . In any organization the man at the top must bear the responsibility. That responsibility, therefore, belongs here in this office. I accept it."

Nixon's distrust of the American people matched their mistrust of him. In the last analysis, both stemmed from his distrust of his inner self. He must never have felt that success could be based on his inner worth alone, that the people would elect him out of warm feeling combined with a belief in his true beliefs. No one, to be sure, relies on these alone without needing support from the outside to fortify them. But there should be at least a base of that kind. This was never the case with Nixon. Nixon's desperate measures in every campaign bespeak his fear that the people would see through him, that they would know, and that he was unconsciously aware of his manipulations of others, and now of history, for one goal—his own good.

Can we go a step further? Was the Watergate his—or their—maneuver to satisfy in Dostoyevsky-like fashion a deep, unconscious sense of guilt? Did they—or he—want to get caught, and did they continue until it happened? Between May 15 and June 17, 1972, the day the men who broke into the Democratic National Headquarters were apprehended, various combinations of this same group of "plumbers" approached or entered Senator McGovern's headquarters in Washington, D.C., four times and the offices of the Democratic National Committee five times —no less than nine chances of this magnitude taken within a month! Several resulted in scares or near captures.

On May 15, James W. McCord, Jr., and Thomas J. Gregory, a college student hired to infiltrate Democratic campaigns, entered McGovern headquarters intending to plant a bug in Frank Mankiewicz's office, but there was not enough time. A few nights later, G. Gordon Liddy shot out a light in an alley near McGovern headquarters. Four break-in attempts into the two Democratic offices failed under dangerous conditions and with almost dire consequences each time. During one of these, on May 26, E. Howard Hunt, Jr., and Virgilio Gonzalez spent the night hiding from security guards, unable to open a door to a staircase leading to the Democratic National Committee offices. A second attempt the following day failed when, at 11:30 P.M., McCord and six Miamians successfully carried two suitcases with bugging and photographic material into the Watergate office building, but Gonzalez was unable to pick the lock on the door to the Democratic National Committee offices. Between these two acts, an overnight attempt on May 26–27 to break into McGovern headquarters was foiled because a man was standing in front of the door. And on May 28 there was a fourth brush with disaster: a second attempt to break into McGovern's headquarters failed when Gregory was discovered there late at night.

One break-in into the Democratic headquarters on May 28 was successfully executed. Five men entered the premises of the Democratic National Committee offices while two others stood guard outside; Hunt and Liddy directed the operation, Eugenio Martinez photographed documents, and McCord planted wiretaps on the telephones of Oliver and Lawrence O'Brien. Afterward the nine men adjourned to Hunt's and Liddy's hotel room for a victory celebration. On June 12 one man, Alfred Baldwin, received a free tour of the Democratic headquarters by posing as the nephew of a former Democratic National Committee chairman. And finally, at 2:30 A.M. on June 17, 1972, five men were caught in the act. Captured by Washington police inside the offices of the Democratic National Headquarters, their surveillance equipment and sequenced hundred-dollar bills were confiscated, the men arrested and charged with burglary.

There was not just one break-in but a series of exposures. For what? When Jeb Magruder, according to his later testimony, gave John Mitchell the Gemstone transcripts of the wiretapped documents taken during the one successful raid, Mitchell complained that there was "no substance to them." He then directed Liddy to correct the faulty tap and get better information. Mitchell later called this allegation a "palpable damnable lie."

The risks taken, the dubious gains to be won, and the steady march toward capture add up to a familiar psychiatric syndrome, a pattern of guilt, risks, bungling, and capture. This is typically followed by dissension among participants, some exposing and pointing to others, and selective punishments, not all according to legal grounds but for various other compelling or adventitious considerations, such as plea bargaining, deals, and other expedient arrangements.

Psychohistory has the same methodological and technical limitations as psychobiography, and both need to be treated with caution and restraint. Neither with a public figure, past or present, nor a group, do we have a subject willing and even eager to break through barriers of defense and to provide the evidence necessary for an understanding in depth. Yet history without psychological motivations misses an essential ingredient. The challenge is to fit the conclusions to the data, not to outstrip the facts, and to limit surmises to reasonable and informed opinions. Evidence may be utilized from other sources which are applicable to present findings. In studies of groups and the historical process, actions may be the only means of communication. These indeed sometimes speak as loudly as words. There are precedents for this in more conventional treatments, as in play therapy with children or in the treatment of disturbed nonverbal adults.

To be complete—this applies equally to individuals or groups—there is another aspect of the etiology of events apart from unconscious motivation. Heinz Hartmann, a leading theoretician in psychoanalysis during the second half of its first century, pointed out that reality is more than man's unconscious. In similar vein, another major theoretical contributor, Robert Waelder, gives a due and proper place to the role of chance. In the case of the break-in, a stream of circumstantial external events conspired to join with the human contributions; without either one, the story would not have "happened" as it did.

Dennis Stefenson, a uniformed policeman who, when the call came through about a burglary at the Watergate, was first assigned to check the suspected break-in, excused himself because he was low on gas and had paperwork to catch up on. The nearest police car available was an unmarked car with three plainclothes members of the tactical squad who answered the call instead. Had the call been answered by a marked police car with a flashing beacon and a policeman in uniform, there probably would have been no Watergate scandal. The car would have been spotted by Baldwin across the street, who would have put out an alarm on his walkie-talkie. Even without this, Hunt and Liddy would have heard the alert and had time to rescue their cohorts in the act. Before this, it was only after the second time he found the door taped open that a guard on his rounds inside the building finally put in a call to the police. With this, Frank Wills, the guard, and the "bum squad" which responded, to quote *The Nation,* "pushed the rock that tipped the boulders that started the avalanche that filled the valley."

II

The Build-Up

The Tapes

The tapes dominate the story that dominates the news of 1973–74. One wonders where the investigation would be without them. And again we must give due credit to the roles played by both chance and the unconscious. Without the confluence of both, there would be no tapes in the picture, and probably no pursuit of Watergate as there now is.

The tapes have brought with them many contradictions and irrationalities. People have become so inured to the repetition of words and actions that questions which are primary are routinely overlooked. Do we agree, for example, with the modus vivendi set up by the president that anyone speaking to him in the Oval Office or the Cabinet Room, at the Executive Office Building or at Camp David, would have his conversation, in person or on the telephone, taped without his knowledge or consent? If the major reason for the existence of this mechanical system was, as Haldeman stated, as an "aid to history," or as Alexander P. Butterfield indicated, "to preserve the history of the Presidency," has this been generally accepted as a new way of observing and recording history? What do we think of a conversation or conference among statesmen who form our history in which one active participant is taping the other or others, unknown to the latter, with one controlling, the other being deceived? Such a method does not record history but creates it. Shaped in accordance with the will of one person, it is

stamped with insincerity at the highest interpersonal level. Both objec-
tivity and morality have been compromised. Ironically, this is what
Nixon—in his old days—used to say was happening in the Soviet Union:
hidden tapes were everywhere!

Why did Nixon so easily admit the existence of the Watergate tapes?
After Butterfield casually revealed their existence in a private session
with the Senate Select Committee on Presidential Campaign Activities,
it was striking how this was immediately—and uncharacteristically!—
confirmed by the White House. One had the impression that this was
done eagerly, even proudly, almost as a mark of honor. The practice of
taping, it was explained, was by now a necessary adjunct to the presidency, which attested to the president's thoroughness and ingenuity.
Not only was the practice of taping *not* an embarrassment, but proved
the president's brilliant foresight; it would—at some later time—exonerate the president from false charges. Moreover—and here was the
only evidence of a possible twinge of regret, perhaps even guilt—the
system was "similar to that employed by the last Administration." The
latter charge was instantly and vehemently denied by inner associates
of both Kennedy and Johnson. While some taping had indeed taken
place—there is usually a kernel of truth in such charges—never was it
on so systematic a basis or on such a large scale.

Why did Nixon tell? He did not have to; he typically does not. Very
few of the men directly associated with the president knew about the
tapes. The question is in the same genre as why the plumbers kept
breaking into Watergate until they were caught. If the tapes are potentially the most incriminating evidence against the president, why did
he not destroy or otherwise dispose of them? L. Patrick Gray burned
incriminating Hunt documents with the Christmas trash. Ehrlichman,
Dean testified, asked him to "deep six," i.e., throw into the Potomac
River, sensitive documents from a White House safe.

Was Nixon suddenly honest in this respect? Did fear now grip him?
Nixon says the tapes will help him, are in his favor. Then why does he
hold them back? A "straight" reason would be that it all isn't so! Nixon's
credibility reaches its lowest point. There is not a believable rationalization accompanying his argument. "National security" has finally
achieved a hollow and depressing ring and does him no good.

Another question in a welter of irrationality: Why would he speak

such incriminating evidence into a tape system? The president was one
of the brilliant lawyers of the country. The recording of history—
whether we accept this explanation or not—is one thing, but the recording of a crime is another. Nixon knew he was recording incendiary
information; why didn't he turn the system off, or not join the conversation? Or separate matters of foreign diplomacy from private conversations about an intragovernmental crime? The crudity of it all is beyond
belief. Did Nixon expect to be able to cover the tapes later, or edit them,
or select parts for his own purposes? Did he feel that safe? Or was he
that careless? Or was he so unthinking? Or was his judgment just so bad?
Did he think he could doctor them and then realize he could not—too
many tapes, too many people, too many conflicting interests involved?
One thinks of some lines from a Robert Burns poem:

> The best-laid schemes o' mice an' men,
> Gang aft agley,
> An' lea'e us nought but grief an' pain
> For promis'd joy!

He must have had a plan—or didn't he? Which could have been even
worse.

Each question leads to an astonishing answer about the president of
the United States. Together they are reminiscent of Freud's story of the
borrowed pot. When accused of borrowing and breaking a pot, the
defense of the person so accused was that he never borrowed the pot,
that it was broken when he got it, and that it was whole when he
returned it. Even rationalizations wear thin.

The president himself has provided a record which might be the only
concrete evidence which can lead to his impeachment. In the absence
of satisfying or credible explanations, the motivations for acts of dubious
logic can only be sought in the unconscious recesses of the mind. Here
contradictions coexist, and motivations operate not by the neologic of
rational adult behavior, but by the paleologic or primitive modes from
earlier periods of psychic functioning.

While the tapes could originally have been set up for quasi-legitimate
and rationalized reasons, they did grow into a practice which suited the
atmosphere of "paranoia in the White House," a characterization made

not by an enemy of the president, but by a self-proclaimed friend, Egil Krogh. Such a use, motivated by such a character trait, is in keeping with the old and permanent Nixon who has existed from his anti-Communist days to his enemies list of today. It fits also with the web of intrigue and distrust, not only between the White House and the country, but between branches of government: tapped phones, bugging devices, secret investigations; the Pentagon putting bugs on Kissinger; the State Department spying against the Department of Defense; crossed wires and sparks between the CIA, the White House staff, and the State Department; Nixon and Haldeman talking of the possibility of Dean's taping the president; the president's tapping the phone of his brother.

Was Nixon building up a defense, as might be characteristic of a paranoid personality? Were the tapes to be used to attack others, which has also been Nixon's way from the beginning? Whom would this be against? Against anyone with whom he was negotiating, from Leonid Brezhnev down to his own inner group? Did Nixon trust anyone? Were the tapes unconsciously set up against himself? A cartoon by Conrad in the *Los Angeles Times* shows Nixon's tapes as a hangman's noose!

Did Nixon record these tapes for unconscious narcissistic reasons, fascinated as an ordinary mortal might be by the sound of his own voice? Could he have just wanted to have the whole record, the good and the bad, to listen to privately?

In narcissistic character types the need for admiration is so strong that the achievement of any one goal does not end that need. The craving continues, and any additional fraction or increment of satisfaction is welcome, even if a heavy price must be paid. Narcissistic rewards can be extracted in spite of events which also bring suffering. This is akin to black humor, something funny emerges out of something grim, like Tom Sawyer's and Huckleberry Finn's enjoyment at being present at their own funeral. A criminal may enjoy seeing himself in a film of his crime even though he was caught.

A number of traits are subsumed under narcissism. Grandiosity, a feeling of omnipotence, exhibitionism are all parts of it. Ambition and a craving for power, in the pathological sense described previously, both traits of high intensity and out of control, accompany the narcissistic syndrome. As mentioned earlier, all of these characteristics, with

narcissism at their center, are the enemies of integrity. When narcissistic pressures erode the capacity of the superego to resist, compromises
of integrity result.

Nixon qualified as having all of these traits. Could narcissism, grandiosity, exhibitionism have played a part in his decision to put on permanent record every word he was to speak? Could this type of personal
push for immortality have led him to install this massive taping system,
and blunt for him any question either of its danger or of its morality?
Narcissistic motivation could have played a large part.

All of these questions stimulate thought but we can provide no definite answers. There is no substitute for having President Nixon himself
honestly, sincerely, telling it all, if one is to have any sense of accuracy
about purpose and cause. Many have wanted and urged him to do so
—Senator Barry Goldwater, for example, or Senator Charles Percy, to
give examples at opposite political poles. Nixon's reasons for not complying with these requests have been as unconvincing and contradictory as all other explanations.

Since the tapes have been discovered, all attention has been on them,
to the general exclusion of other evidence and information. There is a
distorting mechanism similar to that which permitted the first year of
Watergate to be obliterated. The tapes must be kept in perspective and
not blown up to substitute for the whole. The public, the press, even
the investigating committees have acted as if these tapes contain the
only answers to the questions of Watergate. If there is so much on them,
how much must there be which is not? How do we know how many
tapes have been disposed of? And how do we know how much equally
vital material may have been kept off the tapes, as any normal person,
let alone an elite group of brilliant lawyers, would have done? The fact
is, the tapes can prove guilt, but they cannot prove innocence.

For a few months, in February, March, and April of 1974, our attention has been riveted to "the forty-two tapes" requested from and
being withheld by the president. These center around the crucial date
of March 21, 1973, and concern key conversations about the time
when Nixon alleges he first knew about the cover-up: what was said,
what was heard, and what he did at that time. Again, the president
has balked: national security, the institution of the presidency, the
confidentiality of private documents. There has been pressure from

Judge Sirica, Leon Jaworski, and Rep. Peter Rodino, Jr., to subpoena the president. Nixon will give no more; he has already furnished nine-teen tapes and seven-hundred documents. They have all they need. *He* will decide.

With Either One Alone

If we freeze this moment and take a look forward and backward, we might say the following: With either one alone—the figure or the ground, the Watergate event or the Nixon character which brought it about—Nixon would probably have made it through, even as a hero to many. Before the crime itself, Nixon's methods were known to the public and gradually accepted. Similarly, if Watergate alone had oc-curred, on a clean soil so to speak, the embarrassment and shock would have been intense but time limited. Painful but temporary reactions would in time have been successfully outweighed by the real accom-plishments of Nixon, whatever the motivation for those accomplish-ments may have been. The backlash after harsh criticism might even have worked in his favor. People have identified with Nixon's capacity to bounce back after a seemingly lethal blow. He had repeatedly demonstrated this ability and turned it each time to his advantage and success. But both together are another story.

Everything bad which had once worked for Nixon now works against him. Dirty actions synonymous with the name Nixon, which were con-verted into virtues, return in full force. Other presidents have had their trials: Eisenhower his U-2, Kennedy the Bay of Pigs, Johnson the Gulf of Tonkin; and Teddy Kennedy still today has his Chappaquiddick. Defenders of the president will point to these crises hopefully and with fingers crossed. But each of these men had to account for an act, not a way of life. With Nixon it is the accumulation of twenty-five years, one agglutinated memory of his penchant to destroy, his instinct for the jugular, his nothing-is-below-him campaigns in a straight line to the present crimes of Watergate.

When, for internal or external reasons, such a mass (mess) of memo-ries has to be revived, with their original conflicts and accompanying emotions, these may return with greater force precisely because they have been repressed for so long. Old doubts return, joined by the new ones and by the new editions of the old. And the onus for the forced, painful, revived experience is on the one who made and makes this happen—then and now.

For us, the public, the onus is not only on the other; it is also on the self. Such an accumulated, messy mass cannot be remembered without guilt for not having confronted it originally. The widespread anger and disappointment which has overtaken the people of this country is as much a complaint that Nixon made them remember as indignation at the new acts themselves. What happens when further experience shows that original signals were not reacted to appropriately? L. Patrick Gray, we will remember, said that it is the responsibility of each person not to permit himself to be deceived. Does the voting citizen have any feeling of accountability? And if there is little or none consciously, is this necessarily the case unconsciously as well?

Can people be feeling badly without knowing it; can one be disturbed even if he denies it? Affects—the psychoanalytic synonym for emotions—can and do exist in the unconscious. From clinical explorations and studies of human feelings we know that people commonly are not aware that they are anxious or insecure, and that bringing this to light can illuminate and, one hopes, alleviate a great deal of otherwise inexplicable behavior. It takes time for some people to find out that they are depressed and may have been so for years. Repressed "affects" can exist suspended in the psyche, not consciously experienced but producing their effects nevertheless. They can be present for a lifetime, can determine a mood which becomes part of a person's character. One can be a depressive, another anxious, another a cheerful optimist. Repressed emotions can be dormant for years and come up fresh when elicited by current events. In February 1974, a "victory" celebration was held in Los Angeles for Helen Gahagan Douglas, now in her seventies, a quarter of a century after her famous political battle. There were not many dry eyes, and mixed feelings were evident, as fresh as the day she was "defeated" and became more loved than the victor. A mixture of pride and guilt was evident in buttons worn on the lapels of many: "Don't blame me. I voted for Douglas"!

Nixon's characteristics have become more pronounced under pressure, are more definitely Nixon in his times of crisis. As in the days of Vietnam, he does only what he is forced to do, then claims credit for the initiative. An interesting analogy to this type of mechanism appeared in the correspondence between Freud and Jung written some sixty or seventy years ago and recently published in a volume edited by William McGuire. In a letter to Jung written in 1911, Freud says of Alfred Adler, from whose theories both he and Jung were beginning to diverge, "I see now that Adler's seeming decisiveness concealed a good deal of confusion. I would never have expected a psychoanalyst to be so taken in by the ego. In reality the ego is like the clown in the circus, who is always putting in his oar to make the audience think that whatever happens is his doing"! Freud must have liked this metaphor; a few pages later he repeats it, this time adding an observation about a facial gesture which is also relevant to our present study: "Adler's ego behaves as the ego always behaves, like the clown in the circus who keeps grimacing to assure the audience that he has planned everything that is going on. The poor fool!" We have seen the forced little mirthless smile which slips across Nixon's face at times of special stress when it is desirable to convey the illusion of mastery in the face of hopelessness or helplessness.

Contradictions continue to be Nixon's stamp and trade. While claiming to have ordered his own investigation of Watergate and to have himself instigated the government prosecution, his actions toward the investigations and trials which are in progress have been consistently obstructive rather than facilitating. While denying having had any role in a cover-up, he is covering up openly and continuously in the present. And not content with defense, as always he attacks. Instead of answering genuine questions and legitimate concerns about his own actions and participation, he deflects, accuses, and attacks: Congress, his enemies, a conspiracy of liberals, of course the press. He is the Nixon of old.

Facts have been emerging at varying rates and irregular intervals determined mainly by the obstacles put up against them by Nixon. The sequence has typically been: a request for material by an outside agency, by Judge John Sirica, or Archibald Cox, Leon Jaworski, or the investigating committees, or the courts, or grand jury; this is denied by Nixon; the matter is pressed and the issue joined by a subpoena or the imminence of a court test; Nixon then gives in. But his cooperation is partial, never complete. He will provide no tapes, then he gives some; he will give none again, then he gives a few more, never all—all that there are, or all that are asked. The reasons are lofty and patriotic: the security of the nation, the preservation of the presidency, executive privilege, confidentiality, the good of the country, or of the future.

The people, for their part, continue to react with a dual response to unfolding events. One is a relentless and painful change of heart. The other, equally present, is a resistance to this change, a wish against all evidence to keep things as they are. There is a Hebrew song in the Passover story of the Exodus which repeats *"dayenu"*, i.e., "that would suffice," after each of about a dozen reasons why the people of Israel should feel gratitude to God. "Had He brought us out of Egypt and not divided the sea for us, *dayenu* [that would suffice]! Had He divided the sea and not permitted us to cross on dry land, *dayenu!* Had He permitted us to cross the sea on dry land and not sustained us for forty years in the desert, *dayenu!*" And so on down the line; any gift of God would have been enough.

Here today we have the opposite situation: no act suffices; each successive one is overlooked. Act after sorry act which comes to light about the president should suffice for an appraisal and for a final, if agonizing, decision—but does not. Each act is considered—has to be considered—not enough. Strangely, each is also the opposite: too much. Singly or together, they are too much to face. Each incident is passed over, put off until the next.

Nixon appoints Archibald Cox, vows that he will give him whatever he needs for his investigation. He does not. Confrontation; the Saturday night massacre of October 1973; Cox, Richardson, Ruckelshaus go. One would think that would suffice. But non-*dayenu;* it does not. Jaworski replaces Cox. The same promise by the president, in the same sonorous voice, there will be "full cooperation." The promise is broken again. Nixon does not give Jaworski what he wants and says he needs, and what the president had said he would give. *Dayenu?* Does that suffice? No, non-*dayenu!* On to the next, and the next, and the next.

There is a crucial tape on which eighteen and a half minutes have been mysteriously obliterated. This turns out to be of a conversation on post-Watergate strategy between the president and Haldeman on June

20, 1972, three days after the break-in! The explanations given for the
"error" are changing and farcical. The posture assumed by Rose Mary
Woods to demonstrate how her "accident" occurred elicits only a sorry
disbelief. Three sets of experts finally agree: there were five or six
separate "erasures" manually made; the explanations of Nixon and Miss
Woods could not hold. Nixon finally has no further explanation; it is a
"mystery" to him. *Dayenu?* No, non-*dayenu.* Instead, perspective gets
lost. Much more interest ensues in the "how" than in the fact "that" the
tape was erased. By the time an opinion is rendered on the "how," the
"that" is forgotten, or at least dropped. It is too much, too overwhelming to pursue. Another tape of that same day, of a phone call between
Nixon and Mitchell, of similar potential importance, was not hooked
into the taping system. Other critical tapes which could also point to
Nixon's earlier involvement are also missing or do not exist.

During the trial of those involved in the break-in into the office of
Daniel Ellsberg's psychiatrist, Nixon similarly refuses subpoenas, blocks
documents, impedes the administration of justice. Nixon's income tax
problems turn out to be much more serious than they appeared when
first mentioned. Half a million dollars are owed. There are illegal contributions, a fraudulent date, tampering with records. Nixon agrees to pay,
but any errors made were "without his knowledge and without his
approval." Nixon's tax attorney disagrees and states that Mr. Nixon had
a lively interest in his returns and went over them with his advisers
"page by page." As compared with other issues, this matter is absorbed
with ease.

Nixon's actions since March 1973, when even he says he "knew," have
been a monument of obstruction. In another country this would lead to
a vote of "no confidence" and a new election. And I am referring to the
Western world, not the "underdeveloped" world. Willy Brandt resigns,
Pierre Trudeau falls, Harold Wilson replaces Edward Heath, all for
much less reason. When Brandt accepted "responsibility" for an embarrassing scandal of espionage in his midst, even though the spying was
against him and he obviously did not know about it, it automatically
included blame as well, and he tendered his resignation. Semantics
were less devious. Of course this characteristic of our governmental
structure is part of its greater stability. But it is also slower in permitting
the will of the people to be exercised, or perhaps even to develop. "The

problem," says John W. Gardner, chairman of Common Cause, "is not power as such . . . in the Presidency, in the private sector or anywhere else. The problem is power that cannot be held accountable."

But the limitations imposed by our protective Constitution are not what cause people's reactions to lag. More decisive is the nature of the psychological state. Some of the forces operative are quite "up front," in the conscious or preconscious layers of the mind. Among these, a sense of fairness, feelings of compassion, and considerations of practicality play important roles in contributing to an outcome of ambiguity and doubt. And there is simply apathy, not caring about this any more than about anything else. We also cannot ignore, perhaps in more people than we would like to think, the relative lack of discriminatory capacity to sift the complex factors necessary for adequate decision making in this moral-intellectual dilemma.

To be complete, however, there are also the unconscious irrational resistances at work which operate in the service of protection of the self. The identification which has linked Nixon and his public for decades continues to be there, even as it keeps getting weaker. "This could happen to anyone" and "everyone does it" are signatures of the peer aspect of this identificatory process.

An equally universal bond between a leader and the led stems from the early childhood father complex. From the original father of the oedipal period, feelings radiate to other authority figures in life. The outcomes of this early relationship determine many characteristics of later behavior. A president is a supreme transference figure, the only person who serves the entire populace. Love and hate, pride and disappointment, fear and confidence, a spectrum of the unresolved conflicts of life can be displaced onto such an eligible figure.

An end result of the development from child to adult, the "solution," if one can summarize such a complex aspect of life, often adds up to "Live and let live." Such an adaptation acquires strength from two separate directions, the love and fear of the father, the taboo against patricide merging with the patrophilic impulses themselves. Ambivalent feelings remain unconscious, but a workable compromise emerges. This is how the generations live on and coexist.

The same type of "solution" works toward the transference world. While rebellion and subservience alternate in the course of social history, an abnormal "obedience to authority" is the usual baseline condition which exists in an insidious and invisible form. The extent to which this reaches even under placid conditions was frighteningly demonstrated in a series of experiments by Stanley Milgram of Yale University. People were willing to hurt and injure others when given orders to do so by authorities. The subjects, not knowing that they were the subjects, were willing to administer severe shocks to others whom they believed to have heart disease when instructed to do so by the scientist in charge. The experiment showed, under controlled conditions, what we know to be true in life, in war and in peace, from the actions of Lieutenant William Calley to those of ordinary citizens. Whether in a cult or in more disguised political behavior, the voice of authority, distillate of the voices of the fathers of the past, is submitted to more often and more automatically than one is aware. The readiness to relegate authority and to act under its command is an endemic mental disease. Its deleterious effects can be relatively mild and controlled, or, in cults, can reach catastrophic proportions.

As heir to the feelings which flow toward the fathers of the country, Nixon inherits the entire gamut of attitudes which this entails. If the background is ambivalence and the foreground is compromise, the immediate action which stands out as the figure in front of both "grounds" is the instinctual urge to protect the father no matter what. When the father performs and "makes one proud," this is an easy matter. But this is not only for good times; it is also operative when he fails. It might be harder then but there could also be a tendency to rally around him even more. This can be out of love, or guilt, or in spite of his decline, out of continuing fear. They shared in his omnipotence when he was up and may be afraid to challenge it when he is down. It was the people's nightmare as well as Nixon's own from which all hoped they would awaken.

As evidence came out, it was always prevented from touching the president. The actual break-in was kept separate from Nixon and has to this day been little pursued. The cover-up was harder to ignore; if there were no tapes this would be instinctively covered as well. There are those who, even today, would limit the charges against Nixon to "the cover-up of the cover-up." This is the only activity which is overt and cannot be denied. If Nixon had only trusted the people and allowed them to believe him, which they wanted for their own sakes as well as for his, if he had spent more of his energies on this and less against his enemies, he would have received greater long-term rewards. He had much advice in this direction. But it was not like him to listen. He charted his own course through this trouble, the same man who said earlier that he had left his entire reelection campaign to others.

Nixon miscalculated all the way. He apparently had no inner choice. He was a prisoner of his own character, of his suspiciousness, his hatreds, and his resulting preference for isolation. To elicit a sincere counter-trust from the people he would have had to be frank and sincere, which by instinct he was not. To achieve this, he at one point announced "Operation Candor." In his first address under its new aegis, more contradictions emerged which could not be explained, and the "opera-tion" was abandoned.

Perhaps somewhere along the line Nixon would have pulled out if he could. Could it be that he was in it so deeply as to be unable to retract, so that his desperate cover-up might indeed have been necessary? Somehow a rational falsehood might give one a more secure feeling about the president than the present irrational and unconvincing truth. "My God, I'm not that stupid," Nixon told a group of congressmen on a cruise on his presidential yacht, when they asked him frankly about his role in the Watergate break-in. No, not stupid; something else was seriously wrong. It was his zeal which was his doom, the same zeal he attributes to his staff and now blames for his present plight. The ferocity of his ambition, the malignancy of his quest for power, and a specific type of opportunism which permitted these to go unchecked led him into the web in which he finds himself today.

Sometimes neuroses proliferate until they engulf the subject who harbors them. A person who is panphobic may reach a point where he cannot leave the house or even one particular "safe" room. In a compa-rable manner, Nixon has become increasingly immobilized by his state-ments and tricks. No one act has as yet been momentous enough sum-marily to dislodge him from office, such as happened to Agnew for perhaps a lesser aggregate of infringements against the law. But consid-ering them all together, Elliott Richardson feels that "the case is close" as to whether Richard Nixon has engaged in criminal conduct: "I don't think that the evidence is sufficient in any given situation—milk, I.T.T., cover-up of Watergate—to directly implicate the President. But the cumulative pattern of these things surrounding the President, in each case involving somebody next to him in responsibility, creates a really troublesome question."

There is a method of treatment for anxiety known as "flooding" in which the patient is deliberately exposed to his phobic object to the maximal limit which he can endure. By "flooding" him with anxiety, it is hoped that he will be conditioned against the particular danger which he fears. The treatment—a sort of psychological shock therapy—is practiced by some, I do not believe many, psychiatrists. Not only its therapeutic effects but its ethical base are questionable.

The *New Yorker,* which has been very incisive and straight-talking in all things Watergate, has recently pointed out, without naming it, the relationship between current events and the philosophy behind this particular type of conditioning. In the July 1, 1974, issue, its "Talk of the Town" says: "Now the White House has hit upon still another unheard-of tactic in the President's defense strategy. It is to beat the public senseless with more news of Presidential wrong-doing than it can endure. . . . Operation Candor," the *New Yorker* goes on, "had given way to Operation Anesthesia. . . . Revelations that were once damaging serve only to promote the supposed public unconsciousness on which the White House is now relying as the President's best protection. . . . What stands between the President and impeachment is not a scarcity of evidence but a mountainous superfluity of it . . . Once, the bombshells harmed the President's cause," says the magazine, "For the moment it seems that the more wrong he does, the safer he becomes."

The Phenomenon of Pseudo-Stupidity

All who touched Nixon came out tainted. From the government's own early investigation, Assistant Attorney General Henry E. Petersen emerged a broken man: "I am not a whore. I walked through a minefield and came out clean." Another man sacrificed; another defense on a par with the president's "I am not a crook." At a later hearing, Petersen shouted at Senator Ervin, "Do us justice, will you? . . . you have to give us a break. . . . I don't want to sound corny, but I wanted to believe in the President of the United States. I wanted him to come out vigorously." Caught in the same conflict as all the others, Petersen's harshest words were for McCord, whose actions had brought them all to their present plight. "He's the biggest phony of the bunch," Petersen said. "All he did was sit around and see if the case could be fixed. And when it couldn't, he came in crying like a baby."

During the Justice Department Watergate investigation of which Petersen was in charge, Petersen had been approached by Nixon about becoming the director of the FBI! Just prior to that, United States District Judge Matt Byrne, while presiding over the sister case of the *Pentagon Papers* trial in Los Angeles, had been approached for the same position by Ehrlichman and then by Nixon!

By now thirty-one persons have been convicted or have pleaded guilty to Watergate-related crimes, all high administration officials. Many more await their turn. Still others, outside the administration, their characters already blemished, are waiting for the outcomes of various investigations. George Meany feels that Nixon has demeaned an entire honorable profession, the plumbers of America. Not to mention what has happened to the field of politics. Or, more specifically, to the Republican party.

The Watergate defendants who pleaded and, one hopes, felt guilty strike people as more sympathetic figures than those who did not. Magruder, who suffered for his wife and four children as well as himself, was one of those. "I know what I've done," he said. He found it impossible to face the confusion in the eyes of his four children and the heartbreak in the eyes of his wife. He had lost his "ethical compass" somewhere between his ambitions and ideals. Sentenced to a minimum of ten months in prison, Magruder stated, "We were completely wrong. We had private morality but not a sense of public morality. Instead of applying our private morality to public affairs, we accepted the President's standards of political behavior, and the results were tragic for him and for us." There is much to be learned, and he is "confident this country will survive its Watergate and its Jeb Magruders. I don't intend to be destroyed by this experience. I will still have a long life ahead of me, and I think it can be a good life for me and my family."

Donald Segretti also recanted: "I was just a political pawn to be manipulated. . . . With a little luck, I can now start to lead a normal existence." But there was something slightly different about his hind-thoughts from those of Magruder. His came after the tapes revealed how disparagingly he had been talked about at the top level: "He [Segretti] was such a dumb figure," said the president of the United States, "I don't see how our boys could have gone for him." It was after that wound to his narcissism that Segretti spoke out. About his own involvement, "Even now, after all the screaming and yelling, my honest assessment is that my activities amounted to a feather in a hurricane." The sequence of his statements did not sit well with the public. Some objected to his "smugness," did not feel he had a right to it, and admonished him "to wipe that baby smile off his face." He himself feels that "after the catharsis that will and must come, our system will be cleaner, our political leaders . . . will have higher morals, and all of us will have gone through a bone-grinding graduate course in civics." And, while not wishing to put blame on anyone, "I still have a good feeling that the buck stops at the highest level. That is where the responsibility lies, and that is who should accept the heat for not making a more determined effort to nip this whole affair in the bud."

The arrogance which emanates from Ehrlichman in his public appearances results in a stiff reception. There have been some articles describing him as more human privately. But the fact that these articles were considered necessary confirms that his public impression is the opposite. Haldeman, although as adamant in proclaiming his innocence, comes across as less defiant and to that extent fares better with the public. The vulnerability of Martha Mitchell, who has undergone an interesting political and public metamorphosis, helps the image of her stolid and unflappable husband. Considered psychotic at first, she said things which people did not wish to hear. As more and more of what she said turns out to be true, and since she has paid the price of her marriage and reputation, she is emerging as a lovable and independent maverick. Whatever her mental state, it is clear that emotional disturbance does not per se determine the veracity of what a person says. Martha's character softens the image of her stern and forbidding husband, who himself admits nothing. People wish they can believe him, but do not feel that they can.

People wish to believe, if possible. They will also excuse honest mistakes sincerely acknowledged. The instinctive response is to judge others as people would wish to be judged themselves; not because of a moral commandment, but more because it is self-protective. Howard Hunt, emerging from prison appearing sick and pitiful, elicited sympathy. Gordon Liddy, who remains strong and silent, does not elicit an empathic response.

Grown men wept. Interestingly, this happened more with those who escaped punishment than those who received it. Those who go off to serve prison sentences usually go off smiling, almost proudly, with a certain calm. In a sense they are heroes. Punishment neutralizes the guilt, makes for equilibrium. People also feel that to some extent these men are paying for the actions of the more powerful who have been protected. Others who are "let off" cannot discharge their tension and may find escape in tears. Former Attorney General Richard G. Kleindienst, the first attorney general in history to be convicted of a crime, wept openly as he received a suspended one-month jail term in lieu of being tried for perjury. Kleindienst broke down as he heard Chief United States District Judge George L. Hart, Jr., describe him as a man of "the highest integrity . . . who has been and still is universally respected and admired." Kleindienst's failure to testify fully was seen as an act of self-sacrifice to protect Mr. Nixon. Maurice Stans, upon his acquittal, sobbed in the arms of friends and family. John Mitchell, on the other hand, also acquitted but with another trial ahead, walked off stolidly to await his next rendezvous with justice. So far he thinks that the American system is fair and that justice wins out in the end.

The group compliance described here might be seen as a mass stupidity. It was a stupidity, however, born of the group process, an example of what psychologist Irving Janis of Yale has called "group-think." Actually, it is a pseudo-stupidity. Many years ago the child psychoanalyst Margaret Mahler observed that groups and children have much in common; both use primitive mechanisms. Mahler described a purposeful form of "pseudo-imbecility" seen in childhood: because of it, certain children, with the unconscious consent of the parents, are able to don "a magic cap of invisibility"; they are overlooked by adults and at the same time observe and share their parents' otherwise forbidden sexual secrets. If the child assumes a relative stupidity, control by the parent and repression by the child are both rendered unnecessary. Groups also make use of such infantile and childhood processes, unchecked by the individual adult control apparatus. Here, a person's motives to protect himself by sharing and overlooking immoral behavior become invisible behind a similar cloak of pseudo-imbecility. The individual saw nothing, heard nothing, and had to react to nothing.

This aspect of group behavior has always worked in Nixon's favor. Groups react irrationally perhaps more than they do rationally; clarity and logic cannot be automatically expected from the spontaneous reactions of a group. The irrational, which is such a large factor in group decisions, needs to be taken fully into account.

However, it would be incomplete to limit consideration solely to the processes of repression and distortion in the service of internal need. An opposite reaction can be taking place simultaneously. The human ego in its drive for mastery, in the performance of its central function of bringing about an effective stance toward reality, also needs and demands clarity rather than obscurity in assessing the external world. As much as the ego needs to distort to maintain internal equilibrium, and as ingenuous as are the mechanisms of defense at its disposal to achieve this, so does it also have a stake in seeing the world clearly, exactly as it is. Both perceptual modes are necessary for survival, and both have built-in biological mechanisms to achieve their goals.

Emotionally meaningful events are experienced, as they occur, in two ways: the way they are, or approximately so, and the way one wants to see them, with personal distortions added. Both types of perceptual intake may occur in one fused compromise formation, with scenes partially accurate and partially distorted; or they may alternate, or one may be a conscious perception while the other is relegated to the unconscious. Both reactions, of objective observation and of subjective distortion, result in residuals which are retained as memories at different levels of consciousness. Aspects of both may be relegated to the unconscious, where they come to reside side by side. There are no contradictions in the unconscious; opposites exist together in harmony. Now it may be the time for one to come forth, but soon or at another time it will be time for the other.

Recently it took several weeks of analysis for a patient of mine to discover the various layers of perceptions and reactions which had occurred during a meeting he had attended. The atmosphere in the group was one of embarrassed fear under the sway of a witty and somewhat sadistic leader. The reactions of the patient which first emerged were those which represented his compliance to the group under the influence of the atmosphere which existed at the time. Those which came out later, more boldly each day, had originally been repressed but had nevertheless occurred at the time and had found a place within his unconscious. These were his own personal observations, free from the influence of the group. During the meeting his dissent from the group consensus had to be submerged, not only suppressed (more or less consciously or preconsciously) but also repressed (not even consciously perceived). But the feelings were there, kept in suspension. Only later, in a safer atmosphere, after the fear of acknowledging them had been removed, could they be recognized and expressed. His individuality could then assert itself. This small but important example is the sort that happens every day. Its commonness gives it significance.

The nature and intensity of our recent national history has led to a similar dual type of psychic recording. Even where the mechanisms of distortion and denial seemed most prominent, more accurate perceptions were simultaneously registered. These perceptions, moreover, were initially accompanied by appropriate emotions as well as superego appraisals. In simpler terms, there was an appreciation, however fleeting, of the full significance of the facts taken in. The more accurate perceptions were then relegated to the unconscious where they remained in attenuated form but potentially capable of being fully aroused and fully acknowledged later under favorable circumstances.

People "know" more than they know they know. The concept of the unconscious was introduced almost a century ago. Whereas classically this has meant that man is guided by more unknown forces than he realizes, I would have us look at what is equally true. Man also "knows" *more* about what he is doing than he thinks or admits he knows. Cognition is as important in the unconscious as are emotions or affects. What I said previously about unconscious emotions applies to unconscious knowledge as well. What results is an apparent contradiction. The fact that we are guided more than we know by the unknown reduces our responsibility for what we do. The fact that we act more from what we know than we let ourselves know we know, leads to an increase rather than a decrease of responsibility. Both are true and are circular. We know more, as well as less, than we think we know. I will desist from pursuing the large philosophical, moral, and legal issues to which this leads, but will move on to some further empirical data.

Unconscious knowing affects us as individuals and as individuals in groups. We read every day of people who turn their backs on the commission of a crime. On the morning that I am writing this, the *Los Angeles Times* reports the case of a woman bicycling through a crowded park in Chicago, blood gushing from her head, in close pursuit of a man who had just whipped her with a chain. To her shrieks of "Help, call the police!" joggers, bicyclists, and pedestrians stared, then continued about their business. Did they "know"? They "knew" for a moment, then could probably honestly say they did not; their minds did the desired tricks, their knowledge was pushed into the unconscious. But there, I would emphasize, they continued to "know."

The same phenomenon takes place with groups and nations. A populace which did not "know" during a period of trauma turns out to have known all the time. During the fifties, the American people went along, or at least seemed on the surface to go along, with the atmosphere provided by Joseph McCarthy. It is doubtful that what took place could have occurred unless such a mass hysteria had taken hold and had involved the largest part of the population. A few years later, it did not take much convincing or education to assess the nightmarish McCarthy period accurately. The people had "known" all along. The same principle applies when a subject under hypnosis follows the order of the hypnotist but nevertheless retains his own perceptions and the capacity to distinguish right from wrong.

In normal times abnormal impulses or perceptions are distorted, but in abnormal times the more normal and objective mental elements are subjected to repression and distortion—to conform to the abnormal mores of the times. Did the people of Germany not "know" while denying what they saw? Do people not "know" the horrors and immoralities of war as they applaud and march? In times of mass hysteria or panic, objective observations are made but are relegated to the unconscious. They will be available later during more normal times.

During the analysis of an individual, a "new" interpretation which seems to be counter to the patient's lifetime method of thinking is often not really new, but the unearthing of an old observation or a buried attitude or way of thinking of his own. Neurophysiologists as well as psychoanalysts appreciate the fact that the number of neurons in the human brain, astronomical in number, is matched only by the number of memories which reside in the human mind.

Two factors have determined the course of the reactions to Watergate. Quantitatively, there has been a matter of dosage; an increase in the weight of insults and the number of offenses made continuing distortion and minimization less and less possible. Such increases took place in two different ways, by gradual increments or sudden solitary events, "cumulative trauma" versus "shock trauma" which is periodically superimposed. Qualitatively, what determined whether there would be sympathetic identification or a turning away from their harassed leader was the difference between acceptable encroachments on integrity on the one hand and crime on the other. As long as the acts seemed primarily to deal with integrity, empathy prevailed. To the extent, however, that the offending actions crossed over into crime, the people separated themselves from the actors.

"I will tell the whole story of Watergate," Nixon stated on more than one occasion when the pressure reached a minipeak (acknowledging that he had never done this before). But such statements were followed by a replay of the previous sequence, the familiar stalling, obstruction, and the build up of new evidence. What was being revealed daily led increasingly to one conclusion: wrongdoing, of a degree and a nature which could not continue but required condemnation. The gap between what the people were seeing and what they would permit, even of themselves, was coming closer and closer to being unbridgeable.

The Transcripts

On April 29, 1974, Mr. Nixon, sitting in front of the television cameras, pointed with a wave of his hand and his characteristic twisting gesture to a pile of loose-leaf books against a wall on his left. "There," he said, "are transcripts of those forty-two tapes which I have had made. There are 1300 pages of them. I am turning these over to the Special Prosecutor and to the House Judiciary Committee. More than that, I have also decided that these should be available to the American public." After deep soul-searching, and much hard work to edit these tapes so that they could be read without hurting the country, Nixon was now offering them in their entirety to the American public to enable them to be fully informed. There was no limit to how far he would go to see justice done.

A few weeks earlier Nixon had said of the contents of this series of tapes that there was evidence in them which would clearly show his innocence. So convincing was this that both Senator Hugh Scott, Jr., and Vice-President Gerald Ford vouched for the correctness of this statement, and confirmed that there was evidence in the tapes which would exonerate the president. Later, both men admitted that they had not seen this evidence directly. Just before the transcripts were made public, Nixon amended his statement somewhat: the tapes could conceivably be interpreted differently by different people, and some would no doubt even criticize.

The defense mechanism of predicting the onslaught in advance and hoping in this way to mitigate its force proved to be totally ineffective. The effect was what one reporter called a seismic shock across the nation; a new word, "transcripts," sprang to everyone's lips.

Here was Nixon when he was not being watched or judged. This was a person sitting alone in the bathroom, or musing to himself, or taking a shave and thinking out loud. What amazes a psychoanalyst as he confronts this behavior is that Nixon would talk so openly, knowing, as only he did, that the tapes were running! This has a cognitive more than an affective connotation. What it says about his judgment, the base for his intellectual decision making, is frightening to contemplate in a president. It also, however, throws light on the nature of his relationships with others. So sure was he of his aides and staff, so certain that they were tied inextricably to him, with no will or judgment left of their own, that he was indeed able to talk as if alone. This does not speak so much for his trust in them, for his faith in other human beings, as for the complete submission and self-obliteration which he expected and believed he had. And which, for the most part, he did have.

What emerged from this multisided new view was still another Nixon in the ever-changing series. Perhaps this was "the real Nixon," the Nixon behind all the others. This Nixon had no television makeup, showed no studied gestures, no forced artificial smile, no skillful and "sincere" debater's stance. An interesting article was written in this connection by one of the president's speechwriters which made the very opposite point: that the tapes distort the real Nixon. Asking that we achieve a better perspective, Raymond K. Price, Jr., special consultant to the president, pointed out that the transcripts represent only thirty-three out of Nixon's forty-six thousand hours in office. Moreover, Mr. Price felt, these were very atypical hours; the private Nixon, as Price has known him closely for seven years, was a man intensely serious about matters of substance, with his eyes set on high goals and on overcoming the obstacles to achieving them. This could be so. Yet unfortunately this private look presented the very opposite, which meant more in conveying the import of the transcripts than the number of hours the words consumed.

What the people saw and heard were not vision, ideals, a long-range view, a leader and statesman at work, but pettiness, craftiness, immediate goals only. And meanness and gossip; their president was disloyal to those who were loyal to him, dismissing and derogating them with cruel banter. To the extent that Nixon did continue to protect some of his close associates, Haldeman and Ehrlichman and Mitchell—however guilty people thought them to be—he did, I believe, command some unconscious respect.

It was as though the people had been allowed into the Nixon bedroom and saw and heard what went on there. If people's deference to Nixon had been based on unconscious patrophilia and a reluctance to indict him because of their fear of patricide, their sudden letdown at this new behavioral juncture was from having caught the father red-handed. A widespread emotional experience in childhood is the deidealization of the parents which takes place when the child discovers the facts of sexuality and that his parents do it too. Evidence to that effect suddenly come upon, often seen in the analysis of an individual, marks the end of innocence, the beginning of cynicism, and a deep change of heart. This theme was touched on in *Death of a Saleman*, when the sons find their father, Willy Loman, in a hotel room with another woman.

This event is the discovery of the father's id and, to the child, its frightening uncontrollability. The present discoveries about Nixon were of the father's weak superego, of the imperfections in his control which made such behavior possible. An interesting national memory in the same connection appeared in an article by a reporter who recalled early Hollywood and the famous Fatty Arbuckle. Here people got a glimpse of the difference between the public and the private man, between the screen image and reality. The jovial fat man in the movies who specialized in custard pie humor became involved in a messy sex scandal in 1921. Suddenly the real Fatty Arbuckle was no longer the image the public knew and loved but a sexual criminal; his career was ruined. What the Fatty Arbuckle case did to the acting profession, Watergate has done to politics; and the way back will be the same.

This linkage in the unconscious I have pointed to has nothing to do with the specific life of Richard M. Nixon, the person. In fact it is worth noting that the public image of Mr. Nixon as a husband, father, and family man is an impeccable one, and has remained probably his strongest asset. Unlike other presidents and political leaders, this aspect of the president's life has been unblemished and beyond public intrusion or gossip. It seems as if those who are known to be fallible in this area but who maintain ethical standards in general are granted their indiscretions, while Nixon's political conduct, clean personally but dirty in general, is a less tolerable combination to the public conscience. There are some interesting relationships to ponder here. Perhaps this is related to the fact that children do come to excuse the father for his central betrayal as long as he is decent otherwise. It is not as good an outcome the other way around, if the father proved to be celibate or asexual, but otherwise unreliable and untrustworthy in life.

With the transcripts Nixon hit bottom. Criticism was now general and more and more bipartisan. Sen. Hugh Scott, Jr., called the contents of the transcripts a "shabby, immoral and disgusting performance," and felt that they revealed a moral breakdown in the nation's highest office. Attorney General William B. Saxbe, who not long before had himself been appointed by the president, declared Watergate "the greatest cloud in our history" and warned that the nation might not be able to surmount another scandal of such dimensions.

A swell of Republican legislators, administrative leaders, and policy makers called more and more openly for the president's resignation. House G.O.P. Leader John J. Rhodes of Arizona told reporters that "a resignation would probably be beneficial," although "I'm not recommending it." Rep. John B. Anderson of Illinois, chairman of the House G.O.P. Conference, the party's caucus machinery, felt it would be best if the president quit and warned that if he did not leave voluntarily, he would be impeached. Senator James Buckley of New York, while feeling that the president was innocent, asked for his resignation. Senator Marlow W. Cook, Republican of Kentucky, and Rep. Barber B. Conable, Jr., Republican of New York, chairman of the House G.O.P. Policy Committee, felt that the president had to consider resignation. The moral tone of the president as revealed in his inner circle stood starkly exposed, making it difficult for Republicans to continue to defend him.

"Sordid," "squalid," and "moral turpitude" were words widely used. The conservative *Chicago Tribune,* calling for President Nixon's resignation, stated: "We have seen the private man and we are appalled. . . . He is humorless to the point of being inhumane. He is devious. He is vacillating. He is profane. He is willing to be led. He displays dismaying gaps in knowledge. He is suspicious of his staff. His loyalty is minimal. . . ." Newspapers, magazines, media from liberal to conservative across the country joined the call.

Others, while forced to admit the same facts, were more equivocal in their conclusions. Gerald Ford, while he also disapproved of the "tone" of the conversations, after reading the edited transcripts "in their entirety" was "convinced . . . that the President is not guilty of an impeachable offense." This was a bit different from his sweeping pronouncement just before the transcripts were made public, that the president was "totally innocent" and "completely exonerated" by the contents of the transcripts. Republican chairman George Bush, admittedly concerned about the "grubby" nature of the transcripts, nevertheless warned against an overreaction to Watergate. And three Republican members of the House Judiciary Committee, Reps. Charles W. Wiggins of California, David W. Dennis of Indiana, and Henry P. Smith III of New York, while feeling, as stated by Wiggins, that "in all honesty there is information on that tape [of March 21] that might tend to incriminate the President," felt that only the matter of the "hush money" could be a turnaround point in his guilt.

Mr. Nixon's closest friends and supporters, and his special appointees, were forced to admit the new turn of events. Anne Armstrong, chief women's presidential counselor, expressed grave concern. Evangelist Billy Graham found the transcripts "a profoundly disturbing and disappointing experience," and he "could not but deplore the moral tone. . . . We have lost our moral compass. We must get it back. . . . What comes through in these tapes is not the man I have known for many years"; however, Mr. Nixon remains "my friend, and I have no intention of forsaking him." For every such statement another countering one was desperately provided. Dr. John J. McLaughlin, a Jesuit priest on the White House staff, speaking at a White House news briefing, declared that charges of immorality stemming from the transcripts are "erroneous, unjust and contain elements of hypocrisy. . . . These profanities [in the tapes and transcripts] have no moral meaning." They are a "form of emotional drainage, a form of therapy . . . [which is] good,valid, sound. [They contain] a certain disarming function" to help Mr. Nixon search for the truth. Expletives, he added, are healthy! Here again a partial truth is slipped in. Under certain conditions this would have validity. But in this context it is a pathetic defense.

Those associated with the president in affiliation or principle had to disengage themselves from him idealistically if they were to survive politically. "Our candidates are going to have to disassociate as much as possible from the President and take their chances," said Robert D. Grant, Saginaw County Republican chairman, as Republican candidates separated themselves from the president in their bid for office. Their Republican election headquarters displayed portraits of Lincoln, Eisenhower, and Vice-President Ford, but not of Mr. Nixon.

From Nixon's side came a few feeble attempts at explanation, but soon even these ceased; it was as if there was nothing more to be said. But Nixon's actions continued. After the transcripts had been provided as a compromise for the forty-two tapes which had not been furnished, other tapes and material subpoenaed by Special Prosecutor Leon Jaworski were again withheld by the president, tapes containing 64 conversations and 131 documents relating to Watergate, I.T.T., and the milk fund inquiry.

Like the previous statements of Ronald Ziegler's, the pronouncements of Nixon's lawyers on his behalf to the courts and the investigating committees were equally desperate, too much for rational men to accept. Facing another refusal to honor a subpoena from Jaworski, James B. St. Clair, chief counsel to the president, used the same untenable and tired argument which had been the prelude to the firing of Jaworski's predecessor, Archibald Cox. Since the special prosecutor belongs to the Executive Branch, because he works out of the Justice Department, he has no right to subpoena his employer, the president. "It is the President's contention," St. Clair said, "that he has ultimate authority to determine when to prosecute, whom to prosecute, and with what evidence to prosecute." "This," replied Jaworski, "makes a farce" of his responsibilities; while to Judge Sirica the argument "is a nullity." While presenting arguments in Nixon's defense, J. Fred Buzhardt, Jr., special counsel to the president, who had supervised the transcripts of the White House tapes, suffered a coronary occlusion.

Nixon's refusal to surrender this group of tapes elevated the case to the next echelon. Another first in the history of our country: the Supreme Court of the United States will hear a case against its president. It is also uncertain whether or not the president will comply with their decision. He had at one time said that he would abide by a "definitive" decision of the Supreme Court, but later had indicated he might not comply—and then there was silence. The question of whether the president would obey a Supreme Court order is "too speculative" to answer now, White House officials said. Many lawyers and law professors are convinced that the president has deliberately undertaken psychological warfare against the Supreme Court, that this is his way of exerting pressure. The belief of the White House staff is that uncertainty works to his advantage. It is a question of strategy, not a cooperative search for legal truth.

The case goes forward; arguments are presented. Calling on the Supreme Court to disregard "the passions of the moment," Nixon's attorneys warned that a decision by the Supreme Court ordering him to surrender the tapes could alter forever "the complex and sensitive balance of our Constitutional structure. . . . This would nullify the separation of powers and the coequality of the executive. . . . the Presidency will survive . . . [but] it will be different from the office contemplated by the framers and occupied by Presidents from George Washington through today." In a responding brief, Jaworski assured the justices, "Our Constitutional system has shown itself to be remarkably

resilient. Our country has endured through periods of great crisis."
President Nixon's claim of absolute immunity from orders of the judiciary, Jaworski went on to warn, would put him "beyond the reach of
the law, partaking at least in . . . the royal immunities associated with
a king." "The Imperial Presidency" had become more literal than ever
before. Going even higher: "The President is not God," stated Chester-
field Smith, president of the American Bar Association. "The President
has no Constitutional right to defy an order of the Supreme Court. He
must let sunshine go into the inner Oval Office."

Old charges were confirmed. New ones emerged. Jaworski claims to
have substantial evidence that the White House tried to compel the
Internal Revenue Service to harass and intimidate Nixon's political
enemies. Previously denied by the White House (it is impressive how
often the building is blamed or talked about rather than its occupant!
This provided a good column for Art Buchwald), witnesses were now
available to confirm this fact. If true, it would be one of the most serious
of the Watergate crimes. In August and September 1972, shortly before
the presidential election, Democratic National Chairman Lawrence F.
O'Brien was a special target of administration efforts to "abuse and
politicalize" the IRS. In addition, a list of "enemies" was presented to
this agency with the direction that they be audited or otherwise
harassed.

Not to mention the use of the CIA, the FBI, the Federal Communications Commission, and even of congressional committees for smear
purposes. The case had moved from individual to institutional corruption. In 1971, it is revealed in a White House memorandum from Colson
to Ehrlichman, Colson tried unsuccessfully to have the chairman of the
House Internal Security Committee, formerly the House Committee on
Un-American Activities, conduct hearings of his committee at which
derogatory material against Daniel Ellsberg, obtained by E. Howard
Hunt, Jr., in a White House "plumbers" operation, would be allowed to
surface. The chairman of the committee, Rep. Richard H. Ichord, Democrat of Missouri, refused. At about the same time, it now comes out
quietly and unobtrusively, the office of the psychoanalyst of Mrs. Daniel
Ellsberg was broken into in New York, less than three months after the
break-in into the office of Daniel Ellsberg's psychoanalyst in Beverly

Hills. Further, it is revealed, the day after the *New York Times* began publication of the *Pentagon Papers,* the FBI had come to the New York doctor's office to question him about his patient Mrs. Ellsberg and had been turned away.

Looking back at Nixon's 1972 campaign, a staff report of the Senate Watergate committee concluded that violations had "spanned the entire spectrum of corrupt campaign financing" and that some contributions were tinged with extortion and bribery. There was evidence of illegal corporate contributions, huge cash contributions that were "legal and illegal," and unlawful donations by foreigners. The actual legal nature of the president's conduct was elusive and difficult to pin down. While some members of the committee struggled to find a concrete impeachable offense, Senator Lowell Weicker contended that Nixon and his aides had violated the law and generally accepted limits of ethical conduct more than one hundred times, abusing every one of the Constitution's principal provisions. "Several years ago many Americans were willing to silently tolerate illegal government activity against militants, terrorists, or subversives as an expeditious way to circumvent the precise processes of our justice system," Weicker said. "Though quick, it also proved to be only a short step to using such illegal tactics against any dissenting Americans. The result was that we almost lost America. Not to subversives, terrorists, or extremists of the streets but to subversives, terrorists, and extremists of the White House."

The current edited transcripts, which Nixon said would demonstrate once and for all his total lack of involvement, were found to contain such inaccuracies as to make imperative a need for the original tapes themselves. Chairman Rodino of the House Judiciary Committee, to whom the transcripts had been given, stated that they include "misstatements, omission of words, misattributions, additions, inaudibles, and a category we can't define." Persons analyzing the edited transcripts have noted that more phrases were marked "inaudible" when the president was speaking than when his aides were talking. This was attributed by J. Fred Buzhardt to the fact that the president had a relatively deep voice with frequent variations.

One crucial conversation between Nixon and John Dean on March 17, 1973, which might have shown that Nixon knew about Watergate before he said he did, was omitted from the transcripts altogether. In another deleted statement, Nixon was telling Mitchell to "stonewall it, contain it, take the fifth, protect your men. Our goal is containment." John Doar, special counsel to the committee, said that in addition to the deletions, in some instances entire paragraphs were added to the transcripts by the White House. The minority counsel, Albert E. Jenner, Jr., agreed completely with Doar and had "agonized" with him for several days over the inadequacies of the transcripts. But to these concerns Nixon's attorney James St. Clair wrote to Rodino that any suggestion by Doar that these transcripts were not reliable was "gratuitous in the extreme, since he had no basis for making such a statement."

Nixon's emerging strategy to turn the House Judiciary Committee's impeachment inquiry into an adversary proceeding, which would permit his attorneys to cross-examine and call their own witnesses, was denounced by Rep. Walter Flowers, Democrat of Alabama, a conservative member of the committee who had been considered a possible supporter of Mr. Nixon. Representative Flowers accused the president of "playing games with our Constitution, the Congress, the Presidency, and the American people." Here, however, partisanship won out. House Minority Leader Rhodes, Republican of Arizona, backed the plan. In the concurrent Ehrlichman trial, Nixon's refusal to permit access to data led United States District Judge Gerhard A. Gesell to threaten to hold him in contempt. Citing Nixon's broken commitment, the judge stated angrily that Nixon's behavior is "offensive to all our concepts of justice . . . and borders on obstruction."

After Maurice Stans and John Mitchell were acquitted of the first charges against them, the president barred Stans from releasing records which had been subpoenaed to determine whether ambassadorships and other federal jobs had been exchanged for political contributions. Upon Nixon's instruction to Stans, transmitted by Nixon's counsel Buzhardt, Stans took the fifth amendment on this issue. Also brought to light at that time was an "S" list, allegedly maintained by Stans, of persons who refused to contribute financially to the president's reelection campaign. Attorney General William Saxbe stated that Nixon had acted improperly when he disclosed confidential Watergate grand jury information to Haldeman and Ehrlichman who were then under investigation in the case. A former Haldeman aide, Lawrence M. Higby, testified that Nixon spoke of a secret defense fund which could be available to protect Haldeman and Ehrlichman in their Watergate cover-up trials. The actual execution of these plans was denied by "the White House" but not the discussion of the possibility. Later, however, Haldeman, who had consistently proclaimed both his and the president's innocence and that further testimony would vindicate them, indicated now that he would invoke the fifth amendment if called to testify in the impeachment inquiry by the House Judiciary Committee.

There were hints, then confirmations of ethnic slurs, carelessly and naturally flowing from the mouth of the president. The best that could be done was to deny their intention or at least their significance. Nixon's defenders could also of course point to his appointments of Jewish and Italian individuals to the highest posts, including the secretary of state. These were also true. Contradictions and contrasts abounded. Nixon was a practical as well as an ordinary man.

People cannot attend to a long painful story, cannot keep the whole perspective in mind. "Screen memories" are formed throughout life, in which certain events are remembered in vivid detail in order to cover others behind them which can then be forgotten. A "screen memory" is emphasized behind which a "traumatic memory" is repressed. A person may remember a room very vividly in order not to remember what happened inside it. Not only does a screen block access to what lies behind it, it also focuses all available attention on itself, draining it away from everything else. The result is a loss of total perspective, of the long preceding backgrounds of events.

Such a defensive posture has been much in evidence throughout the years of Watergate, where commonly every new or dramatic uncovering took the place of all that had gone before. When the existence of the tapes became known, testimony of mere witnesses was lost sight of, hardly pursued. And when a particular tape or set of tapes was subpoenaed, it became the all-important one, obliterating other tapes which preceded it or what was not on tape at all. For a time it was the tape of March 21 upon which all eyes were riveted and upon which everything seemed to hinge. And just as the tapes, when their existence became known, took the place of the whole of Watergate, so now did the transcripts, which were only a small part of them, replace the whole of the tapes in the people's interest.

Not only did the transcripts supersede the tapes, but after the transcripts themselves were absorbed and integrated, two or three phrases were isolated and emphasized over the rest. It seemed as though the entire Nixon case and the future of the administration depended solely on the interpretation of these few crucial phrases. What did Nixon mean by "that's for sure" or by the phrase "then get it"? Did he mean "get the hush money" or "get the signal" to Hunt? Did he mean "that's for sure, he would get it," or did he mean "that's for sure, they certainly wanted the money"? To three Republicans on the House Judiciary Committee, Charles Wiggins, David Dennis, and Henry Smith III, as late as during the Memorial Day recess of the committee the only evidence which could directly incriminate the president in the Watergate cover-up depended on the correct interpretation of these phrases.

The mechanism of screening is used unconsciously by all individuals in the service of self-defense. During these unprecedented times, in addition to this use by the general population, the same mechanism has been made use of in a more devious way, forced by some upon others with conscious intent for the same purpose of self-defense. The White House (I too find myself using this distancing euphemism, referring to the building instead of its occupants) has at this juncture complained about and tried to focus attention on "leaks." Give the people a screen, it is intuitively felt, and those who are looking for one will use it.

It seems true that there have been some premature escapes of information in the administrative arms investigating Nixon. And it is certainly true that it is not correct to do so. But the purpose of this new deflection is a patent one, to introduce a false scent and draw the pursuit as far away as possible from the impeachment proceedings and the monumental task of the House Judiciary Committee.

It is ironic, as depicted in a recent cartoon: an administration which has caused a flood complaining about someone who has caused a leak. The fact is that leaking information has been second nature to the administration, and Nixon for many years has been a skilled practitioner in leaking news for his own advantage. The transcripts showed the president suggesting a leak of "IRS stuff" to discredit political op-

ponents and leaks of testimony before a grand jury. A conversation
with Haldeman revealed the president's predilection: "We could easily do that," says the president to Haldeman, "Leak out certain stuff.
We could pretty much control that." And in handwritten notes of conversations between the president and Ehrlichman, Nixon is quoted by
Ehrlichman as saying that damaging information on Daniel Ellsberg
must be leaked to the press, "Leak stuff out. . . . that is the way we
win." And by way of confirmation, Nixon advised Ehrlichman to read
the Alger Hiss chapter in his book *Six Crises,* observing, "It was won
in the press."

But Nixon, his lawyers and staff are now irate about the leaks which
they claim emanate from the House Judiciary Committee. These are
made equivalent to and given greater claim to outrage than the Watergate affair for which the impeachment proceedings were instituted. It
is like someone caught in a murder and complaining that his captors
scratched him in the process. Peter Rodino, who in his opening instructions initiating the investigation, as well as in the manner in which he
has carried it forth thus far, introduced a note of seriousness and impar-
tiality which has received widespread respect, reacted as though stung
by the sharp accusations. Confronted by charges not only of leaks but
of foot dragging, Rodino showed a greater degree of embarrassment
than Nixon did to all of Watergate, or than was outwardly apparent in
the array of witnesses who pleaded guilty to immoral acts. A conscience
ready and available shows. Motivated to keep the committee image
untarnished, Rodino scheduled an unusual Friday session, which was
out of the committee's regular routine, to conclude presentation of
documentary evidence in its impeachment inquiry.

It has been pointed out that leaks of information have at times been
to the public's advantage, even if against the wishes and to the embarrassment of their leaders. The *Pentagon Papers,* the biggest leak of all,
alarmed the administration because it was a leak of the truth. Leaks
have been used over the years from George Washington on, by politicians of every persuasion and from every party, sometimes for good
causes, sometimes for bad. Half facetiously, James Reston of the *New
York Times* observed recently that one of the biggest leakers in recent
history has been Alexander Solzhenitsyn.

A sudden demand comes from Nixon's corner to open the doors to the impeachment inquiry, to counter the committee's "prejudice" and to ensure an impartial inquiry. The man who for years has jealously guarded confidentiality, secret negotiations, national security, executive privilege, and the intense right to operate in private, now insists that the impeachment hearings by the House Judiciary Committee be open to the public. Suddenly he is against secret sessions; a completely open policy can serve the public best. What is "right" never seems to be what primarily motivates Nixon in his attitudes or decision making. This time it was Rodino who replied that the committee would continue to meet behind locked doors, with armed guards standing outside, until it had heard all grand jury materials and other evidence covered by committee rules of confidentiality.

The word "perspective" cannot be overemphasized as a desideratum. Every time another crucial issue or dramatic piece of evidence pushes out front, it is seized and drowns out all others. Eugene McCarthy is quoted as having jokingly said that "the popular attention span doesn't go past ninety seconds." James J. Kilpatrick, the columnist whom Nixon was to choose later for his only private interview in fifteen months, felt that McCarthy exaggerated, that the popular attention span for public affairs is actually closer to two minutes and fifteen seconds. A political theme has to make its point and be absorbed, he says, in from 90 to 135 seconds or it will be met by "a monumental yawn."

A public stance in which one retains perspective long enough to see the whole picture is rare enough to be noticed. House Republican Leader Rhodes expressed such a position when he said, "The Committee [House Judiciary Committee] has been mesmerized with tapes long enough." The best evidence, he went on, was not the tapes but the individuals involved in the conversations, who should be called and cross-examined. The statement went unheeded, perhaps unheard.

One also has to be sure of what this suggestion meant. In this instance, it fitted Rhodes's stance that this be done; it had been used by Rhodes as an argument for the committee to stop demanding White House tapes. It certainly should not have meant that the tapes were to be ignored and witnesses substituted. The goal, one hoped, was to add witnesses to the evidence of the tapes.

Kissinger

Henry Kissinger, who remains the cleanest and most respected of the staff, was also one who fixed on a leak and was indignant because of it, to the exclusion of relevant surrounding circumstances. It mattered little that the leak involved was a leak of the truth! The incident had to do with the bugging and surveillance which was ordered and executed because of a leak of the news of the secret bombing of Cambodia. Neither the bombing nor the secrecy was legal or moral. But Kissinger was indignant because the news had been leaked. To him and to those who agreed, this was the most salient issue. To one who always covers, the truth is a leak.

The Kissinger story is itself noteworthy from the point of view of the inner psychic components we are tracing and pursuing. Against the background of recent events and the activities of the administration of which he is a part, many perplexing questions of morality and responsibility can be asked about Kissinger as well. An example occurred on June 11, 1974, at Salzburg, Austria, where Kissinger reacted with an angry outburst when a newsman questioned him, based on evidence which had been reported, about the accuracy of previous testimony given by Kissinger to a Senate committee.

It turns out that the previous fall, when the Senate Foreign Relations Committee confirmed Kissinger as secretary of state on September 17, 1973, it knew that according to FBI documents Kissinger had requested wiretaps on some of his subordinates whom he considered possible sources of national security leaks. In his testimony given at that time, Kissinger had denied this under oath. In a tape of a White House conversation (of February 28, 1973), John Dean, referring to the *Time* magazine story which had revealed these taps, is heard telling the president that they had denied the story completely. "We are stonewalling totally here," Dean said. "Oh, absolutely," the president replied.

Questions about Kissinger's role had existed for years. When the issue now came up again, Kissinger, with a loss of emotional control which shocked even the presidential party, quickly replied to the newsman's question, "I do not believe that it is possible to conduct the foreign

policy of the United States under these circumstances when the character and credibility of the Secretary of State is at issue. . . . And if it is
not cleared up," he added, "I will resign. . . . I cannot conduct my office
if I have to devote my energies to disproving allegations of perjury, nor
do I believe that the United States can conduct an effective foreign
policy with a Secretary of State who is under such attack and, therefore,
I am simply stating a reality."

Kissinger has amassed a truly enviable record. Does this in itself make
it offensive, or impolite, or worse, disloyal, to question other aspects of
his activities which should rightly call for this? It was Kissinger, as well
as Nixon, to whom Charles Colson pointed as having given him the
go-ahead to get information on and defame Daniel Ellsberg. Kissinger's
subsequent denial not only of Colson's charge but of knowledge of the
existence of the White House plumbers themselves was flatly contradicted in a written statement by John Ehrlichman, the boss of the
plumbers' outfit. There is other evidence of Kissinger's contiguity to
this operation which refutes his denial. A tape of an investigation conducted by David Young, who was a member of Kissinger's staff as well
as the number two man in the plumbers' organization, is said to have
been played for Kissinger. Kissinger has never satisfactorily accounted
for this, nor has he ever asked Young to supply clarifying information.

And now the wiretaps and Kissinger's role in them which has been
hanging fire since 1969. One former member of Kissinger's staff, Morton
Halperin, has sued Kissinger and other government officials for damages allegedly caused by a tap on his home telephone. Kissinger's part
in this wiretapping of thirteen administration officials of the White
House, the State Department, and the Pentagon, including some of his
own staff, along with four of their supposed journalistic accomplices—
a series of taps which followed the "leak" about the secret bombing of
Cambodia—has long been suspected and questioned, with never a satisfactory rebuttal. Among the products of these wiretappings, Haldeman
had received FBI summaries of wiretaps on two former Kissinger aides
after they had become advisers to Senator Edmund Muskie, a candidate
for the 1972 Democratic presidential nomination.

In light of documents which prove the accuracy of these allegations,
Kissinger's personal outrage and angry threat to resign, was not only a

regrettable reaction but a curious stand on morality—a peevish gesture certainly not calculated automatically to exonerate him from suspicion. The incident was a dramatic demonstration of the power of one's own ego interests and its effects on poise and emotion—of how wide a gap there is when the self is involved as compared to the interests of others. There was a remarkable change of mood in Kissinger; it was the only time he lost his famous cool. No longer was there his normal joking with the press. There was always great humor when it was the honor of others, including his chief's, which was at stake.

Did Kissinger feel that it was possible for the president of the United States to conduct foreign policy when his character and credibility were at issue, whereas the secretary of state could not? If it were not possible, which his statement clearly indicated about himself, and if he did not feel it was his prerogative to advise his beleaguered superior to resign as he himself had threatened to do, how was it possible for him to continue to operate as secretary of state under a president whose basic character was under such question? Kissinger's humanness was showing. It was not against him, but it also makes him subject to normal checks and balances.

Rep. Joshua Eilberg of the House Judiciary Committee reiterated, after Kissinger's threat, that there was direct evidence in the hands of the committee from White House and FBI memoranda that Kissinger had initiated these wiretaps. "There are seventeen taps and Dr. Kissinger participated in initiating some of these taps," Eilberg said. In the White House tape of February 28, 1973, in a section which had been deleted from the president's transcripts, but which was heard directly by the House committee, Nixon told John Dean that Kissinger had asked that these wiretaps be instituted. "Henry . . . asked that it be done. And I assumed that it was. . . . But the taps," the president went on, "never helped us. Just gobs and gobs of material: gossip and bullshitting . . . very very unproductive. . . ."

It was not a question of impugning Kissinger's "honor," nor was the public as ungrateful to him as he felt. They had in fact treated him with uncritical adulation. But not to investigate properly would be to include this issue with the many others which have been treated with neurotic passivity. The charges against Kissinger were not vague innuendoes voiced by "unnamed sources" engaged in "defamation of character." Such qualities and activities have usually come from the direction of the administration.

The charges were specific, and concrete questions remained to be answered. The acknowledged wiretapping had occurred after William Beecher had reported in the *New York Times* on May 9, 1969, that American B-52 bombers were secretly bombing inside Cambodia without protest from the Cambodian government. This was another revelation which, like Watergate, received far less reaction than it deserved. Between March 1969 and April 1970, the United States had mounted 3,620 B-52 bombing runs at Cambodian targets, disguising all of them from Congress by a double-entry reporting system that listed them as taking place elsewhere. Because of that cover-up, of which the wiretaps were a part, Nixon was able on April 30, 1970, to justify sending American ground troops into Cambodia on the basis that Communist sanctuaries there had been immune from attack. It was not until 1973 that the administration admitted that the bombing had started in 1969, and that the invasion was required because the military results were "not satisfactory."

We had "scrupulously respected the neutrality of the Cambodian people," Mr. Nixon had said before July 1973, and had done nothing "to violate the territory of a neutral nation." That this was false was known to the Cambodians, the Communists, Kissinger, and everyone but the American people. When the falsity of the reports to Congress was revealed a year ago, Kissinger had said that neither he nor the president "ordered nor was . . . aware of" the deception. This was flatly contradicted by General Earle Wheeler, then chairman of the Joint Chiefs of Staff, who said that Mr. Nixon had told him "at least a half-dozen times" to "make sure the tightest security is maintained" on the raids. Wheeler also quoted Kissinger as telling him that the deception was appropriate because he had told the truth to six pro-administration members of Congress and then pledged them to secrecy.

The issue is again not the question of guilt or innocence—this cannot be determined here—but of accountability, which can be. Should Nixon and Kissinger have to answer? The deep moral question is: Are even "the best and the brightest" beyond suspicion, beyond questioning, and therefore immune from accountability for their actions? Kissinger's challenge laid down at Salzburg, if it were allowed to prevail, would establish a principle which would be welcomed by anyone in high places under pressure of scrutiny. His outburst is already said to have caused private elation among the White House staff and antiimpeachment strategists who saw in this a weapon with which they could take the offensive against the impeachment inquiry.

Kissinger's threat worked. People, Congress included, reacted as groups usually do, not on the basis of clarity and resoluteness but of guilt, emotions, and wish fulfillment. When the *Washington Post* printed J. Edgar Hoover's memo that Kissinger had requested telephone surveillance on a member of his own National Security Council staff, Senator Goldwater impulsively denounced the publication of this document as treason. Later, to further information that the memorandum had been obtained in an entirely legal fashion, he amended this and stated it was doubtful that the treason statute would apply. But Goldwater chided Congress, the media, and people in general for questioning Kissinger and called for a halt to their "incessant nit-picking" against him. Ronald Reagan pointed out that Kissinger's Middle East achievements were much more important than any possible question of wiretaps. Gerald Ford stated that news leaks about Kissinger's role in wiretapping activities were given to newsmen "on a selective basis, I think with some ulterior motives."

On June 12, 1974, one day after Kissinger made his threat to resign at Salzburg, a resolution was introduced in the United States Senate expressing confidence in him in this wiretapping controversy. By nightfall of the next day, this resolution had fifty-two senators, a majority of the Senate, as signers and cosponsors. This prompted Sen. William Fulbright, chairman of the Foreign Relations Committee which was to study the matter, to declare the resolution premature. "This raises a serious question as to whether it is worthwhile to continue the review by the Foreign Relations Committee" which, he pointed out, was to be undertaken at Kissinger's request. The sponsors of the resolution, Fulbright said, "no doubt intended it to be helpful, but it can only have the opposite effect. . . . A majority of the Senate are now apparently willing to resolve these issues without seeing a shred of additional evidence. This is in the interests neither of Dr. Kissinger nor of restoring public confidence in the credibility of government." Declaring that he too was an admirer of Kissinger's diplomacy, Fulbright nevertheless stood for restraint and a more rational approach and urged "everyone in this distracted city" to calm down over the weekend.

The committee proceeded with its "investigation" under the cloud of Kissinger's threat to resign, which he would withdraw, he had said, only if the committee gave him a full vote of confidence. This was the atmosphere in which the committee was to determine the "truthfulness and completeness" of Kissinger's previous testimony, which he had defined as the issue before the committee.

Even the deceased J. Edgar Hoover was now being "used" in Kissinger's behalf. Attorney General William Saxbe said that Hoover might have "used" Kissinger as an unwitting front for his own wiretapping of White House enemies. Several senators agreed with Saxbe—with no further evidence. It was a question of who was using whom. Later, when the air was cooler, Kissinger himself joined in pointing a finger at the ex-FBI chief. Volunteering an opinion which may have been a clue to his own ego ideal, Kissinger stated that Hoover was always against him because he was a "Kennedy-type Harvard professor." This statement could have carried another message: not to tie Kissinger to this present president in trouble but to a previous one, John Kennedy, Nixon's own ideal and rival.

In the meantime, in June 1974, Kissinger was charged with having negotiated a secret arrangement which allowed the Soviet Union more offensive nuclear submarine missiles than in a formal SALT agreement on nuclear arms limitation signed in Moscow on July 24, 1972. The dispute was touched off by the resignation of Paul Nitze, a former deputy secretary of defense, from his post as Nixon's chief negotiator at the Strategic Arms Limitation Talks. Nitze told Senator Henry Jackson's Subcommittee on Arms Control that he quit because Kissinger had agreed to secret proposals, not submitted to Congress for approval, of which Nixon had not been informed.

Kissinger's first reply, given at a press conference on the eve of President Nixon's departure in June for the summit talks in Moscow, came in his typical fashion: "Those arguments are totally false in every detail—they have no merits whatsoever." This answer usually ends the discussion forthwith. But in this instance Senator Jackson, interviewed on "Meet the Press," on July 14, 1974, referred to documentation showing negotiations of this secret deal which had allowed Moscow a "loop-hole" for seventy more sea-based missiles than permitted in the published treaty. Kissinger's explanation, Jackson said, was "dead wrong" and "the American people will be shocked to find the Administration did not make a full disclosure of the facts." To this new fact, that Jackson would now release evidence, Kissinger's next statement was also typical. "I can only assume that there was a misunderstanding on the part of some of the witnesses, or on the part of some of the Senators who heard testimony. . . ." After first a denial, Kissinger's next tactic is not like Nixon's, to attack, but is characteristically more diplomatic, to give and take a little; when wrong and proven wrong, "there was a misunderstanding." Testifying later before the Senate Subcommittee on Arms Control, Kissinger acknowledged the existence of a loophole in the arms pact. This time, however, he declared that the loophole was unintentional, that he had not known about it at first, and that it had been closed last week.

The pot story again. It seems to have been invented for this administration. "There is no truth to it. I did not know about it. I corrected it last week." Credibility is not enhanced, but the heat is off. Kissinger is in the clear again.

Is this how things were achieved by Kissinger in his secret negotiations, in the Soviet Union, in China, in North Vietnam? It would be unfair to think so automatically. But in the face of the contradictions which have followed whenever the facts have surfaced, not to consider the possibility of such maneuverings is to exhibit a passive compliance which is neither straight nor rational.

Richard Holbrooke, managing editor of *Foreign Policy* magazine, notes the contradictions in the political Kissinger and the difficulties in arriving at a unified assessment; there is "the technical and legal level" and "a deeper and more basic" one. Reviewing the moral dilemma of Henry Kissinger, Holbrooke wonders for the public whether Kissinger was "the one clean man in a school of skunks" or "another member of the team, involved in some kind of 'White House Horror' " of his own. He must be "somewhere in between," Holbrooke concludes.

The fact is that the superego, in the same individual, can have varied, even opposite ingredients. Each side or cluster can have its day, or its weeks or years, and produce its separate sets of outcomes. And credit for one side does not—or should not—preclude accountability for the other.

Much has been written this past year about our "sick society." The suffering endured needs to be carefully dissected and understood to separate the pathological from the healthy and reparative aspects. Just as grief and mourning can be normal and adaptive, so can guilt, anxiety, or shame be appropriate, not pathological reactions. Guilt appropriate to the circumstances is restitutive and bodes well for the future. Its absence can be more cause for concern. Insights gathered from studies of individuals in analysis, microscopically pursued for more than three-quarters of a century, need to be applied to the understanding of the behavior of groups, from the small to the large, to the nation, to the world.

The will of the people is by no means always rational, and certainly cannot be automatically counted upon. This is no new revelation; the following lines are from Ibsen's *An Enemy of the People,* also written at that same turn of the century from which so many penetrating insights seem to have come.

HOVSTAD: The majority always has right on its side.

BILLING: And truth too, by God!

DR. STOCKMANN: The majority *never* has right on its side. Never, I say! That is one of these social lies against which an independent, intelligent man must wage war. Who is it that constitute the majority of the population in a country? Is it the clever folk or the stupid? I don't imagine you will dispute the fact that at present the stupid people are in an absolutely overwhelming majority all the world over. But, good Lord! —you can never pretend that it is right that the stupid folk should govern the clever ones! *(Uproar and cries.)* Oh, yes—you can shout me down, I know! but you cannot answer me. The majority has *might* on its side—unfortunately; but *right* it has *not.* I am in the right—I and a few other scattered individuals. The minority is always in the right. *(Renewed uproar.)*

HOVSTAD: Aha! so Dr. Stockmann has become an aristocrat since the day before yesterday!

III

The Rush

Following the transcripts which revealed the contents of the tapes, which are now unavoidable evidence, Nixon's involvement has become so thick that his most intimate colleagues are turning against him one by one. The most recent of these is Charles W. Colson, "Mr. Tough Guy," creator of the "enemies list," and regarded as chairman of "the department of dirty tricks." Dubbed "the cobra" by Herbert G. Klein, and "an evil genius" by Magruder, Colson—about whom it was said he would "walk over his grandmother" to help reelect Nixon—had been the most vociferous during the first year in proclaiming the innocence of the president and himself. Now it is Colson, after he has found religion and overcome his "damnable pride and ego," who in June reveals, in the most damaging evidence yet to come against the president, that Nixon urged him to discredit Ellsberg and his attorney, thus obstructing the flow of justice.

It was not only a religious conversion that Colson underwent; he also volunteers evidence of a new introspection and insight. Explaining why he moved against Ellsberg, on June 21, Colson tells Judge Gerhard Gesell, as the judge sentences him to a one- to three-year prison sentence:

> I had one rule . . . to get done that which the President wanted done. And while I thought I was serving him well and faithfully, I now recognize I was not . . . at least in the sense that I never really

questioned whether what he wanted done was right or proper.
. . . I rarely questioned a Presidential order. Infrequently did I
question the President's judgment.

These two things, unquestioning loyalty on the one hand and a
feeling of self-sacrifice on the other, caused me to lose sight of some
very fundamental precepts. . . . I lost my perspective to a point
where I instinctively reacted to any criticism or interference with
what I was doing or what the President was doing as unfair and as
something to be retaliated against.

In this self-assessment and self-recrimination Colson joins Magruder
and Segretti. Others are more like Herbert Kalmbach whose explanation, at least outwardly, upon receiving his sentence to prison is simply
that he was used by the White House. Inwardly it is likely that more
goes on, but the incentive for public display and for a public acceptance
and lavage is not the same in all.

Colson also informs the House Judiciary Committee lawyers that he
had alerted Nixon to high-level complicity in the Watergate affair in
January and February 1973, two months before Nixon admitted having
known of this.

Hints and allegations of a possible earlier involvement of President
Nixon than on the March 21, 1973, date upon which he presently stands
continue. A major discrepancy was discovered in two different versions
of the transcripts of a tape of September 15, 1972. In the White House
transcript the president was shown as having had a conversation on that
day with John Mitchell, who had resigned as director of the president's
reelection campaign the previous July. The House Judiciary Committee's version, however, showed that the conversation was held with
Clark MacGregor, Mitchell's successor as campaign director. This was
one of the discrepancies which raised questions about the accuracy and
completeness of the transcripts made public by Nixon.

In the House committee version, the president, speaking to MacGregor, makes a reference to "bugging" a full six months before the president says he was told the facts about Watergate. Speaking to MacGregor, the president asks, "Did you put that last bug in? Huh?" This
referred to a second bugging device discovered inside Democratic National Headquarters earlier that September. There was no such remark

in the White House–edited transcript. When asked about this reference, MacGregor said, "If the President used the word 'bug' in that
September 15th conversation with me, I'm sure that he was joking."

In his book *An American Life: One Man's Road to Watergate,* Jeb
Magruder expresses the opinion that Nixon demanded and received the
full story of the Watergate break-in immediately after it occurred, and
had kept "in close personal touch" with it and with the cover-up of it
ever since. James McCord goes even further, saying in his book *A Piece
of Tape,* in the same vein as Colson did about Ellsberg, that it was the
president who influenced his break-in into the Watergate offices.

On March 28, Sen. Lowell Weicker disclosed a memorandum on
White House stationery from John Caulfield to John Dean in July 1971,
eleven months before the Watergate break-in, describing how a break-
in could be performed at the office of the Potomac Associates, a Washington think tank. According to "a leaked charge," Colson had suggested fire-bombing the Brookings Institution, a charge which his
lawyer called false and malicious and denied at his trial. The famous
eighteen-and-a-half-minute erased gap involves a conversation between the president and Haldeman just three days after the Watergate
break-in, which might well have pointed to a very early initial involvement of the president. Is the president's word sufficient to turn off all
suspicion or investigation on this point? Or to limit the questioning only
to a date named by him? Have any findings made it inappropriate to
wonder who was responsible for the initial planning—and how much
the president may have been involved? Would he not more naturally
have been indignant at those people for their crime when he finally did
find out about it? There would have been two motivations fused into
one—abstract principle and personal safety. But Nixon's anger and
derision in the transcripts were consistently about the bungling, never
about the crime. This would fit if the crime had belonged to them all
but had been executed badly.

I am not passing on innocence or guilt but attempting to understand
attitudes and behavior that are otherwise bizarre. As previously noted
with regard to the ending of the Vietnam War, not to consider such
obvious possibilities is to exhibit a passive compliance that reaches the
proportion of a pseudo-imbecility.

"Deniability" was a key word in the Nixon White House. Every projected activity could be disowned if things went wrong. Above all this was a requisite for the president: he could, if necessary, be kept isolated, or appear to be kept isolated, ignorant and uninvolved. For a long time this ploy worked, almost forever. But then the armor fashioned around the president began to give way. One astute observer, Walter Pincus, posed a question which was much deemphasized by the rest of the country: "My review of the edited White House transcripts suggests that the initial question should not be what did Mr. Nixon know, but rather what did the President *want* to know between June 17, 1972 when the burglars were arrested, and the following March 21st? And what did he want to know after that date?"

The same question needs to be asked of the people as well, of the broad population base. Is not the possibility that their president is guilty of protecting wrongdoers (which has a redeeming human quality) more acceptable than the possibility that he is a wrongdoer himself? The investigating apparatus has operated with impeccable correctness; Nixon can have no justifiable complaints. But one must ask whether all of us in the collective are willing actively to pursue evidence which might lead toward complicity of the president from the beginning.

The committees, for example, never attempted, nor was any pressure put on them, to call Martha Mitchell as a witness—Martha, who early in the story, when distraught and flushed with the first anger and excitement, faced a television camera and, rolling her eyes, said, "You know who is responsible. You know who gave all the orders, that S.O.B. at the top. John is taking the rap for him." This was a simple statement, and Martha had some closeness to what was going on. But she was never called. At one time she was reported to have been forcibly given an injection, held in a motel room for two days against her will, and treated for an acute disturbance. A public image of instability might have been used by us all as a rationalization for not listening to whatever she might have said. As a psychiatrist, I would have to say that her mental condition would have had nothing to do with consideration of her testimony. The mental conditions of others were not considered deterrents to their having to reveal what they knew. Not that anything that Martha might say now would definitely settle this tender issue. The moment may have passed. A protective metamorphosis seems to have taken place. She has become a co-hostess on a TV talk show, seems more happy, conciliatory, and self-interested, and now jokes about Watergate.

We might go further. If no tapes or transcripts had become available —concrete documents which miraculously survived and which recorded the president's later knowledge of the break-in—the same fate probably would have befallen the cover-up. That too in the early stages, without "hard" evidence which could be read or heard, would have appeared shameful, indelicate, even unpatriotic to pursue. It was not a subject about which to press unwilling witnesses. If the case had devolved solely between conflicting human witnesses, John Dean would by now have been the most disgraced and lonely figure in America. Every witness was lined up against him, and all would have stayed that way if they could—unless an unconscious sense of guilt had led someone to exposure.

There is another matter to which Colson points: there was a plane crash. Early, when evidence was mounting but still being "contained," a plane went down and a large sum of cash, part of the original hush money, was found in the wreckage. Is it inappropriate to note, more quizzically than has been the case, that in the midst of an incredible web of operations, a commercial airliner crashes in Chicago with hush money on the person of the wife of a principal in the case? A patient of mine has a habit of saying, when data in an analytic hour keeps piling up, "It's all just too much, too much."

In two strange evening confessionals just days before he pleaded guilty on June 3, Charles Colson made a series of startling allegations to Richard L. Bast, a Washington private investigator, statements which Watergate investigators said later that Colson had also made to them. One was an enigmatic statement that the circumstances surrounding this plane crash, which had caused the death of Dorothy (Mrs. E. Howard) Hunt in December 1972, should be looked at more carefully. This suggestion was, however, part of a larger agenda to cast suspicion on the role of the CIA about broader Watergate affairs. Thus Colson joined the alleged concerns of President Nixon who, Colson had said, "was out of his mind over the C.I.A. and Pentagon roles" in Watergate.

Other evidence, however, from witnesses and tapes, had substantiated the fact that suspicions had been cast upon the CIA, early and throughout the period of Watergate, to deflect from the role of the White House itself. The CIA, it was shown again and again, was being used by the accused to draw away attention. Nevertheless, the plane crash remained a crash, and the tainted money had been aboard.

Explanations themselves are now in conflict, but should suspicion lift? Did Colson also try to deflect? Would Watergate have been investigated . further if those two feisty *Washington Post* reporters had been willing to take no for an answer? Were not their suspicions a more "normal" reaction to the news item of June 17 than the combined reactions of two hundred eleven million other Americans?

Questions remain unanswered. Some always will. The hanging matters pointed to here, the time of the president's initial involvement and the death of Mrs. Dorothy Hunt in a United Airlines plane crash, may well deserve another Bernstein-Woodward nose-grinding, nit-picking investigation. But more likely these questions will remain open-ended, areas that will never be penetrated. This is the more usual course of history.

Art Buchwald

The only person deriving benefit from the existing conditions, and even having legitimate fun while he was at it, was Art Buchwald, Washington-based syndicated columnist. Humor, at least his brand, had a heyday. He told the truth as if it were fiction, but told it exactly as it was. When serious media told it straight, the result was irony, bitterness, even tragedy. The *New Yorker*'s "Talk of the Town" was somewhere in between, with tongue in cheek. But Art Buchwald or Mort Sahl twisted the daily news into a pretzel. It came out funny, hilarious, unbelievable. No, this could not be the way it was; it must be a joke. The relief of tension is what makes for humor; it brings on the tension discharge of laughter. One had thought the tension had no place to go. Suddenly it was out and away; one laughed with a "thank God."

Buchwald wrote many classic pieces during this, for him, fertile period, writings which should go down in the annals of humor. His format was to reprint news of the day, with his selection, twists, and editorial comment, and with his inimitable play on words and names.

In one column there is a negotiation going on between St. Clair and

John Doar over which tapes and evidence the White House will turn over in answer to a subpoena by the House committee. Here are some excerpts:

"Now look, Doar, we want to be reasonable down here and we're willing to give you everything you've asked for."

"You are?"

"Yes, with the only exception that it doesn't harm the Presidency or violate the Constitution. As Mr. Nixon's lawyer I believe I'm in the best position to know what is relevant to your impeachment hearings. I've sifted through every piece of evidence, and I give you my word a lot of the stuff you're requesting is not worth fighting for."

"How do we know that if we haven't heard the tapes?"

"I heard them and the President's heard them and H. R. Haldeman's heard them. Why can't you take our word for it that there is absolutely nothing on them that can contribute to Mr. Nixon's impeachment? What on earth would we have to gain by keeping evidence from your committee?"

"I'm certain, Mr. St. Clair, that what you say is true, but there are some members of the committee who have a thing about presidential tapes. Now are you going to turn them over to us?"

"That's what I'm calling about. We're willing to give you 42 tapes as requested."

"Then we don't have a problem."

"But the President feels he should have the right to decide what 42 tapes to give you. That's only fair."

"I don't get you."

"The President is offering instead of the Kleindienst telephone conversation of April 15th a tape of his call to congratulate Don Shula of the Miami Dolphins for winning the Superbowl. The President says it's a much jazzier tape, and he's sure the entire House committee would enjoy it. . . . Furthermore, he is throwing in a tape of a personal message he dictated to Secretariat when he won the Triple Crown. . . . Believe me, Mr. Doar, the ones you people have asked for are dull and repetitious and you'd be bored to death. . . ."

"Thanks, Mr. St. Clair, but no thanks. We still want the tapes we asked for."

"OK Doar, the President asked me to give you a message if you refused his generous offer."

"What is that?"

"He told me to tell you 'That does it. No more Mr. Nice Guy.' "

Another column involves an I.Q. test: "Watergate has been going on for so long that it is now time for the first Watergate trivia test. Anyone who gets every answer right will be given Executive clemency."

Some of the questions: "What was the name of the man who ran against Richard Nixon for President in 1972?" "Nixon had two Vice-Presidents during his second term in office. One was Gerald Ford. Who was the other?" "President Nixon has insisted from the very beginning that he never had any knowledge of Watergate until March 21, 1973. What football games did he watch while the cover-up was going on?"

"What two buttons on a recording machine would you have to push down at the same time you put your foot on the pedal to erase 18 1/2 minutes of a crucial White House tape?" "Most of the people involved in Watergate have been lawyers. What subjects did they take in law schools which made them believe that they were not doing anything wrong?"

A third column considered the plight of the building, the White House, which has served the likes of Washington and Lincoln and is now blamed for the doings of its present occupant. In another, Art Buchwald goes to see a psychiatrist; he tells him about an idea that he has of breaking into a building called the Watergate—and all that he would do—and repeats in summary what has been done. Of course he is passed off as seriously ill.

One column concerns a White House press briefing: "Alice's Adventure in Briefingland." Alice is invited by the March Hare to go to a press briefing:

"That is where they deny what they have already told you, which is the only reason it could be true."

"It sounds like fun," Alice said.

A chess pawn was standing at a podium.

"Who is that?" Alice asked.

"That is the press secretary. He talks in riddles. Listen."

"Why can't we hear all the tapes?" The Mock Turtle asked, "so we can decide for ourselves who is innocent and who is guilty?"

. . . The press secretary replied, "If you heard the tapes it would only prove the innocent are guilty and the guilty are innocent and it would serve no purpose but to confuse you. Besides, what you would hear is not what you have read and what you have read is not what you would hear, so it's better not to hear what cannot be read. Isn't that perfectly clear?"

"I feel I'm back at the Mad Hatter's tea party," Alice said.

"Now I will give you some important news today," the press secretary said. "This is on the record. 'Twas brillig and the slithy toves did gyre and gimble in the wabe: all mimsy were the borogoves, and the mome raths out grabe."

Everyone wrote it down.

"What did he say?" Alice asked.

"Nothing," the March Hare replied. "He's just stalling until he can go to lunch."

There is the column about a committee hearing which was debating the articles of abdication, "Resolved that the Emperor violated his oath of office when he paraded down the streets under a canopy with no clothes on."

"That he made false and misleading statements to the effect that he was wearing clothes at the time, and that he was party to a cover-up and interfered in a lawful investigation as to whether in effect he did on said day parade in the nude."

The courtier from Grazinda asks a question "that could affect the empire for generations to come . . . did the emperor know he had no clothes on and what did he do about it?

Let me review the evidence. . . . we can all agree that he spent all the taxpayers' money on clothes for himself. . . . from the emperor's own parchments we know that on June 17th two cheats arrived and claimed they were weavers who would make him . . . magnificent clothes. . . . On March 21st the emperor himself went to the weavers and saw with his own eyes that there was no cloth; there were no trousers; there was no robe. Did he arrest the weavers? Did he report them to the justice minister?

"No, Mr. Chairman. He praised them as two of the finest men he had ever known and told the country they had woven him a magnificent set of clothes. That, gentlemen, was the beginning of the cover-up."

Says the courtier from Tearturnia, "Mr. Chairman, I can't believe that I have been sitting here for six months and heard the same evidence as my learned friend from Grazinda. If you read the emperor's parchments as I have done, you can only come to one conclusion: The emperor was wearing clothes on the day in question."

The evidence he quotes is too long to repeat, but it is taken from the pages of today. "Let us remember that at this point in time the emperor was busy with affairs of state and could not devote time to his clothes." And at the end, after a bit more, "Mr. Chairman, if the Emperor says he had clothes on, it's good enough for me."

In a banner end-of-the-year report at the annual stockholders' meeting of the Watergate Industries, Sherlock Springbinder, chairman of the board, reported a windfall profit of two billion dollars. Watergate Industries is a conglomerate that deals in all aspects of the Watergate affair, from providing legal talent to selling memoirs of Watergate personalities.

Springbinder told the happy stockholders, "Watergate should be one of the best growth stocks of 1974. . . . The legal profession alone has earned $30 million, and very few of the trials have begun. By the time all of the indictments are handed down, we expect to have 30,000 lawyers working full-time on motions. After the trials we will have another 5,000 producing appeals. Estimated net income from this division should bring in $100 million. dollars."

There was a great deal of applause.

"Our book division is also showing a great profit. . . . we believe there will be 670,000 different books published this year, and the advances alone will come to $20 million. If President Nixon decides to write his book of what really happened, I could see another $10 million in added revenue."

"The movie rights for Watergate are going very briskly. . . . Several . . . movie producers are readying projects, including 'Gidget Goes to the Watergate,' 'Last Tango at the White House,' 'The Tapes of Wrath,' 'The Life of Bebe Rebozo,' and 'Confessions of a Jesuit Priest.' . . . We now have a record division where we intend to produce the hit expletives from the transcripts. . . .

"Watergate Industries is happy to announce it is going into the employment agency business, since it is estimated there will be 345,890 White House aides looking for jobs in the next 12 months. . . .

"Our . . . printing plant is now working 24 hours a day and we just received a multimillion-dollar contract from the House Judiciary Committee, which should keep us busy for 2 more years." Springbinder got a standing ovation.

"Are there any questions," he asked.

"Why aren't there more women involved with Watergate," a militant stockholder shouted from the floor.

Springbinder answered nervously, "It's true that Watergate was strictly a white male affair, with very few exceptions. . . . Women don't seem to be physiologically or mentally able to cope with all it takes to be part of a Watergate scandal."

In one of his wild but sad fantasies, Buchwald engages in a soliloquy while sitting on the headstone at the graveside of the late Mr. Checkers, the Nixons' cocker spaniel. "You saved him once, but you can't save him this time," he tells Checkers as he muses over his master's doings. "He did some great things, Checkers. Even his worst enemies acknowledge that. . . . The whole world picture changed for the better under him.

"But at the same time he tore the fabric of his own country to shreds. . . ."

Buchwald reviews all that Nixon and his people did, then how he covered it all up:

"I'm not making this up, Checkers. It's all in the tapes . . . oh, you don't know about the tapes?

"Well, you see, soon after your master took over the Presidency, he decided to record the conversations of everyone he came in contact with— without their knowledge, except for H. R. Haldeman. . . . the tapes were the only evidence that could convict Mr. Nixon and he turned some over to the justice people. . . .

"I know what you're going to ask, 'Why didn't he burn the tapes?' Nobody knows the answer to that question, Checkers. Either he was stupid or he was so contemptuous of the laws of this country he didn't believe anyone would ever get to hear them. . . .

"But do you want to know the worst thing your master did? He lied to the American people. He lied to his friends, his lawyers, his own party, and everyone who believed in him.

"Why, Checkers, why? You knew him better than we did. . . . Was it scorn for us that made him do it? Was it some insecurity in his character that kept him from playing by the rules? Or was it simply a case of a man who was a born loser even when he became President of the United States?

"Well I've got to be going now. The country will survive, Checkers. We're much better than your master thinks we are, and we do have some consolation. If things hadn't worked out the way they did, Agnew might have become President and then we would have had to impeach him."

And in a helpful mood toward Vice-President Gerald Ford, who "has been zigging and zagging on the question of impeachment for some time," because Buchwald admires the vice-president very much he writes a standard speech for him which should cover all the bases. Since Ford has to give so many speeches, it has been hard for him to remember what he said the day before. [Actual news: During this difficult period, Ford has so far outdone Nixon in talking to both sides of every question, particularly on the question which is most burning to people's minds.]

The speech goes something like this:

My fellow Americans,

I would like to say before I begin that I am neither for impeach-ment nor against impeachment. . . . on the basis of all I have read so far, the President is not guilty of any impeachable offenses. At the same time, if he is withholding evidence which could show that he should be impeached, then he should turn this evidence over to the House Judiciary Committee. . . .

I have talked to the President on this very subject and ex-pressed my views quite clearly. He has expressed his views to me. It's quite possible that on the basis of our discussions we may dis-agree.

But the fact that we disagree does not mean that we do not see the question in the same way. . . . Because the President is stone-walling Congress does not mean that I do not support his efforts to do the right thing no matter if I personally believe it's the wrong thing.

I feel the House Committee has enough evidence now to judge whether the President is guilty of high crimes and misdemeanors and they shouldn't ask for any more evidence, unless they believe they need the evidence to find out if the President is guilty or not. . . . I can tell you though that every time I have met with the President, he has been in excellent health both mentally and physi-cally and I am impressed at his ability to see everything so clearly, although at times it doesn't seem very clear to me.

In conclusion, I would like to say that I will continue to support the President, although I may disagree with him. And I know he supports me. . . .

As things get worse, Buchwald prints a Dr. Seuss rhyme with "Rich-ard M. Nixon" substituted for "Marvin K. Mooney" in the book title *Marvin K. Mooney Will You Please Go Now?* A few of the sequences:

> Richard M. Nixon
> Will you please
> GO NOW!
> You can go on stilts.
> You can go by fish.

You can go in a Crunk-Car
If you wish.
If you wish.
You may go
By lion's tail.
Or stamp yourself
And go by mail.
Richard M. Nixon
Don't you know
The time has come
To go, go, GO!
Get on your way!
Please Richard M.!
You might like going in a Zumble-Zem.
You can go by balloon . . .
Or broomstick.

Or

You can go by camel
In a bureau drawer.
You can go by Bumble-Boat
. . . or jet.
I don't care how you go.
Just GET!

And there were many more until:

Richard M. Nixon!
I don't care HOW.
Richard M. Nixon
Will you please
GO NOW!
I said
Go
And
GO
I meant . . .
The time had come

So . . .
Richard WENT.

Humor, or pathos, or truth, or premonition?

There were so many others, it was almost a daily report. One column was about the interesting technical difficulties of the secretaries who were typing the various White House documents, just who decides what will be left in and what deleted. One was about Rose Mary Woods and her trials and tribulations trying to get into the complicated and difficult gymnastic position necessary to erase eighteen and a half minutes of a particular tape. One sad essay was on Pat's need to return the emeralds and jewels given her by the king of Saudi Arabia. And one tragicomic column was on the many faces of Nixon, with the conclusion that the new Nixon has been a fake all along to cover up the old one. A humor column, it reverberates to the "big mechanism" described earlier as a psychic defense mechanism and is not far in content from the "scientific" description I gave then in a more serious vein.

I am quoting liberally from Art Buchwald's output, not frivolously, not only for relief—although to be sure I welcome that—but because the content fits so snugly into my straighter and more serious theme. The line between truth and fantasy, between fact and fiction, was always so thin, so tantalizing as to make the country unsure whether to laugh or cry.

The Tide Turns

But the serious case grinds on. It can be laughed at, but cannot be laughed away. Slowly but now surely, opinion—in the media, in public life, and in polls of the people—has been declared against the president's continuing in office. Most newspapers and magazines throughout the country have openly called for his resignation or impeachment, itself a first in American history. In this conservatives join liberals, and at its most telltale point, the middle of the middle of the population curve. The trade union movement, which in recent years had been behind Nixon, has switched. Three thousand United Auto Workers

Union delegates voted virtually unanimously to call on the House of Representatives to vote for impeachment.

This is not to say that the majority is convinced that the president has committed a high crime or misdemeanor; technically it is a moot point whether one impeachable crime actually occurred. However, Nixon's character and mentality, his motives and morality, his low level of behavior have revolted and outraged the country. These traits are human—unfortunately, we must agree with Father John McLaughlin that they are—but the question is whether these aspects of being human should be excused in the leader of the country. Whether a man who says, or even thinks, "Jew-boy, Wop, and bullshit" at that level of national crisis should be the role model for the young, and in a position to decide the nation's fate, has weighed on the public conscience too openly and for too long. Indeed a new conflict has arisen: What is more important in judging the qualities of a president, one isolated culpable act or a diffuse characterological mediocrity (or worse) over a lifetime of behavior?

Polls reflect the hardened mood; the popularity of the president has reached a new low. In a poll in early May 1974, 69 percent felt that he was obstructing justice and 55 percent felt that Nixon knew and approved of the Watergate affair in advance, i.e., in the planning stage! Only 8 percent believed that he knew nothing at all about Watergate. The president who a few years back had received the second greatest landslide in history has now come closer to impeachment—whatever the final outcome—than any previous president in history. The mechanism of screens and blocked perspective is failing.

The turning of the tide is now bipartisan across the board. The Republicans have turned; whether for reasons of principle or expediency is hard to tell. The Democrats, who seem to be soft-pedaling resignation and at times impeachment as well, are not necessarily being guided by higher principles either. They are actively against resignation, it is thought, because they wish to play the dominant part in Nixon's demise. And as far as impeachment goes, might it be, some wonder, better to face Nixon in 1976 than a Gerald Ford with a few years behind him? Republicans or Democrats, they are all subject to human frailty.

As low as Nixon sinks, there is still something about him with which people can identify. There are those, no small number, who empathize with his failures. "Anyone could have become hopelessly involved," it goes. Everyone has a fear of reaching the top, his own top, and then falling off, or of falling from whatever height he has already achieved. There is a universal fear of ultimate punishment based on a universal wish to throw off all the shackles. Everyone can identify with helplessness based on the desire for omnipotence and with failure which results from a gamble to achieve it. Nixon has a bead into people's minds as the helpless Everyman who lost.

The president was right in feeling he need never give up, that there was always a chance. A Gallup poll conducted between May 31 and June 3 showed a slight upward trend again in Nixon's favor after a long decline. The same refrain that has operated at every point at which inner evaluation is called for can and does persist: "Nothing is wrong with what Nixon did. Everyone does it. Let's get off his back and get back to business as usual." Which means our business too. Keep everything as it was. Whenever there is an absence of external change, even if only for a short time, the people opt for the stand-pat position. Maintenance of the status quo has precedence in mental life in accordance with what is known as "the constancy principle." There is a biological base for this mental quest. The nervous system, like the psychic system which derives from it, aims for homeostasis, wants to restore the condition of placidity that existed before stimulation and excitement and upset impinged. This is both a biological and psychological principle, which operates in the regulation of psychic as well as physical life.

However, there is an opposing force at work. Constancy and change are also at odds with each other; duality exists in every aspect of mental life. Not only do stimuli from the outside continuously press for change; there is also a "stimulus hunger" from within demanding it. Boredom, the absence of stimuli, can be a special kind of trauma in itself. The reactions to Nixon also change with this psychic oscillation within those congressmen and senators who are to judge.

There is another pendular dichotomy in the behavioral arc, between the living-out of satisfying only the "self" and the alternating ascendancy of conscience and "otherness." This is based not only on guilt and the yearning for restitution, but on the fact that two sides of human character exert their pressures and each has its day in court. The "me" generation will inevitably be followed by a return of the work ethic and religion. The ego has to live with its ever-present superego, its close companion throughout life. The two live on variable terms. Sometimes they do not speak, but sometimes they are "best" friends.

Periodically, perhaps every decade or two, after years of double-talk and camouflage, the people need a purge. It is "time for a change," but of a specific kind. The chronic strain on integrity which exists in all yields to an opposite push, a hunger for "straightness." Just as I said that external need and the readiness of science coincide, so is there a convergence from within and without. At the moment that people are ready, a fresh voice, a special type of person appears on the political scene. Along comes an Adlai Stevenson or a Wendell Willkie. This phenomenon is nonpartisan; the need for purification follows the activities of both parties; it is as necessary after a Democratic Tammany or Pendergast machine as after a Republican Harding or Nixon administration.

Joseph Welch was suddenly there to clear away the stench and shame of the fifties. Today, when such a cleansing is again needed, there is an Archibald Cox or an Elliott Richardson to be looked to for rejuvenation. Sam Ervin is today's Joseph Welch, and there is a Peter Rodino for good measure. When Ervin came to the testimony about Hugh Sloan's having left the gang in the middle of their nefarious operations, this recalled for him the old adage that "an honest man is the noblest work of God." How welcome it is when candor is introduced into public statements in even the smallest way; Senator Charles Percy's candor in saying that he would run for the presidency is refreshing. Should not every candid-ate be at least "candid"?

Early in the history of the psychoanalytic movement, Freud, lamenting the difficulties he was encountering in the earliest groups, wrote in a letter, "I am not lying on a bed of roses myself. . . . My guess is that the insides of other great movements would have been no more appetizing if one could have looked into them. There are never more than one or two individuals who find the straight road and don't trip over their own legs."

Truth is the balm when the falsehood gets out of hand, the ingredient necessary to counteract the type of strain the country has undergone. "Intrapsychic integrity," a term I have used in describing the goals of psychoanalysis, is a capacity for "straightness," which is striven for in the training of analysts and then routinely in their treatment of patients. Intrapsychic integrity is a prerequisite for interpersonal integrity. To be honest with oneself, at least to a necessary degree, is a prerequisite to being honest with others. Is this not essentially what we mean by character? Freud himself, who had to overcome his own inner resistances in his discovery of basic psychic truths, wrote in a letter to Stefan Zweig: "Insofar as [my] achievement is concerned, it was less the result of intellect than of character."

Not only does a hero appear periodically when needed, but often, in the absence of this, one is resurrected or reconstructed. Harry Truman is being built up today. The Truman revival is directly parallel to the fall of Nixon. It is time now not for brilliance or intellect but for a blunt voice to speak the truth. In his characteristically salty way Truman, quoted in Merle Miller's book *Plain Speaking*, who knew Nixon in much earlier years, expressed a point of view about Nixon that is relevant today:

"All the time I've been in politics there's only two people I hate, and he's one. He not only doesn't give a damn about the people; he doesn't know how to tell the truth. I don't think the son-of-a-bitch knows the difference between telling the truth and lying. . . . Nixon is a shifty-eyed, goddamn liar and people know it. I can't figure out how he came so close to getting elected President in 1960. . . . He's one of the few in the history of this country to run for high office talking out of both sides of his mouth at the same time and lying out of both sides."

Here is an additional observation about the psychology of the two faces. It is not as if one side tells the truth and the other lies. The credibility of both must be questioned. In contrast, Truman goes on, "It's a most interesting study to find out that the Presidents of the United States have all up to now been honorable men, whether you like them or agree with them or not. Not a corrupt man among them."

What is being written today about Harry Truman may or may not be the truth, at least not to the extent being described. One can smell an idealization, a counterreaction. In 1961 and 1962, tapes and conversations obtained from Mr. Truman for a TV series on the Truman presidency failed to materialize for lack of interest and because Truman was at that time "too controversial." Today, in the backlash of Nixon and following Truman's death in 1972, his time has come. A number of biographies which have appeared in the last few years have reached the bestseller lists.

The comparison between Truman and Nixon is an interesting one. Sharing as they do their modest origins, the identification of the people with them and their achievements takes on a special intensity and a similar quality. But there the common ground ends, and their public histories diverge. While Truman proved that humble origins can be overcome, Nixon proved that this is not automatic. Lowly beginnings are compatible with but do not guarantee greatness. Truman also bore the stain of the Pendergast Machine in his early political background and overcame it. Nixon, at age eleven, was so outraged by the Teapot Dome scandal that he pledged himself to become a "lawyer who can't be bought"; he went on to become the opposite of that.

One characteristic deeply wanted now is the quality of sincerity. The measure of a leader yearned for above all others is to have him say what he means and to be able to believe him. Sincerity is to be distinguished from credibility. A man's credibility is whether he can be believed by others. His sincerity is whether he believes himself. While the two run parallel, they do not always overlap. What is at issue in judging and reacting to a man's sincerity is the distance between his inner and outer dialogues, between what he thinks and feels inside himself and what comes through his censor and is heard by others.

Nixon lacked both, although this was overlooked for long periods of time whenever it served the public to do so. Watergate brought to the surface a buried observation, forced people to look at it when it could no longer be denied. Consider the following, which we owe to Fawn Brodie from an article in the *Los Angeles Times:*

Frank Nixon died in 1956 while his son was in the midst of his second vice presidential campaign. The funeral ceremonies were private, and after a few days the candidate resumed his speech-making. In Buffalo, New York, Mr. Nixon paused in the middle of a speech, apparently groping for control. "I remember," he said, "Father telling me a long time ago: 'Dick,' he said, 'Buffalo is a beautiful town.' It may have been his favorite town." This reference was repeated in the next two speeches, each time in a quivering voice, but on both occasions Mr. Nixon took care to substitute the names of "Rochester" and "Ithaca" as needed.

It is human to have an inner dialogue and the privilege of a private world. And it is human and normal to have a filter between inner mental processes and the products which appear on the surface. This is a psychic fact of living and is necessary for survival. But there should not be an unbridgeable gap between the two. Nor should there be a process which converts what goes on inside to the very opposite when it comes out; or else—and this has been the most doleful characteristic of the last few years—which fashions the inside to whatever the outside wishes to hear.

There is a hunger for heroes. There is for example a new love for Goldwater in the land. Not because he was right, but because he meant what he said and would do what he meant. Goldwater, it is not forgotten, was for bombing Hanoi and mining Haiphong Harbor while Lyndon Johnson was for bringing our boys back home and letting "Asians fight on Asian soil." After which, Johnson did what Goldwater said! Nixon was neither the first nor the only one who did what his opponent said; nor was this characteristic limited to one party. But Nixon perfected the mechanism. Johnson was later rejected for this, or at least felt pressured enough not to run again.

Now Barry Goldwater is cheered in colleges and wherever he appears. "In your heart you know he's right" appears on posters, and makes for a nostalgic sentimentality. Not because Goldwater *was* right —he proved as wrong as Johnson was later judged to be—but because you know he means what he says and can be trusted to carry it out, even if wrong. He can be trusted—this is the characteristic held in common by Truman and Goldwater, neither of whom ever had much love for the other. When, as Nixon's troubles began to mount, Goldwater kept urging him "to come out with the truth, to tell all there is to tell about Watergate," this, combined with his past record, was sufficient for a revival of the hero label for Goldwater himself. Since that time, to the extent that Goldwater has gradually drifted back to the Nixon defense, the label seems to have been somewhat withdrawn.

From the same need, Governor George Wallace has risen considerably in the esteem of the American people. This is not because the public as a whole believes in what he stands for any more than they did at the beginning. It is, rather, a gut feeling about his consistency and straightness. A recent Harris poll showed that 61 percent compared to 17 percent of those polled considered him "a man of high integrity." Eighty-six percent answered in the affirmative that "Wallace has the courage to say what he thinks." Blacks supported Wallace's recent victory as governor of Alabama; and Charles Evers, the black mayor of Fayette, Mississippi, voiced support of him for vice-president of the United States! To quote Evers, "I guess it boils down to the fact that I can respect Wallace. . . . even if it is just cold politics, if it works and we get results, that's what we need—not empty promises and broken dreams. We've had them too long now." Evers does not speak, of course, for all black voters. Six prominent black officeholders have declared flatly they would not support a presidential ticket that included Wallace. "If Jesus Christ were nominated as President and George Wallace as Vice-President, I would vote against Jesus Christ," said Percy E. Sutton, president of New York's Borough of Manhattan.

Herbert Hoover is also being polished up. In this centennial year of Hoover's birth (he was born in 1874), Hoover history is being rewritten. Rexford G. Tugwell, a member of President Franklin D. Roosevelt's brain trust and the leading proponent of the New Deal, said, "We didn't admit it at the time. But practically the whole New Deal was extrapolated from programs that Hoover started." Described now as "the unluckiest man ever to be elected president of the United States," Hoover is being recognized "as one of the most activist presidents in our history, an immensely capable, honest, hard-working administrator." "Before his defeat in 1932," revisionist historian William A. Williams writes, "Hoover had pulled out every anti-depression tool the progressives ever owned."

The hero's time is limited—at least for the savior who rides on a moral beam. Wendell Willkie lifted the spirits of people for a short time and then lost. So did Adlai Stevenson, twice. For completeness of view, it should be noted that neither of these men ran against discredited opponents or easy marks. The winners in each case, FDR against Willkie and Eisenhower against Stevenson, had their own charisma and timing and would have been difficult, even impossible, for anyone to defeat.

People need complex, not one-sided representation. Both or all sides of their inner struggles need to be satisfied. Goldwater, who although of an opposite political stamp from a Willkie or Stevenson is equally consistent and unambiguous, was swamped by as much of a landslide as there was against McGovern in favor of Nixon. The political process is becoming increasingly such that it is only the middle—in fact the middle of the middle—that counts. A candidate has to sit astride the heap from which he can survey and claim allegiance from all sides. No one has yet achieved the dead-center as well as Nixon, who has emerged as a conservative liberal, liberal conservative. No longer can we have a McGovern on one side or a Goldwater on the other. A Robert Taft on today's scene would be out of the question.

No dalliance of Nixon's is the final straw, no stubbornness of position the last resort. Nixon can defy prosecutors, court orders, Senate committees, grand jury requests, the Internal Revenue Service, the urging of friends and the pressures of adversaries, the House Judiciary Committee and both houses of Congress; with each move, his defense goes on. After a continuous series of such obstructive moves, a petition twenty feet in length is presented in his defense. This is signed not by official backers or political leaders but by the apolitical, middle-American, middle-opinioned public. "It's great country," the president said of Southern California from where such a petition has just come. "It's Nixon country," replied one of the signers, "the whole country is Nixon country."

There seems to be a rock bottom in negative criticism beyond which the people will not go. This can almost be quantified. No matter what evidence comes out or how many charges go unanswered, roughly 25 percent, from any poll or measuring device, stays with the president and continues to defend and support him. I find this "bottoming out" a fascinating and telltale statistic. Perhaps these are the same 25 percent who do not "see" a crime, even a murder, committed before their eyes. There is a definite number who suppress or repress such perception, or else, permitting the perception to be registered, deny its significance and react as though they were looking at a painting or a movie.

Perhaps this ratio *among* people also reflects a similar proportion *within* people. Could it be that 25 percent of each person identifies with antisocial behavior up to any point? Who could not identify, perhaps with this quarter of his psychic equipment, with the following Nixonian behavioral constellation: doing the right things for the wrong reasons; doing wrong things and giving right reasons; saying one thing and doing another; doing one thing and saying you did another; calling things by their opposites; hating or disliking whom you say you're for; being close and friendly with those you say you're against; being the opposite of what you say you are and of what you're supposed to be. This is the stuff that dreams—and fantasies—are made of. It is a dream lived out in life.

If such a cynical appraisal causes unease, there is the consolation that the other 75 percent within each individual is against such behavior. This is what keeps people, and civilization, going—and is also what keeps the 25 percent repressed. But the continuous pressure of this repressed minority makes for awe, fascination, and unconscious admiration of one who succeeds in living by such methods.

Nixon has been nurtured on crises, lives familiarly among them, has always advanced in their atmosphere. Crises have followed him in his travels at home and abroad. When they have not existed, he has created or fanned them. His one excursion into "literary ranks," his political autobiography, was on that subject. From the danger and crisis of communism at his political birth through Alger Hiss to the Vietnam War, in repeated military crises during the war, and during the prolonged crisis of the ending of the war, Nixon has always used crises to his political advantage and has learned how to extract from them an unfailing advancement of his "self" interests. Crises do not overcome him; they stimulate him; and he needs them.

Nixon relates to either side of any conflict. His automatic unconscious linkage or readiness to be linked not to one, but to both sides of any dichotomy is an asset, if not to his character at least for his "success." Nixon has learned to ride the alternating and contrasting currents as a surfer rides the waves. He can wait for the trough, knows when it is coming, and can get maximum mileage as it makes its way back to the crest. People could at this moment, if they had the chance, vote for him again because he "agreed to pay" the half-million dollars in back taxes which it is said he owes. Nixon can wait for the counterreaction and ride it from the depth back up to the height.

He is best—or at least thus far has always been best—with his back against the wall. This capacity was perhaps the first visible trait which cemented a bond between Nixon and the people on a national scale. Reacting to the first real crisis which threatened to nip his fast-moving career, Nixon's response was automatic. Confronted with the exposure of an illegal campaign fund which jeopardized his remaining on the ticket with Eisenhower, his tactic was instinctive. He faced the nation on TV, struck a clean, all-American Dick Merriwell pose, and with chin forward grappled with the charges directly. He was brilliant, disarming, winning. His defense and general appeal as epitomized in the famous "Checkers" speech, which was spontaneously born for that occasion, took the form and tone of "I am not guilty. You all could be as guilty as I. They are after me and after you. I am as small and helpless against them as are all of you." From this model, which he was to use many times later, he elicited a national reaction on which he rode back to safety and victory.

I recently had the opportunity to see and hear that history-making performance again. The Checkers speech of 1952, listened to in 1974 against the backdrop of today, was an uncanny view into a forerunner of history: "My fellow Americans, I come before you tonight as a candidate for the vice-presidency and as a man whose honesty and integrity has been questioned." Nixon is before us again in the same way two decades later.

A questionable slush fund—exact prelude of what was to come! He plunged into it directly. "It isn't a question of whether it was legal or illegal, that isn't enough. The question is, was it morally wrong? I say that it was morally wrong—if any of that $18,000 went to Senator Nixon." He uses the third person, the same distancing device as when he was to talk about the president or the presidency in 1974. "And now to answer those questions, let me say this: not one cent of the $18,000 . . . went to my personal use. Every penny of it was used to pay for political expenses that I did not think should be charged to the taxpayers of the United States." He didn't do anything. And he was doing it for us, in the national interest. And not one person received any political favors in return for contributions, nor, he went on to say, would any person during any administration of which he was a part.

"I then turned to my second job" he wrote later in his *Six Crises*, and did more than was necessary, more than he was asked for, "a disclosure

of my entire financial history so as to discredit any future smears." In
his speech he said:

> There are some that will say . . . 'How can we believe what you say
> —after all, is there a possibility that you got some sums in cash? Is
> there a possibility that you might have feathered your own nest?'
> . . . And so now what I am going to do—and incidentally this is
> unprecedented in the history of American politics—I am going at
> this time to give to this television and radio audience a complete
> financial history, everything I have earned, everything I have
> spent, everything I own. . . .
>
> I should say this, that Pat doesn't have a mink coat. But she does
> have a respectable Republican cloth coat, and I always tell her that
> she would look good in anything.
>
> One other thing I probably should tell you, because if I don't they
> will probably be saying this about me, too. We did get something,
> a gift, after the nomination. . . .
>
> It was a little cocker spaniel dog, in a crate . . . sent all the way
> from Texas—black and white, spotted, and our little girl Tricia, the
> six-year-old, named it Checkers. And you know, the kids, like all
> kids, loved the dog, and I just want to say this, right now, that
> regardless of what they say about it, we are going to keep it.

This statement became forever related to Richard Nixon. The tone and
the subtleties of it aroused strong feelings, feelings both pro and con.

> But let us not only defend; let us look at the other side. I don't agree
> . . . that only a rich man should serve the government. . . . I believe
> that it's fine that a man like Governor Stevenson, who inherited a
> fortune from his father, can run for President. But I also feel that
> it is essential in this country of ours that a man of modest means can
> also run for President, because, you know—remember Abraham
> Lincoln, remember what he said—"God must have loved the com-
> mon people, he made so many of them."

"And then," he says later in his *Six Crises,* "I went over to the
counterattack":

I would suggest that under the circumstances both Mr. Sparkman [Governor Sparkman of Alabama, Democratic candidate for vice-president] and Mr. Stevenson [Adlai Stevenson, governor of Illinois, Democratic candidate for president] should come before the American people, as I have, and make a complete financial statement as to their financial history. And if they don't it will be an admission that they have something to hide.

Nixon now sets the ground rules; and he does not ask this of General Eisenhower, who was the only one he left out.

I know that this is not the last of the smears. In spite of my explanation tonight other smears will be made. Others have been made in the past. And the purpose of the smears, I know, is this: to silence me, to make me let up.

Well, they just don't know who they are dealing with . . . I intend to continue to fight.

Why do I feel so deeply? . . . I think my country is in danger. . . . I say, look at the record. Seven years of the Truman-Acheson Administration and what's happened? Six hundred million people lost to the Communists.

This was then followed by attacking in the vulnerable area in which he had been charged. "Take the problem of corruption. You have read about the mess in Washington. Mr. Stevenson can't clean it up because he was picked by the man, Truman, under whose Administration the mess was made." Guilt by association is still automatic, long after Hiss. It must be noted that Richard Nixon was later to select Spiro Agnew as his vice-president. Tens of others whom he was to choose were also later to be indicted.

His insincerity was palpable, but not yet recognized. Nixon found the formula early: hammer away at the hysteria of the hour. The response was immediate, in Nixon's words, "the greatest immediate response to any radio or television speech in history." Between one and two million telegrams poured in; overwhelmingly, he says in his book, "to keep Nixon on the ticket. . . . The effect was to lift my name to national prominence and to give me a national political following which helped

in the years ahead to give new stature to the office of Vice-President."
The Checkers speech also worked where it counted the most. General
Eisenhower, watching the telecast from the manager's office of the
Cleveland Public Auditorium, where he was to address a rally, re-
marked, Nixon writes, "I would rather go down in defeat fighting with
a brave man than to win with a bunch of cowards."

On that same recent occasion I was also able to hear again the Kennedy-
Nixon debates of 1960. Here, too, one of Nixon's permanent characteristics was evident—aggression smoothed with balm. With the same earnest voice and self-effacing posture, reaching for the most lethal arrow
of the moment, he smilingly, repeatedly, doggedly kept reminding
John Kennedy of his softness toward the Chinese. Kennedy had been
in favor of surrendering the offshore islands of Quemoy and Matsu to
the Red Chinese, in contrast to Eisenhower's contrary policy, Nixon
insisted. "If only you would admit that you were wrong, I would be the
first to drop this issue," he kept pressing. Admitting one had been
wrong—this was to become quite a test of Nixon in the years ahead.

But here Nixon met his master, someone with pure style who met his
pure pose. Kennedy did not ruffle, and patiently presented to Nixon and
the audience a more accurate version of what he had said, along with
the reasons and the logic for the varying positions he had taken as the
issue had unfolded. Writing later about the Kennedy debates, which is
generally considered to have cost Nixon his first attempt at the presidency, Nixon, with a characteristic defense against insight, stated, "I
recognized the basic mistake I had made. I had concentrated too much
on substance and not enough on appearance. I should have remembered that 'a picture is worth a thousand words.' " His version was that
he had been too straight, too rational, too honest. Later, after he had
learned his lesson, he reverted to gut talk.

Nixon has harnessed himself to the rhythm of the mind of man, and
can swing with it in any direction, at any phase of its cycle. He can make
of himself whatever is popular or appealing at the moment—in fact, at
opposite moments. In the spring of 1974, Sen. Henry Jackson accused
President Nixon of being soft on Communism! And just as Nixon has
always been in the past the bête noire of the liberals, so now, in more
liberal times, do conservative elements dislike and distrust him. Speaking to a meeting of the revived John Birch Society in March 1974, at one

of the largest political banquets in Los Angeles in recent months, Robert Welch called Richard Nixon "one of the ablest, shrewdest, most disingenuous and slipperiest politicians that ever showed up on the American scene." Describing him as a would-be dictator, Welch said, "From Alger Hiss to Richard Nixon, every Communist or 'Insider' has a knowing fear that although he is a peacock today he may be a feather duster tomorrow." The circle had closed.

It is still intuitive with Nixon, even after his unprecedented troubles and with all eyes upon him, to say nothing straight. Confronted with the fact that a Democrat had just won a congressional seat in Michigan held by the Republicans for sixty-four years, the same seat occupied by Gerald Ford for the last twenty-five years, Nixon attributes this victory not to Watergate, as does everyone else, but "to the political situation." As people wait in long lines for gas during the 1974 energy crisis, he declares that the "crisis" is over, only the "problems" remain. People are so used to this behavior that they are not even offended.

Nothing is below Nixon; no contradictions embarrass him. In a speech at Annapolis in June 1974, explaining his opposition to pressing for a freer Soviet policy on Jewish emigration, Nixon declared that we have no right to intervene in the internal domestic policies of foreign countries: "We would not welcome the intervention of other countries in our domestic affairs and we cannot expect them to be cooperative when we seek to intervene directly in theirs," the president said. "We cannot gear our foreign policy to transformation of other societies." The president's memory did not present to him for consideration our long history in Vietnam, or in Korea, or Rhodesia, or more recently in Chile, or elsewhere in South America—and who knows as well as he where else. Capable of nimble balancing acts where necessary, when he returned to the White House in the early afternoon on that same day, Nixon met with seven United States Jewish leaders to express his support for Israel in the military, economic, and political fields.

It was Nixon, yes, Richard Nixon, who recently abolished the attorney general's list of subversive organizations, and who declared the protection of privacy to be a national priority. In doing this he espoused the thought expressed in the famous funeral oration of Pericles twenty-four hundred years earlier, extolling Athenian democracy in the fifth century B.C.: "Many things are necessary to lead a full, free life. But none of these is more important than the most basic of all individual rights, the right to privacy. A system that fails to respect its citizens' right to privacy, fails to respect the citizens themselves."

It is ironic that the administration which more than any other in this century placed American citizens under surveillance should be the one to claim for itself, as an operative principle, the protection of privacy. Speaking with deep concern about the invasion of privacy which has come with the increase in technocracy and with the misuse of computer data banks, Nixon now proposed to create a cabinet-level committee to protect this right of citizens. "Until science finds a way of installing a conscience in every computer," the president said, "we need personal human safeguards."

Anytime you need it, "Here I am, another Nixon." Many consider him a pragmatist for this trait; different terms could be used. When one listens today to his complaints about congressional investigators and his insistence on the ultimate supremacy of executive privilege, it is shocking to read in his *Six Crises* of 1962 how, when he was a member of a House investigating committee, he espoused the need for congressional investigating bodies to check and force the executive branch. Not only the executive: "We did not trust the Justice Department to prosecute the [Hiss] case with the vigor we thought it deserved." Ten years later he entrusted the Watergate case to the Justice Department as a reason for Congress to stay out. Nor has there ever been a statement that a previous position was wrong, as Nixon gyrated repeatedly from one position to its opposite. This was the man who, in the early television debates, had asked Kennedy, "If you would just say that you were wrong, I would drop the issue completely."

Insight, self-awareness, contradictions are not apparent or available to him. In his book he writes how Eisenhower, in backing him against Kennedy in 1960, attacked Kennedy's "appeal to immediate gain and selfishness" and, declaring himself "completely committed to the election of Dick Nixon," Eisenhower called for "woodshed honesty" with the American people. "Personal interests" and "political expediency," Nixon wrote then, were two motives he would not tolerate in himself or others in his political life. "Selflessness," he went on, "is the greatest asset an individual can have in a time of crisis. 'Selfishness' (in its literal rather than its lay sense) is the greatest liability." I also, interestingly

enough, have used "selfish" in "other than the lay sense"—in quite a
technical sense—but have come to an opposite conclusion about
Nixon's status with respect to this criterion of character.

When asked at a press conference whether he would be willing to put
his present case before the people in a referendum, Nixon declined for
the reason that "the President must not be encouraged to do something
for popularity. Some of the most unpopular Presidents have turned out
to be the best ones." His ability to say anything that would benefit his
cause, in total disregard of facts and the accumulated weight of evidence, continues now as it has from the day he entered politics. Just as
he assured the American people a few years ago that both the beginning and the end of the Vietnam War were honorable, so now does he
calmly declare that everything that has been said against him is "all a
lie." The Watergate matter, he says, "has been overpublicized." On the
eve of the impeachment meetings of the House Judiciary Committee
in July 1974, Nixon issues a blanket statement that Watergate is the
broadest and thinnest scandal in American history: "If I was guilty of
any of those charges, I would not serve as President for one day."

It is so "thin" that its base occupies thousands of pages of documents,
reports, and data, a labyrinth of charges which continue and grow
worse. That the IRS and the CIA and other government agencies have
been used to harass "enemies," or even simply the opposite political
party, is now a proven and documented fact. But Nixon's brief statement is supposed to supersede all this. And it can. An easy, simple,
confident, unequivocal statement has its effect on the collective mind.
The people, for example, came to accept two years of Watergate as one.

Nixon invites regression. His appeal is to the emotions, not to logic;
to gut reactions, not to fine discrimination. His communications, his
affect, the content of what he conveys and the manner in which he
delivers it, encourage in the listener what psychoanalysts call "primary
process thinking." This is a type of cognitive and intellectual activity
which is irrational rather than rational, and which occurs in a variety
of regressed conditions. In normal life this type of thinking takes place
in sleep and in dreaming, in daydreaming, in reverie states, and in
fantasy life. In these states thought processes proceed without being
checked by reality, by the requirements of rationality, by the limits of
external life. The same type of mentation takes place in abnormal states

as well, as under the influence of drugs or hypnosis, or in more overtly disturbed mental states as deliria, schizophrenia, or other types of psychoses.

"Primary process" thinking characterizes the normal irrationality of the unconscious, where contradictions and inconsistencies exist side by side. It is governed by the "illogic" of easy and labile associations, by the combining and condensation of psychic elements, and the displacement of thoughts and emotions from one element to another. All of these result on the outside in fuzziness, lack of clarity, ambiguity, or confusion. Suggestibility is increased. In the sum total of messages, speeches, communications, and warnings Nixon delivers to the people, he invites them to think and respond at these levels of psychic functioning. With this type of receptivity, they are more likely to be with him as he wants them.

"Secondary process" is the opposite mode of thinking. This is the more rational, cognitive process of life in which the ego is more in command than the id. Logic predominates, judgment and discrimination are finer, contradictions and ambiguity are discouraged and less in evidence. This crisper and clearer type of thinking is not characteristically appealed to by Nixon in his public communications. Nor does he particularly want or aim at it. With this mode predominating, people would think for themselves, would never have served him well in his times of crisis.

It is interesting to note that after his first Kennedy debate, which it was generally conceded that Nixon lost, he felt that he had paid too much attention to content, not enough to emotional appeal. He apparently felt he had slipped on that one occasion. He never did so again. I believe that on that occasion he was impressed and made anxious by Kennedy and the crucial nature of the event. The debate was perceived by Nixon as a high point and a braking (not breaking) point in his career. He rose above himself for a moment. Then he slipped back.

In the service of achieving the regressive state, Nixon is a master of the cliché, the slang expression, the catchy phrase. He makes ready use of "clang associations," where sounds, not thoughts, convey the message. Words and phrases are sing-song, alliterative, and tend to lull the listener. Nixon brought the POWs home "on their feet and not on their knees." He admonished the country to "let others wallow in Watergate"; that "those who drag out Watergate, drag down the country." Such phrases and slogans, and the mass reactions to them, he felt instinctively and from past experience, would lead him out of his troubles.

These metaphors conjure up in the mind concrete and visual imagery of a type that exists in dreaming, a state in which abstract thinking and critical judgment are little in evidence. Nixon's script writers are of course of great help to him. Nixon is protecting the presidency, not the president; the government, not his own interests. Resignation, he says, would be "an easy cop-out" that would lead to "weak and unstable Presidencies in the future. . . . The nation and the world need a strong President. I will not be a party to the destruction of the Presidency of the United States." If he leaves or is forced out of office, "the government, the executive office, the sensitive political balance will be weakened and fail."

Words replace things and names are substituted for people. This is another mechanism borrowed from disturbed mental states. In schizophrenia there is a reification of the word, the symbol, the label. Words and names become concrete objects in themselves; they replace the original objects which they are supposed to designate. To a schizophrenic the word "chair" becomes an object in itself and not a symbol to designate a thing to sit on. The schizophrenic then plays with and distorts and takes off from the word; the object, the piece of furniture, is lost. The presidency, national security, executive privilege become living things in themselves and come to replace what they were originally designed to connote. The people get dizzy and sleepy and feel taken care of. There is a deep and strong pull to go along.

Words are used to avoid facts, not to convey them; to deflect the listener, not to inform him. Unrealities result and absurdities occupy the surface. One cartoonist depicted a robber putting a gun to a victim declaring, "This is not a stick-up." Non sequiturs are offered, and accepted. Nixon, the accused, will decide how many tapes and which tapes and documents the prosecution needs for its case against him. He gave them 19 tapes, "which is all they need"; then he withholds 42, then 64, then 131 conversations, documents, and tapes. A suspect can tell a judge, "I will tell you where I was on Tuesday, not on Wednesday; that is all you need to know."

Nixon is not the first to use slogans, words, and phrases which dull perception and dampen judgment. Nor was "peace with honor" the first cliché in history to lull people into a passive compliance with a course of action which a determined leader was bent on bringing about. There is a long tradition for this, and history is a succession of such verbal ruses. There was a very bloody "war to end all wars" to which the people marched willingly. The phrase was catchy and nipped any discontent in the bud. In our more recent history there was the "New Deal" and later the "New Frontier." The mechanism is again a bipartisan one. And it is not limited to political life. It borrows freely from commerce and industry and from the highly developed professional fields of advertising and other forms of mind persuasion. Sometimes, it is to be hoped, the words of persuasion carry some substance, and do not necessarily tout a negative product even if their fronts are catchy. But with Nixon any such coincidence is purely incidental. Nixon's sales formulae generally have been devoid of value, bear only the remotest relationship to the social good. Characteristically they have been of value to his "self" interests; and in the most recent period to his political survival.

After the mammoth illegal tax deduction Nixon took for his vice-presidential papers, evidence gathered by a congressional committee showed that he had held back the papers of greatest value. These included correspondence with such figures as Kennedy, Churchill and Queen Elizabeth, Khrushchev, Ben-Gurion, Konrad Adenauer, and Albert Schweitzer. These letters, which his appraiser had informed him would be of most future value to historians and autograph collectors, were removed from the files and set aside for personal use as much as a year after Nixon had donated them to the government (before the July 25, 1969, deadline for taking income tax deductions on charitable gifts of papers). Folders containing the letters and related correspondence are being held in special storage for him in a high-security room in the Archives. One cynical theory about the reason Nixon set up the taping system in the first place was to have another tax deduction later, since he had already given away his earlier papers. With all that has happened since, this theory is no longer difficult to entertain.

With mounting criticism, Nixon does not seem touched or personally fazed. His ability to appear resilient, to go on with optimistic predictions and high-sounding speeches is part of the character armor with which he goes through life. As the prospect of impeachment presses, he can make a speech on Memorial Day expressing sincere and deep wishes about the respect we owe to the dead. Warning the country against taking peace for granted by weakening its military strength, Nixon goes on, "Lasting peace can be achieved only through lasting awareness, lasting preparedness and lasting strength both physical and moral." It is hard to put this together with the man who was speaking in the transcripts. In a speech at a Republican congressional fundraising dinner, without mentioning Watergate, Nixon predicts a Republican election victory in the fall and a revival of the economy by then. "We're going to win in the fall," he says.

Yet in spite of his aplomb and seeming equanimity, he is no master of tact or finesse, is in fact astonishingly guilty at times of the opposite. Attending the memorial services for President Georges Pompidou in Paris, Nixon exhibited unbelievably gauche and clumsy behavior which strongly offended French officials and the French people. Plunging into the crowds with smiles and handshakes to acknowledge cries of "Bravo Nixon," he was later criticized in high French official circles and by leading French journalists as having "shamelessly substituted a publicity campaign for the mourning of an entire nation." "Noblesse oblige," wrote Le Figaro, "but power also obliges." Other newpapers reported his behavior as characterized by "discourtesy and clumsiness." One commented: "The United States President forgot he came here for a national mourning and behaved as though it was the liberation of Paris." This incident, spontaneous in its occurrence, supports a view of many abroad of Nixon's intrinsic lack of empathy and insensitivity to the feelings of others, traits in keeping with his accumulated record of behavior at home.

When in Doubt, Travel

Nixon's tactics are repetitive; some uncanny repetitive series have occurred during the course of his volatile political career (Checkers and Watergate are one). I have described how, just before Election Day 1972, Nixon sent Kissinger on an eye-catching trip to Paris, Saigon, and

Hanoi. He achieved his goals. The Vietnam War was brought under control, the Watergate threat hovering over Nixon was dispelled, and from the combination of these Nixon was handed a third, the biggest trophy of all, his reelection.

Now, as the threat of Nixon's un-election day mounts, a similar situation presents itself. And instinctively, as if by rote, the same plan is set into action. Again Kissinger is sent traveling by Nixon, at the same relative time to an impending personal threat for the same type of mission, this time to the Middle instead of the Far East.

As before the reality is a mixed one, and the motives are fused and blurred. Again there is the principle of the multiple function of behavior. Realistic requirements cannot be overlooked. There was a war going on in the Middle East, as there had been one in the Far East, and it was as laudable as before to try to mitigate or end it. But unfortunately, just as with the ending of the Vietnam War, so was the ending of this war by Nixon and Kissinger as important to Nixon at this particular moment as it was to Israel, the Arab countries, the United States and Russia, and to the world. Nixon's record by now is such that nothing can be believed. This was also close to the time that he put the air force suddenly on alert in a supposed military crisis in the Middle East and had to undo it at once because of public suspicion and opposition.

A frantic travel schedule, by now familiar, was set up. This time Kissinger started moving on April 28, 1974. The transcripts were released April 29–30 (his Paris-Hanoi movements had begun one day before the *Washington Post* article appeared in print). Kissinger's luminous and well-covered mission took place during the time that the posttranscript fever was at its most acute. In thirty-two days of high-powered diplomacy that involved almost daily shuttles between Jerusalem and Damascus, meetings with Soviet Foreign Minister Gromyko in Cyprus and Geneva, and stops in four other Arab capitals, Kissinger clinched and delivered to the American people and the world—but also to Nixon and to the headlines he so crucially needed—the Syrian-Israeli disengagement pact.

Upon Kissinger's return to this country, Nixon, who was originally scheduled to make his own Mideast trip on June 27, accelerated his plans. A separate trip was announced; Nixon, along with Kissinger, would leave for the Middle East on June 10, returning to Washington on June 19. As "election politics" were denied in 1972, so were "impeachment politics" denied now. But a White House aide, while insisting that "impeachment politics is not being played," acknowledged the acceleration in travel plans and that Mideast developments "could well make some Congressmen realize the foreign policy successes of this administration which, as the President said, have brought us closer to peace in the Mideast than at any time in the past generation." Other senior aides said that back-to-back visits had never been planned; but there was little doubt that the schedule was suddenly accelerated.

Nixon's critics, inside the Congress and out, questioned whether the trip could accomplish anything of substance and asserted that he was using foreign policy for partisan political ends. The people themselves reacted with muted—but only muted—criticism. Again it would be churlish to object, at least too strongly. Who does not wish peace at this time? But Nixon's defenders were vocal. And he responded to their loud and unbridled support in his usual manner. At a luncheon of cheering, chanting supporters just before he left for the Mideast, Nixon said he was embarking on his "long, difficult and very important journey" with the hope of helping to build an era of peace in the troubled region. He intended to serve his full term, he reassured them, and to leave his office in January 1977, "with our heads held high." Nixon's appearance was before the National Citizens' Committee for Fairness to the Presidency, a group whose purpose was "to serve notice on the radical-liberal media and legislators that their vendetta against the President will not go unchallenged."

Hitting again on a theme he was sounding repeatedly in his efforts to blunt impeachment, Nixon said, "A strong American President is essential if we are to have peace in the world." The 1400 guests struck up a chant of "God bless Nixon." A fierce loyalty to the president and a hostility to the news media occasionally erupted into boos and fist-waving directed at the press covering the luncheon. "We of the Citizens' Congress," said Rabbi Baruch Korff, chairman of the committee, "are deeply concerned with the climate of hysteria being engendered by members of the press and electronic media in a massive attempt to reverse the overwhelming mandate given the President by the people of the United States." Sen. Carl Curtis, Republican of Nebraska, told the group, "I criticized the firing of Archibald Cox. My criticism was that it wasn't soon enough. Lynching hasn't stopped in the United States. It's just that different people are doing it."

Nixon's trip to the Arab countries resulted in a tumultuous welcome and intense Arab adulation. In a gargantuan and frenzied reception, a crowd of two million hailed the president in Cairo alone. Similar greetings awaited him on a trip through the Nile delta to Alexandria, in Amman, Jordan, in Damascus, and in Saudi Arabia. He was hailed as a peacemaker in the Holy Land.

Just as Vietnam turned all eyes away from the *Washington Post*'s revelation of Watergate, so now was the edge taken off Nixon's troubles at this near-climactic phase of the Watergate investigation. A criminal in his own country, he was a hero in another. From President Sadat he received Egypt's highest award, the Grand Collar of the Nile.

Nixon carried his traits with him to these distant continents. In a sudden move known at first only to himself, he handed over a nuclear reactor to Egypt along with an offer of United States aid in developing nuclear power technology. To the wave of protest which was immediately forthcoming when this was announced in the United States, Nixon assured the country that this atomic know-how would be used only for peaceful purposes. We have their word for that, he said! Later, to balance things as usual, he made a similar gesture in his subsequent visit to Israel. In another burst of generosity, it was revealed that Nixon personally presented to Egyptian President Anwar el-Sadat a two-million-dollar helicopter from the presidential fleet after Nixon and Sadat had flown in the craft from Alexandria to Cairo. It was difficult to be sure whose interests were being primarily served.

To Sen. Henry Jackson, who more and more was becoming the spokesman for the Democratic opposition, Nixon's Middle East trip was "fraught with danger" and "will be more cosmetic and ceremonial than it will be substance." But the reactions of others were epitomized by Governor Ronald Reagan, who said that what President Nixon and Secretary Kissinger were doing in the Middle East was "far more important than anything the Rodino Committee is going to produce. ... The government of the United States and the President are the only anchor holding world peace together," Reagan told a Los Angeles Area Chamber of Commerce luncheon at the Los Angeles Hilton.

It is interesting to note that when Syria refused to sign an agreement to oppose terrorist activity within its borders, Kissinger persuaded Israel to accept the agreement without the Syrian signature on the strength of Nixon's *word* that he would support the Israeli cause on this issue in the United Nations. Thus Nixon's word, discredited in his own country, was accepted by Israel under pressure.

Those who cared to look closely at this time could have observed that the president had started to limp. A minor reference was made about this medically: the president was suffering an acute thrombophlebitis in the left lower extremity. It was not clear what medical advice or treatment he had received. Any physician would agree that such a condition made a trip of this nature not only undesirable but risky. The condition has within it a danger which is more serious than the local inflammation itself. An embolus, a clot, can break off and lodge in the heart or lungs with catastrophic results up to sudden death. If anything, the trip could have been legitimately postponed or even cancelled, certainly not accelerated. Or it could have been stopped en route. It is not clear when this condition began. But whatever Nixon was told, on this occasion the president kept moving; this trip meant a great deal to him. I think we can say that no matter what happened, he felt he had something to gain.

Following the Mideast trip and after a week or two at home, Nixon was off again, this time to Moscow and the third summit, his second in the Soviet Union. A warm reception awaited him, the friendliest yet received by Nixon in the Soviet Union. A personal greeting at the airport by Communist party leader Leonid I. Brezhnev himself, with big smiles and a back slap, was regarded in international circles as a particular sign of favor. Brezhnev had not met Nixon upon his arrival in 1972 for the first summit meeting. And there had been fewer people then at the airport and on the streets along Nixon's motorcade route. Self-interests determine not only the course but the mood of international diplomacy. The ego over the superego by a landslide. They like Nixon in Russia now. He is their favorite American.

Immediately upon arrival, Nixon emphasized the "personal" relationship between himself and Brezhnev. It was this rapport, he stressed, which produced and maintained Soviet-American détente. In his first public statement after arriving, Nixon emphasized that agreements reached in the previous two summits were possible because of this personal relationship. And again during a Kremlin banquet toast, he said, "Because of our personal relationship, there is no question about our will to keep these agreements and to make more. . . ."

A stir was created the next day when, in the official Russian translation of the toast, the word "personal" was left out. In the Russian translation distributed by Tass, the Soviet news agency, printed in *Pravda,* the official party paper, the word "personal" *(lichnoye)* was omitted. The Russians, it was suggested by some diplomatic sources and reported by several news agencies, were preparing themselves for the future. Soviet officials, they felt, wished to deemphasize the importance of these personal relations in the future development of ties with the United States. A diplomatic debate ensued as to the meaning and motive of the error. The director of Tass and some Soviet officials privately denied any deliberate intent. The Russian text, they said, would be changed by the afternoon edition of *Izvestia,* the government newspaper. "It is a non-issue," said Ronald Ziegler. But no conclusion was reached. And *Izvestia* made no change in the Russian text.

The meetings and travels and discussions continued; it was difficult to say what was accomplished or even what was intended. But no doubt Nixon would have liked to visit a series of such areas, trouble spots to which only he could attend personally and which would take him out of the country for the remainder of his term. In another one of his timely treatments, Art Buchwald wrote a column about Nixon as a mobile target moving from country to country. He is in touch by telephone with Kissinger who is similarly on the move.

Secret diplomacy was again the mode. The double purpose of the trip and the desperate need for success made this imperative. And with it, as Senator Jackson continued to warn, came the possibility of secret agreements. While the impeachment proceedings were approaching a climax at home, Nixon's dramatic activities abroad were deflecting attention. The result for the people was the same conflict, doubt, confusion, and guilt as had existed during the diplomatic flurries in Vietnam. In each area, the results were reported to be immediate but with each the future remained unknown. To appreciate the flavor of each political journey one needs to retain a vertical as well as a horizontal view. It is the longitudinal history which gives clues to the methods and casts a shadow over the current performance. The present alone can seem simple and right.

The picture of Nixon at the walls of the Kremlin, placing a wreath at the Tomb of the Unknown Soldier, or of Nixon with Comrade Brezhnev aboard Brezhnev's yacht on the Black Sea can produce peculiar gastric effects in many Americans with a strong memory. Those without such acute and lingering recall are in a sense better off. Memory, especially the full-blown variety, available not only in its cognitive form but with its appropriate accompanying emotions, can produce psychosomatic effects, even quite severe ones. The capacity to forget, or a good repressive mechanism, can protect against such experiences.

During the trip, Nixon casually presented Brezhnev with a third American car to add to his collection—he had given him two others at their previous meetings. One other observation: Nixon was again limping, this time a bit more. Getting on and off planes and moving among crowds, he walked with some effort on his affected and obviously tender left leg. But he smiled and waved and walked and did it all. Following Nixon's return, Kissinger stopped at other European capitals on his way home, needing to allay the anxieties of our allies and to tie up loose ends.

People respond positively to Nixon's perseverance, his industriousness, his fight upward as the underdog. Nixon himself volunteers a piece of his past history to explain this aspect of his character. "I am not a quitter," he has said in more than one speech when things looked bad, and attributes this trait to his parents who taught him that "when things look the worst, you work the hardest." John Mitchell gave similar advice to Hugh Sloan, Jr., when Sloan was advised by Jeb Magruder that he might have to perjure himself: "When the going gets tough, the tough get going," said Mitchell.

Nixon has other sympathetic traits, although they are more difficult to see now. Mrs. Jeb Magruder stated in a recent television interview, "Nixon was a shy man and meant well." This could have been true, on top of, or below, everything else. If only Watergate could have gone by unnoticed, or, better still, if Nixon had allowed himself to be reelected without it, perhaps in his second and final term he could have let himself do what the best of him wished. He might yet have recorded a presidency to be proud of; if, that is, there can ever be a top limit to neurotic and insecure ambition.

If Nixon's achievements as president are judged only horizontally, with no concern for questions of reliability or the past history of motivations, there is no doubt that they rate high. Even by the standards of the liberals he always opposed, he did do in actuality everything they labeled good. He did acquire much expertise in international affairs in spite of what he stood for originally, or perhaps because of it. Détente and cooperation, which he accomplished openly, were as strong on his record as the spying, bombing, and militancy which he always stood for and sneaked into action. What his secretary of state accomplished on the international scene must also be credited to the president himself. The many faces of Nixon do not preclude that some of them may be good ones, just as he probably meant at least some of the idealistic phrases he wrote and spoke on his way up.

People do grow in their jobs; and this is especially true of the presidency. Truman grew with it; so did Johnson, and many others in the past. Nixon grew as well, and did accomplish much. No doubt he could still grow if given the chance; he has a tough capacity to overcome obstacles and go on from there.

I mentioned earlier the process of "change of function," that behavior undertaken for one motive may be diverted in transit to another. While many instances cited were from the idealistic toward the personal, the same mechanism can operate in the reverse. A shift can be made from the personal to the altruistic—particularly after the personal has been achieved. This is what often happens with "growth in office." And to some extent it can have happened with Nixon too.

A time to be careful is when one reaches his goals. It was Nixon himself who wrote in 1962, "The easiest period in a crisis situation is actually the battle itself. The most difficult is the period of indecision —whether to fight or run away. And the most dangerous period is the aftermath. It is then, with all his resources spent and his guard down, that an individual must watch out for dulled reactions and faulty judgment." Did he presage his Watergate a decade in advance?

Nixon is a Rorschach to the American people; they react selectively to whichever of his faces they wish, reflecting their own inner prefer-ences or attitudes toward life. To many, everything Nixon says now is suspect. Even the actual good, it is continuously feared, stems mainly from personal motives. On any specific issue now they may be doing Nixon an injustice, even if this is of his own past doing. As the fate of the boy who cried "wolf" too many times, too much has been imprinted.

Others display the opposite reaction; to them the same Nixon can inspire. Nixon's contacts with his audience have always been as much with his assumed faces as with his "real" ones. In March 1974, before the transcripts but after the tapes, Gov. Winfield Dunn of Tennessee was both accepting of and convinced by Nixon in a speech to the nation's governors. Following Nixon's speech, Dunn said: "I have never been more inspired, I have never been more elated, I have never been more confident. I'm going to break my neck to keep him in office." Asked if he shared Dunn's views, Gov. James E. Holshouser, Jr., of North Carolina replied, "Yes, sirree." Other governors who were more dubious about the president were also impressed with his form and performance. Gov. Tom McCall of Oregon, to whom the evening was "something ecstatic," said that the cruelty was "when you see what life could be like in Washington. . . . I wish we'd get back to it, not just for three hours but for three years." About President Nixon, whom he still opposes, he said, "I just hope he gets a little surcease from this agony."

With regard to what Nixon achieved and the ways in which it came about, the people must share the responsibility for both. This was what they wanted, and the ways they wanted it too. Did they not turn down other men who were more unequivocal, who stood for the same goals more openly and would have pursued them in a straighter path? Did the people ever acknowledge that they wanted these particular international achievements? If anyone had run on the platform of a close relationship with China or the Soviet Union in 1968 or 1964, or 1960, would he have gotten off the ground? He would have had no chance, would have been defeated soundly. One had to run against these ideas; only then could he put them into effect. Deep down the people knew that these directions were right. So did Nixon; so did Kissinger, who was advising him. But all were in collusion at each stage, unwilling to acknowledge directly, but only in gradual increments, that cooperation and mutuality with the other half of the world was called for; a true one, not a condescending one. It was a national as much as a personal narcissism which directed the method.

Jacob Burckhardt, in *Reflections on History,* speaks of the "mysterious coincidence between the egotism of the individual and the communal will." Every nation, historians point out, must bear the responsibility for its own history. There is, in the preconditions for an historical event, a unique conjunction between individual and general prerequisites. The age and the man must intersect, as do the leader and the led. This is true not only in dramatic and fulminating national events, but in more subtle developments as well.

Joachim C. Fest, in *Hitler,* a sensitive analysis of Hitler and emergent Nazism, emphasized the interaction between Hitler and the German people in producing the most catastrophic events of our age. The clue, Fest says, lies not in the differences which Hitler projected between himself and his people, but in his "typical" and "normal" aspects: "He was not so much the great contradiction of the age as its mirror image." What Fest wished mainly to express for mankind in the twentieth century is the significance of tendencies which go beyond the specific circumstances of Germany, to pre-Fascist conditions present with variations everywhere in the world today. In a review of Fest's work in the *Los Angeles Times,* Robert Kirsch writes that the screens must be stripped away between people and recent history which shield them from events which both fascinate and repel them.

From a demographic point of view, one might say that the ambivalence described toward Nixon, the amalgam of attraction and repulsion, applies not to all the people but only to the large silent majority, the undecided bloc in the middle which determines the outcome of every election. It is true that this duality exists mainly within this central distribution. At each end of the bell curve of the population people are more decided, on opposite sides. Yet the principle of ambivalence and internal splits is not that sharply limited to some and not to others. In the deepest layers of the personality there is conservative in the radical and radical in the conservative. History shows repeatedly how close together the opposite poles can be.

It Could Have Gone Either Way

It is now the latter part of July. The House Judiciary Committee is expected to present its bill of impeachment in about two weeks. It is not known at this time what the recommendations will be.

Although these words will be read after the decision, they are being written before it. As much as that dramatic decision occupies center stage at this moment, the conclusion and the terminal thrust of this analysis is separate from the outcome and can in fact only be obscured by it. The central empirical fact upon which the accumulation of events of the past two years converges is that it could have gone either way. Only this is the complete psychological truth. Neither side of the final arguments now being presented, whatever the conclusion to which they may lead, will of itself tell the whole inner story. Neither of Nixon, nor of the people who are his ultimate judge.

One final event or impassioned speech or summation can tip the mood and switch the heart of the people, the Congress, the judges, the jury. And the decision can be swept either against Nixon, toward the first impeachment in our history; or to drop this whole sordid matter and continue our national history with an officially unblemished record. A last emotional push can cast the die and afterward make it look as if it were even one-sided. If we lose sight of this, we will lose the lesson of Watergate, especially since the basic cause will survive either impeachment or Nixon's escape from it.

In pausing to survey this moment before the decision, however it goes, we can see that a tragedy equivalent to Sophocles' *Oedipus Rex* has already transpired and run its course. The final fate of Oedipus could also have gone either way, and the tragedy would have had an equally general applicability. As many people escape final retribution as pay the price. The same is true of the present drama which involves not the id but the superego as its fulcrum. The agony has already been experienced on the public stage no matter how it ends.

With the evidence available, if Nixon is impeached, as when Oedipus was blinded, a need for reparations will probably set in along with a reaction of guilt and shame. Oedipus also did not "know" what he was doing; the information was also kept from him. As long as Nixon says this about himself, a sliver of belief remains because he said it; and to those who still believe him, Nixon would be eligible for martyrdom. If Nixon is not separated from his office, anger and outrage can result, followed by a gradual rationalization, return to normal, and even apathy about the whole experience. Guilt and shame under the present circumstances can be present with either outcome. And in either case, restitution and reconstruction will follow.

Even with the final arguments, substantive data keeps appearing. The Nixon administration used the Internal Revenue Service to investigate contributors to the McGovern campaign, as well as those who failed to contribute to Nixon's own treasure chest for reelection. Two former directors of the IRS testified that they resisted direct pressure to do this and resigned from their positions as a result. A comparison of the tapes in the hands of the committee with the transcripts edited by the president shows omissions, additions, and changes which invariably, in the committee's version, puts Nixon's knowledge about the cover-up in a more damaging light. In one such new version, the president says to Dean and Mitchell, "I don't give a shit what happens. I want you all to stonewall it, let them plead the Fifth Amendment, cover-up or anything else, if it'll save it—save the plan. That's the whole point. . . ."

The case for a definite legal breach against the president is becoming more probable. Witnesses have spoken of earlier and earlier involvement by the president: Colson—that he had told Nixon of the cover-up two months before the president says he heard it; Magruder—that Nixon knew of the Watergate involvement shortly after it happened; McCord, in his book—that the president set in motion both the break-in and the cover-up. March 21, 1973, has been left far behind. In the evidence we are getting closer and closer to the actual day of the break-in. A partial transcript of a tape of June 30, 1972, thirteen days after the break-in, quotes the president as telling Haldeman and Mitchell that he hoped nothing else would "come out" on Watergate. "I'd cut the loss fast," the president says. "It would make anybody else who asked any question on it look like a selfish son-of-a-bitch."

The chief administration witnesses give shabby performances. "Mitchell is trying to get the benefit of the Fifth Amendment without using it," commented Rep. John Seiberling of the House Judiciary Committee. "He's a genius at not recollecting," stated Rep. Hamilton Fish, another member of the committee. Sen. Sam Ervin had earlier commented, during his own committee hearings, how many witnesses had, wherever it could serve them, "a good forgettery." This was not uncommon. It applied to Ehrlichman and many others. Mitchell had speed forgetting. Vice-President Ford, asked to comment on what Colson had revealed just a few days before, prefaced his bland denials of their serious implications with "If I remember rightly what he said . . ."!

Both the majority and minority counsels of the House Judiciary Committee are now emphasizing the gravity of the matter and the "extreme seriousness" of the case against the president. And official reports have now come out which document the damaging case against him. A three-volume, 2,217-page report by the Ervin committee has concluded that the cause of this "most tragic happening in American history" was a giant abuse of the power of the president which had been "viewed by some in the White House as almost without limit." While stopping short of blaming the president, Senator Ervin, when asked about the president's specific role, replied in one of his better aphorisms, "We have drawn the picture of a horse. We did not have to say it was a horse." In a four-thousand-page sister document, a massive report of the House Judiciary Committee, let out before the committee turned to articles of impeachment, details a White House campaign of stonewalling, perjury, hush-money payments, and other strategies which add up to a sweeping cover-up of the Watergate scandal. A cold encyclopedic account, devoid of passion, judgment, or even suggestion, it draws no conclusions about impeachment, which is now left up to the committee members.

Meanwhile, outside the hearing room, repugnant developments continue. It has now come out that American firms are offering to sell Russian police the latest equipment for bugging, night photography, and other devices for personal surveillance. United States companies have been invited by the Soviet Union to display at their fair, Krimtekhnika 74, the world's most sophisticated print analyzers, lie detectors, identification systems, surveillance devices, and similar gear. The United States now would supply the Soviet police with devices to tighten their control over minorities and dissenters! A swell of protest against this has caused the secretary of commerce, Frederick B. Dent, to discuss with the State Department whether such export sales should be allowed.

It is now revealed that in 1970, only a year after Nixon's first election, he was using half a million dollars in cash from his reelection campaign to stop George Wallace, a potential opponent in 1972, from winning the governorship of Alabama. Reacting to this news. Wallace carries the thought even further, ties Watergate politics up with the recent assassination attempt which has left him paralyzed. More potential enemies for Nixon: in the transcripts Nixon calls William Rehnquist "a clown"; and Herb Klein "should get his head screwed on." Even on the international front his gifts and promises are going sour. The helicopter he left in Egypt cannot be used; there are no technicians to maintain it. And in Israel, Kissinger's image has dropped 15.5 percent from June to July. The majority in that country are now against him.

Within the committee, the president's counsel, James St. Clair, in his final summation on the president's behalf, shocked and offended the committee members by producing "new" evidence which he stated supported the president from selected transcripts of tapes which the president had heretofore refused to submit to the committee upon their request. There was no explanation as to why this new revelation only now came up. This contemptuous attitude worked in reverse and embarrassed and further alienated Nixon's judges.

But Nixon still has a segment of support. Within the committee, Rep. Charles Wiggins regards the data as "most assuredly not an overwhelming case" and would "reserve final judgment because it required analysis." To Rep. Wayne Owens, another member of the committee, the evidence is "damaging" but "interspersed with materials that could be exonerating." Rep. Walter Flowers sees it straight down the middle. The committee has heard "some things very damaging and some things [which] tended to support the contentions that have been made by the White House." Many polls, public and private, show that the president has bottomed out and is sometimes actually on the rise. The committee is generally counted against the president; the House less so; the Senate the least. Republicans tend to consolidate behind him, partially because of what they hear from the voters back home. Plain proof of criminality has become the impeachment test. Hence, writes Joseph Alsop, putting it all together, "As of today, it comes out to an even bet."

There are other clues to public sentiment which are relevant, not so much regarding which way the decision will go, but how it will be, no matter what the outcome. In a speech in Los Angeles on July 25, Nixon is given a standing ovation when he urges business and labor leaders to "act responsibly." The president is greeted warmly at Oklahoma State University where he delivers a commencement address. One day later, John Kenneth Galbraith, speaking at the commencement of the neighboring University of Oklahoma, is interrupted by boos and shouting whenever he criticizes Nixon or his administration. Agnew is cheered when he enters a theater. Goldwater receives loud applause at any university or other public appearance. A patient of mine, sophisticated in political and economic affairs, today, in July 1974, assesses President Nixon as "the best president the United States ever had. Just look at his record."

The father has a secure and protected berth. It is ironic that Nixon did not know this and make better use of it from the beginning. "Impeachment," not called by that name, fails to come about when deserved more often than is realized. Leaders and chairmen and presidents and chiefs, in business, professional, and academic life, who may in the course of their careers qualify for dethronement, generally escape it. Only rarely does it come to pass: when the wrongdoing has gone over the brink, or when the people in a position to carry it out are distant enough to separate themselves from the leader. Even then it only happens when their own fortunes are in jeopardy. For every revolution which comes off, hundreds do not.

There is another factor which has always worked for the president: the spreading of the guilt. Almost everyone who touches the case becomes contaminated. Plea bargaining itself has a questionable moral base, and the finger is pointed on this score at Leon Jaworski, Judge Sirica, and others, the most moral on the scene. Three lawyers recently resigned from Jaworski's staff on that account. The American Bar Association recommends reforms of the plea-bargaining process by federal and state courts. Committee leaks add to the doubts and confusion. Public criticism is widespread. Attempts are made to equate these flaws with the monumental misconduct for which the committees were set up in the first place. Rodino is accused of having predicted a vote for impeachment by his committee in advance, a charge which he indignantly denies.

Sen. Edward Gurney, the member of the Ervin committee most supportive of the president, has himself been indicted on charges of bribery, conspiracy, and perjury in a scheme to collect kickbacks from housing contractors, the first sitting United States senator to be indicted in fifty years. Former Secretary of the Treasury John Connally, the only Democrat to serve in Nixon's Cabinet, and at one time thought to be Nixon's choice as his successor, is indicted on five counts in a milk fund case.

Everyone in the case will be put to the test, first the members of the committees, then of the House, then each individual senator. Ironically, each of them faces the same dilemma which confronted the original inner circle—the conflict between expediency and principles, between personal gain and what is right. The Watergate case has a recurrent theme. Everyone who plays a part has to take an agonizing look inside himself, and detach himself from considerations of what might serve him best. Republicans who look as though they might swing are already receiving hate letters. Rep. Robert Mathias expressed it for California's nineteen Republican congressmen: "No matter which way I go, people aren't going to like it." The conflict is different for both parties but exists in all.

There is a crucial difference in the case of the judges which did not exist for those being judged. The original group made their decisions in private. The test today is being conducted in public. The pens of scholars are poised to record the present votes as history. It is easier now to do what is right; the pressure, in fact, is in that direction. If the Nixon trial were a private affair, there would be less doubt as to which way it would go.

It is hardly possible to transport oneself into the oval room with the president of the United States and to vouchsafe from one's present position what one would have done. Conversely, there is little doubt that if Mitchell, Dean, Magruder, or Colson were sitting on one of the investigating committees today, deciding on the same moral questions in full public view, they would be bearing the same miens as Senators Baker or Weicker or Talmadge or Gurney. In fact, it was when their dilemmas were illuminated that they did "go straight." The case presents human beings under the conditions of a natural experiment.

The same conflict operates up and down the population scale, from the original dilemma of the current defendants to that now facing the succession of judges to, by a more distant and diffuse identification, the inner feelings of the people of the country in whose name the judges are facing their tasks. Just as the ultimate individual is inwardly divided, so do the compositions of the committees vary from a Jerome Waldie at one end, out and out for impeachment, to those at the other like Rep. Charles Sandman or Rep. M. Caldwell Butler who do not see that the president has done anything wrong. Between the two are those who know matters to be serious but who, in addition to waiting for evidence, are waiting to see which way the wind blows.

And how is it blowing? How is the universal test going at the base of the population pyramid, the broad bottom upon which the judges stand and from which they derive their power? How is it playing in Peoria? That is the question first posed by Agnew and later used by Ehrlichman, each as a source of hope for his cause. It is the great heartland that counts, not the academic or intellectual world. And it is from there that the president and his men hope that he will be transfused back into health.

The answer does not have to be guessed at; we can know exactly. In true American style, a poll has just been taken in none other than Peoria, Illinois. And how is it playing there? The answer on the eve of the decision is that it is playing both ways, pretty evenly. The president "is not playing nearly as well as he was a couple of years ago in this Republican stronghold." But at the same time many Peorians are deeply troubled by the possibility of impeachment: "President Nixon is a victim, whether of circumstances, of mistaken loyalty to his aides or the hostility of the media." "People in Peoria believe in patriotism. They want to be able to look up to the President." "If you don't have loyalty to God, to your party, to your country, to your President, then what do you have?" "I hate it," said one respondent, a Democrat, "It's the worst thing I've ever had to watch. He's come up the hard way. He's a family man. He's got kids. I don't want to look but I'm forced to see. This is hurting us badly." There are few loud voices demanding the president's resignation or impeachment. Yet teenagers even in Peoria do not want their parents to paste bumper stickers on the family car urging support of the president. They fear that their friends will laugh at them.

The public test shows a split, collectively and individually. A biopsy of this division can be seen in the jury which has just acquitted Mitchell and Stans on the charges of conspiracy and obstruction of justice. The jury split quickly down the middle, with five voting for conviction, five for acquittal, and two undecided. A quantitative symbol of the ambivalence present, an exact division between guilt and innocence. In the American system of justice a split such as this generally results in acquittal, giving the accused the benefit of the doubt. That is what has taken place in this smaller trial, preliminary to the big one.

The issue on Nixon is not yet joined. One-third plus one is necessary for acquittal. It is now not fifty/fifty but probably two-thirds to one-third. Nixon lost in 1960 by less than 1 percent of the popular vote, and won in 1968 by the same margin. The margin today is again that close, after Watergate, the same as when he started.

There is speculation about the state of the country if Nixon should stay in by one vote. This is not considered an impossibility; sixty-six senators for impeachment and thirty-four against would do it. Nixon himself seems to be playing "one-third plus one politics" by encouraging his support among conservatives in the South. If this succeeds, he will join Andrew Johnson, who stayed in office by one vote. Johnson was "acquitted," but ruined; he lingered in office eleven months. Should Nixon stay, Americans would work under a disgraced president for over two years.

The White House staff is glum but hopeful. The consensus is that an impeachment recommendation may come from the committee and an impeachment vote by the House; but there is every hope in the pro-Nixon world that the Senate will fail to convict. The number by which this will happen seems to them to be in doubt, but it is getting smaller with every count.

Nixon is counting on the ambivalence of his judges, the official ones and the masses who stand behind them. Nixon has had experience in overcoming crises; he had six of them before and overrode them all. If he outwaits this one, a backlash in his favor might come again. In the past time has always been on his side. Will it be this time? Or has ambition and anxiety pushed Nixon to his final rendezvous with crisis?

Art Buchwald has caught the mood. As he sees it, now that the House is going to vote on impeachment, every congressman is feverishly at work writing a speech which will be seen and heard not only by two hundred twenty million Americans but, more important, by his own constituents. Since their political futures are hanging in the balance, most congressmen ask for all the help they can get. Buchwald helps his good friend Congressman Turntable write his impeachment speech.

He supplies him the phrases: he has to make "the most agonizing and painful decision of his life," "wrestle with his conscience," and "search his soul." He has a "sacred" obligation and "must face up to a momentous question which has troubled him for over a year: Can this great nation survive when criminal acts by those in high power go unpunished?"

> "But when do I get to say, 'on the other hand'?" [Turntable asks].
> "I'm coming to that. On the other hand you have to have evidence. What kind of evidence, Turntable?"
> "Beats me."
> "Clear and convincing evidence."
> "That's the best kind," Turntable agreed.
> "Now, who are you going to ask for guidance in this grave hour of crisis, when your vote will affect future generations of Americans for all time to come?"
> "My wife?"
> "Try again."
> "My campaign manager?"
> "God, Turntable, GOD."
> "Of course," he said happily, "why didn't I think of that myself?"

It is a cliché to say that truth wins out. It does not always. But sometimes it does. In this instance, it hangs by a hair. "From good to evil," says Solzhenitsyn, quoting a Russian proverb, "is one quaver." "If it were only so simple," he writes. "If only there were evil people somewhere insidiously committing evil deeds and it were necessary only to separate them from the rest of us and destroy them. But the line dividing good and evil cuts through the heart of every human being. And who is willing to destroy a piece of his own heart?" The human mind, in one and in all, is divided on issues such as this.

The first body from whom a decision can be expected is the Supreme Court. Their decision can well be the one which will tip all the others. As Nixon waits, so waits the nation. No matter what the outcome, the president elected by one of the greatest landslides in history is fighting not to be the first to be removed from his office.

Also waiting in the wings is Gerald Ford, now the vice-president of the United States. The president is by tradition "the people's choice." For better or worse they choose him and must take what he gives. But the man who stands next in line now happens to be, literally, not the people's but Nixon's choice. And if Richard Nixon has to go, Gerald Ford, his own named successor, stands ready to take over.

Here again we come to an incremental series of *dayenus*. That this vice-president—who could be president when this book is read—was named by one man, and not elected by the people, should of itself raise questions. It would suffice for that; *dayenu*. That the man who did the naming had earlier selected the previous vice-president, Spiro Agnew, who happens to be the first in our history to have had to leave his office in disgrace—*dayenu!* That the man who had this unprecedented choice was the same man, most of whose appointees and intimate staff, cabinet members included, have been indicted, with some already in prison, *dayenu*—that alone would suffice. And finally that the same man who exercised this privilege was himself on his possible way out for illegal behavior—was that not already over the brink?

This procedure of vice-presidential succession is of course totally within the Constitution as it exists. But should not irrationality spur a spirited reassessment of the rules of legality? There are no public discussions, no town meetings to protest, no extraordinary sessions of Congress to analyze and correct faults. Perceptions are obliterated or their impact denied again in the service of defensive avoidance. This aspect of vice-presidential succession has not been mentioned among the future reforms which are discussed.

These considerations say nothing about the particular appointee but the method by which he was chosen. They applied before the choice was made. They are not against the legality of the process but the rationality of it.

Now let us take a look at Gerald Ford the man. He has been vice-president for half a year. And what do we see? We see whom President Nixon has selected and perhaps why. We often get to know later why Nixon did things earlier. The presence of Ford rather than another can prolong but cannot hasten Nixon's departure. Everything Ford is and says seems to bear this out. Perhaps Nixon could not be that sure of someone else in this respect. Few believe that merit or qualifications or supreme ability dictated Nixon's choice.

As Nixon needed to say "I am not a crook," Ford has felt the need to say "I am my own man." Both remarks speak for their particular problems at the time. Ford was chosen by Nixon, is obligated to Nixon, and, during this time of waiting, has been trained by Nixon. The vice-president is anything but inspiring in the department of "talking straight." He may change later, but his present performance will not be forgotten. More accurately, it may be forgotten, but it will be part of his history. Ford has learned from Nixon, at least during this fragile period, how to unify opposites, to bridge and straddle conflicts, to speak simultaneously from both sides, especially on the most controversial subject of all, that of Nixon himself. Since December 7, 1973, when Ford was appointed to his office, his special task has been to be against Watergate and for Nixon, against what Nixon did while for who Nixon was. He has learned this well, and has become proficient in expressing opposite ideas with equal conviction.

Drawn into the same vortex as the president's original men, Ford, like them, was for allegiance first. In his first public statements after his elevation to the vice-presidency, he went through the same internal process and came to the same outcome as the others. Echoing Nixon's words, "left-wing elements" were dragging out Watergate. Nixon, Ford knew from the beginning, was innocent. There was documentary evidence, he maintained, that Nixon had no role in the cover-up. In the face of evidence to the contrary, Ford admitted that he had never seen the evidence but had received the president's assurance that it was in the files. A month later, after the transcripts became part of history,

Ford repeated his original view: "I admire and I have affection for the President of the United States. . . . I have diligently read the transcripts and I think the overwhelming weight of the evidence proves the President is innocent of the charges."

As evidence against the president mounted and criticism of Ford's stand began to be heard, Ford, needing to demonstrate his independence in addition to his loyalty to the president, began to moderate his remarks: "If you newsmen can make corrections so can a Vice-President," he told the White House Correspondents Association at a dinner. Expediency and self-interest were now competing with his personal obligation. It was no easy task to combine the two, but he tried valiantly. The president, he believed, was innocent of involvement in the break-in or cover-up, but "I want the Constitutional process to continue as rapidly as possible with as much evidence as can possibly be made available." Nixon should turn over relevant information to the House Judiciary Committee, and "the sooner the better." Yet when tapes were turned over as evidence, Ford stated that he did not listen to them because he should not be involved in judging the president.

Ford was preparing himself. He tried humor; he tried humility; and he traversed the country many times. Referring to himself as "the nation's first instant vice-president," he and his men clocked the mileage he had traveled since his appointment as vice-president, some two hundred thousand miles. He mingled well, saying with perfect blandness to friend and foe, "Hi, how are you? Nice to see you." "I don't think he hears what they are shouting at him," one reporter commented. And from Nixon and others he has learned the art of the cliché. "Vote Republican to save New Federalism" is a slogan which, in the words of one reporter, "makes the eyes glaze over." While defending he attacked, urging support for Henry Kissinger and Richard Nixon, "the greatest Secretary of State and greatest President for peace in our history, against those trying to destroy them by innuendo and leaks." From the audiences to which he says this, it gets the loudest cheers.

The closest Ford came to asserting his independence was when he denounced CREEP, his (and his speechwriters') new name for C.R.P., the Committee to Re-Elect the President. The alliterative and phonic slogan, which invites regression, did not pass him by: "Never again must Americans allow an arrogant elite guard of political adolescents like

CREEP to by-pass the regular Republican Party organization." These remarks had not been cleared with the White House, he answered to questioning: "I spoke as my own man." Did this then divorce him from President Nixon's philosophies? "Not at all. I simply said CREEP did a great disservice to the Republican Party." Although the reelection committee was authorized by Nixon and chaired by John Mitchell, one of the president's closest advisers, his remarks, Ford emphasized, should not be interpreted as criticisms.

In times past, such assurances as "I am my own man" or "I am not a crook" or "I am not a whore" (Henry Petersen's contribution to this series) did not have to be made. Now each bespeaks an insecurity as to what the person might be, which then has to be denied.

Ford continued to walk a tightrope across the country. When Colson testified that he and the plumbers had acted against Ellsberg on the president's orders, Ford pointed out that there was "a big difference between a smear and a break-in." Then was he condoning a smear, he was asked? No, he was trying "to draw a legalistic distinction between a smear and breaking and entering."

Mr. Nixon would prove to be "the peacemaker of this century. . . . I think a lot of Republican candidates will be darn glad to have him come in and help them [campaign] this fall." Like Nixon, Ford attacked, although without the vitriol. He did not have Nixon's instincts; in many respects he was imitating. News leaks about Kissinger's role in wiretapping activities, Ford said, were given to newsmen "on a selective basis, I think with some ulterior motives. . . . I think generally the people who are leaking this kind of information are pro-impeachment." Acknowledging that a contempt-of-court citation against the president, if it had to be issued, "could be interpreted in the minds of some as an impeachable offense," he was not ready to pass judgment since "you could argue both ways on that." He deplored violations of professional standards of conduct; "moral discipline" was the most significant safeguard of the honor of the legal profession. But no developments in the Watergate case had in any way shaken his confidence in the president.

In general the people were tolerant of Ford's behavior. While it made many uneasy—it was too much like déjà vu—it made others feel secure. The instinct after a trauma is towards self-preservation, to return to the last previous state of security before the trauma occurred. What the people wanted now was Nixon before Watergate, before they had to ask themselves whether they had done anything wrong. With Ford, they came as close to this wish as they can.

Ford instinctively plays it safe and airy. The platitudes come in rapid succession. "So long as I have the physical capability and so long as I can contribute to the climate of reason and truth in this country, I will remain my own man, fly my own course, and speak my own convictions," he vows. The Watergate scandal, he tells the United States Junior Chamber of Commerce, has the nation "spinning its wheels." The initiative and energy which achieved diplomatic breakthroughs in the Middle East should be turned to resolve the "impasse" caused by Watergate at home. "There is too much deadlock here at home—too much acrimony and animosity, frustration, faint-heartedness." Watergate should not become "a cop-out" for inaction on domestic programs: "The time has come for bold domestic diplomacy to negotiate a return to pride in America."

Ford's windy phrases receive standing ovations. His speechwriters are busy turning them out; and these phrases are paying off. A poll just taken shows Ford to have moved away from the field as the top choice of Republican voters for their party's nomination in 1976. In close contention at the beginning of the year, he is now far in front of Reagan, Rockefeller, and Goldwater.

Like everyone else, Ford has been affected by his linkage to Nixon. From his past, however, and what he basically is, he does seem at the core to be sincere. At a deeper level than his vice-presidential actions, this is reassuring to all and will help.

IV

The End

Last Days of the Administration

July 24, 1974

The Supreme Court, with three Nixon appointees sitting (the fourth, Justice William Rehnquist, disqualified himself), has announced its historic decision: eight to nothing, unanimously against the president's position; neither the doctrine of separation of powers nor the president's need for confidentiality was reason enough to withhold evidence from a criminal trial. Executive privilege did indeed exist, but "cannot prevail over the fundamental demands of due process of law in the fair administration of criminal justice." Mr. Nixon must "forthwith" turn over the tapes of sixty-four subpoenaed White House conversations to Judge John Sirica. Eight hours later the president's attorney, James St. Clair, reads a statement for Nixon that the president will "comply . . . in all respects."

The thirty-one-page opinion was low keyed, measured, almost subdued. It was delivered by Chief Justice Warren Burger, Nixon's first appointee to the high court. The justices who listened to it appeared grim. Like Ford, they were judging a Nixon whom the majority of the people had turned against. The collective superego which now had to be heard leaned in the same direction as their own professional consciences. The result was inevitable: unfavorable to the president.

The House Judiciary Committee opened its formal debate on articles of impeachment the same day that the Supreme Court delivered its opinion. An eleventh-hour attempt by Republican members to delay the procedure had been made but had failed.

Following the Supreme Court's decision, it took just four days for the committee to come to its first decision. Republican members defected daily. By a vote of twenty-seven to eleven, with six Republicans joining the twenty-one Democrats, the committee approved article 1, recommending that the House impeach President Nixon for directing a criminal conspiracy to cover up the Watergate scandal. The same night, adding another Republican to the majority, the committee, by a vote of twenty-eight to ten, passed article 2, to recommend impeachment for the president's misuse of the powers of his office. A third article, recommending impeachment for refusing to comply with four requested subpoenas, was approved by a vote of twenty-one to seventeen, predominantly along party lines.

While three articles of impeachment were approved, two were not. By a vote of twenty-six to twelve the committee rejected one article which would have accused the president of income tax evasion and another of constitutional violations in the secret bombing of Cambodia. Not that it was so clear-cut that Nixon was innocent of these, but each side of the contesting internal forces had to have its say.

Even now, the national ambivalence had to be taken into account. While Ford was declaring that "the odds are such" that the president might be impeached, he continued to express his belief that the president was innocent of any impeachable offense. The Republican members of the Judiciary Committee who had defected were nervous. Republican Rep. William Cohen of Maine admitted that he had agonized over the possible adverse effects the decision might have when he runs for reelection this fall. Rep. Thomas Railsback, Illinois Republican, along with other Republican "swing" members, received many critical messages from his constituents. Some were behind him, many opposed. Packages containing rocks were received with the message "Let him who is without sin cast the first stone," and one letter contained three dimes with the message, "Judas got thirty pieces of silver—here are yours." Alabama Democrat Rep. Walter Flowers, whose conservative district had been thoroughly behind the president in the past, believed that he might be putting his political future in jeopardy by his vote for impeachment. "He called me from Washington," his mother told a reporter, "and said as a consequence of his vote he might be a private citizen again."

But the futures of all were quickly foretold. In Maine, Cohen was immediately nominated as one of the ten outstanding young men of the year by the Bangor chapter of the Jaycees. Impeachment in the House seemed more and more certain, and the situation in the Senate was growing increasingly serious. Republicans were now changing sides fast. Prior to transmitting the requested tapes to the court, Nixon insisted on listening to them once more alone. A few days earlier, James St. Clair, jolted by a question from Judge Sirica about his not having personally listened to the tapes before—not having been permitted by his client, the president, to do so—had promised the judge that he would review the contents of each tape himself before they were transmitted. Again a peripheral exchange proved crucial.

Wednesday, July 31

St. Clair received the transcripts of conversations held between Nixon and Haldeman on June 23, 1972, just six days after the Watergate break-in. The contents were devastating to Nixon's defense. Nixon knew of the crime and authorized the cover-up at that time. The CIA, the president says to Haldeman, should tell acting FBI director Patrick Gray "to lay off" the investigation of the Watergate burglary: "Don't go any further into this case, period!" There is a reference to an even earlier discussion, almost certainly the June 20 conversation which had been expunged by the famous eighteen-and-a-half-minute manual erasure.

A "smoking pistol" had turned up in the rubble. The awesome revelation is passed from St. Clair to Haig to Kissinger. It was apparent to all that this was the end. St. Clair confronts and braces Nixon. The damaging information has to be released. St. Clair will have to resign from the Nixon defense if his advice is not taken. Fatalistically, Nixon concurs.

Friday, August 2

Rep. Charles Wiggins, the president's strongest defender on the House Judiciary Committee, after having been given a sneak preview of the "smoking gun" transcript by Haig and St. Clair, recognizes the likelihood of impeachment and agonizingly calls for Nixon's resignation: "The country's interest, the Republican Party's interest, and Richard Nixon's interest would be served by resignation." Wiggins cancels the briefings he had called for the Republican defenders of the president in the coming congressional hearings. He does one thing more: he calls House Minority Leader John Rhodes and Vice-President Ford and warns them against making any further public statements in support of the president until a briefing with Haig and St. Clair can be arranged.

A mini-drama is now also taking place. Today John Dean has been sentenced by Judge Sirica to a one-to four-year term in prison, a penalty regarded by court observers as surprisingly severe and which has left Dean and his attorney stunned. Prior to the sentencing, the two men had thrown themselves on the mercy of the court, pleading for compassion and sympathy for the role Dean had played. Could there be a touch of revenge here, a special punishment for the man who had "caused" it all by telling about it? Is there an unconscious backlash, more sympathy at this moment for what is happening to Nixon, and a reactive anger at the man who exposed him and who split each individual in two? For John Dean the timing of his day in court, at the very moment that what he said was proving true, might not have been propitious.

Saturday, August 3

Nixon travels by helicopter to Camp David where he will map his final strategy. Resignation is not to be considered, he says; he will "go down to the wire."

Sunday, August 4

Nixon calls in five of his aides—St. Clair, Haig, Ziegler, Price, Buchanan. He stiffly resists their talk of resignation, is not at all certain that the effect of the newest tape disclosure would necessarily be fatal. Raymond Price is drawing up a statement to accompany the release of the transcripts. St. Clair insists on a paragraph making it clear that previously he had been unaware of the damaging evidence.

House Republican Leader John J. Rhodes, warned by an ominous call from Haig, postpones a press conference he had scheduled for the next day to say how he would vote on impeachment. Senate Republican Whip Robert Griffin, regarded as a Senate bellwether and canny head-counter, sensing that impeachment is inevitable, begins to nudge Nixon toward resignation. He himself, he warns Nixon in a letter sent to the White House by messenger, will vote to convict if Nixon withholds subpoenaed evidence from the Senate. Griffin tells Nixon he is circulating copies of this letter to other senators. Congressional support is shaky and shrinking.

Monday, August 5

Senator Griffin, having learned in the meantime that there is adverse news coming, goes a step beyond his previous warning and now urges Nixon to resign: "It's not just his enemies who feel that way. Many of his best friends believe now that this would be the most appropriate course." Haig informs Cabinet members and one hundred fifty members of the White House staff of the coming revelations. St. Clair undertakes the more difficult task of informing the ten Republicans who had stood by Nixon and opposed every article of impeachment. They are shocked and devastated.

Why should they be so shocked? One answer might lie in the statement of Ohio's Republican congressman Delbert L. Latta: "We'd put our trust in the President. We felt he was telling us the truth. I think every American has that right." Another answer might be that their minds had been impervious to facts and dominated by wish—for weeks, months, and years.

The transcripts are released late in the afternoon. Nixon's accompanying explanation has the present version of what has been characteristic for twenty-five years: no credibility. He had forgotten the June 23, 1972, conversation with Haldeman, he explains, until he reviewed the tapes in May of 1974. Contrary statements had been made from memory, and he had not told his counsel or the Judiciary Committee because "I did not realize the extent of the implications which these conversations might now appear to have." His case had been argued before the committee, and judgment passed, he admits, "with information that was incomplete and in some respects erroneous. This was a serious act of omission for which I take full responsibility and which I deeply regret." Again full responsibility but no guilt, and especially no accountability. The tapes, he concedes "are at variance with certain of my previous statements," a new euphemism for lying. "Inoperative" had been the word before.

The cover-up is adhered to blandly to the end. It is as if no new evidence had just been revealed. "When all the facts were brought to my attention," Nixon drones as before, "I insisted on a full investigation and prosecution of those guilty. I am firmly convinced that the record in its entirety does not justify the extreme step of impeachment and removal of a President." At a Washington press conference the previous March 6 Nixon had agreed that "the crime of obstruction of justice is a serious crime and would be an impeachable offense."

The "old Nixon" is still hanging on with blind faith that continued perseverence will gain him his ends. Is he out of touch with reality? This question passes many a lip, appears here and there in the press. It is a question that may never be answered. No psychiatrist who was not there can make a diagnosis. But there is no evidence, either from Nixon's public utterances or remarks by those who passed these last days with him, of a delusion or a "break." Nixon was not out of touch with reality but in touch with it and pushing it away, not like a psychotic but like a desperate man trapped. He never achieved the peace either of a confession or of a psychosis. His was, in fact, a less human feat, more difficult for the average mortal to identify with. It was this which kept him separated from the people and prevented the compassion which might otherwise have come to his aid. He would have been understood more readily and with more empathy had he "cracked."

The members of the House Judiciary Committee are outraged. The Republicans who stood by Nixon feel deceived and betrayed. To a man they declare that they will reverse their votes and now vote for impeachment. Rep. Wiley Mayne now finds the "direct" evidence which was needed and Rep. Charles Sandman, Nixon's most vocal champion on the committee, the "specificity" he had declared lacking in the evidence.

Tuesday, August 6

Nixon calls together his Cabinet to rally their support. In a grave and strained ninety-minute session he recalls and justifies his entire political career. Still reported as remarkably composed, he recounts the Vietnam War and his diplomatic breakthroughs in China and the Soviet Union. He then returns to an old refrain as though to explain his memory lapses by emphasizing how preoccupied he had been as his reelection campaign of 1972 approached: "One thing I have learned is never to allow anybody else to run your campaign."

His timing is astonishing. As an additional piece of information, if anyone was still inclined to believe him, the newly released transcripts have just revealed evidence relevant to this old chestnut of reelection. In contrast to the portrait of an above-the-battle president that Nixon has always sought to present, he has in fact just been shown to have been painstakingly concerned with personal and political minutiae throughout his campaign. He worried about helicopter prop wash spoiling the coiffures of his wife and daughters at the Miami GOP Convention. He weighed the political advantages of posing with southern Democratic congressional candidates. And he cautioned his advisers against trying to stage "nonpolitical" cultural events because of the supposed influence of Jewish left-wingers in the arts.

Nixon continues to bolster his determined opinion not to resign. In a fifteen-minute monologue to a silent Congress, he states he will not resign because it would set a precedent! The motive is still a lofty one, still for others and the country, not for himself. "In my opinion and in the opinion of my counsel, I have not committed any impeachable offense." Therefore, he insists, "the constitutional process should be followed out to the end . . . wherever the end may be." An aide calls him "an incurable optimist."

So ingrained is the feeling that Nixon could conceivably survive that Art Buchwald can still take a chance with humor on the president's day of decision. In a column written on August 7 (and printed in the *Los Angeles Times* on August 11) Buchwald gives the president one last opportunity. President Nixon, he says, intends to hang tough, stonewall it, and stay in office no matter what anyone says. Many people have wondered how he can do it—how can a man whose own party has disowned him, whose credibility has sunk lower than Ron Ziegler's, hope to survive his term in office?

The answer is quite simple. Mr. Nixon has one last trump card. He has the Button. "Button, Button, Who's Got The Button?" the piece is called. Nixon refuses to leave the White House without taking the Button with him, "the only one that can set off World War III."

"It's my Button and if you want to toss me out of office, you're going to have to get another Button."

A delegation of senators and congressmen argue: "The Button belongs to the American people. It's our only defense against the enslaved nations of the world." After much back and forth, at the end, after making a deal for sixty thousand dollars annually, plus twenty thousand for Pat and ninety-six thousand for expenses above the pension, and a promise of immunity from criminal prosecution, Nixon reveals that he cannot return the Button.

> "I wish I could, but I can't," Mr. Nixon said.
>
> "Why the hell can't you?" the congressmen screamed.
>
> "Because I sold it," Mr. Nixon replied sheepishly.
>
> "Why did you sell it?" someone shouted.
>
> "I needed the money to make a mortgage payment on San Clemente."
>
> "Good grief!" the senator said. "Whom did you sell it to?"
>
> "Howard Hughes. He's always good for a buck when anybody in our family gets into a jam."

At this point Vice-President Ford finally begins the process of separation. "The public interest is no longer served," he explains, if he continues to make statements in defense of the president. "I understand," Nixon states when he hears this. The president then abruptly shifts to a discussion of the economy, employing the maneuver of deflection which has served him well in the past. He suggests setting up a domestic "summit meeting" to grapple with inflation. He was always best at the top, felt safer there, as far removed as possible from the base. He wants this meeting to be held immediately. When Attorney General William

Saxbe ventures, "Wouldn't it be wise to wait until next week anyway
. . . until we see what's going to happen?" Nixon stonily replies, "No,
this is too important to wait."

Those around him watch closely for signs of emotional instability. But
there were no "Captain Queeg" mannerisms, Saxbe reported later,
"We were all looking for something like that. He was calm, in control
of himself, and not the least bit tense."

At a regular weekly luncheon meeting of the Senate Republican
Policy Committee held on August 6 on Capitol Hill, Senator Barry
Goldwater reaches the limit of what he can justify or rationalize. "There
are only so many lies you can take," he tells the assembled senators,
"and now there has been one too many. Nixon should get his ass out of
the White House—today!" Senator Rhodes announces he will vote for
impeachment. The senators whom Nixon can count on in an impeachment showdown are now seen as no more than nine or ten, far below
the thirty-four required for his survival in office. Goldwater is chosen
to confront the president about the odds against him. As rumors of
resignation run wild, the Dow Jones average rises twenty-five points. By
the end of the day Nixon has told Rabbi Korff privately that he is
seriously considering resignation. Ray Price is already working on a
resignation address. Talk is now turning to the transfer of power and
possible immunity for the president from further prosecution.

Today, August 6, by a unanimous vote of the Senate Foreign Relations
Committee, Kissinger is cleared in the investigation of his previous
testimony regarding his role in wiretapping. Said Senator Fulbright at
the conclusion of the hearings, "He did not, in my opinion, initiate the
program." While there was little doubt that the committee, which was
generally sympathetic to Kissinger, would clear him, some members
privately express concern that Kissinger might have been less than fully
candid during the confirmation hearings. Robert Anderson, spokesman
for the State Department, states that Mr. Kissinger is "gratified" by the
report of the committee, and "no longer sees any reason for resignation."

Wednesday, August 7

Haig calls Ford to the White House ostensibly to discuss the situation. In fact Ford is told to prepare to assume the presidency. Republican leaders, unaware of this development, worry about what Nixon might do when facing the final truth. These fears later prove unfounded. "I read this morning," one senator declared, "about the North Vietnamese getting close to Danang, and I was concerned about what he might do."

The family gathers in the White House. The Dow rises another twenty-four points. Nixon agrees to see Goldwater but asks that Rhodes and Scott join them as well. The meeting "to assess the current situation" is postponed by Nixon from late morning to 12:30 P.M., then to 2:00, 4:00, and then 5:00 P.M. Finally, in the Oval Office, Nixon is amiable, puts his guests at ease. After chatting about the Eisenhower years he comes to the point, asks them about his chances. "Very gloomy," his friends inform him. "It's damn gloomy," he agrees. "Whatever decision I make I'll make entirely in the national interest." He asks for no advice and receives none.

For more than half an hour, sitting at the head of the table as always in the Cabinet room, the still-president reminisced about his youth and his presidency. Choking up frequently, he recalled his days in track and football at Whittier, how hard he had to fight to stay ahead, how he had to struggle to keep from being twelfth on a twelve-man track team. Here was a brief glimpse into the origin of his deep insecurity, as well as of his determination and dogged capacity to overcome it. If he persevered, if he just kept showing up, he could stay on.

Even now his defenses continued above the pain. There was no comment on the evidence against him, only that he was leaving to spare the country the agony of a Senate trial. This, he told his audience through his tears, could last six to eight months. Others had said it would last two. He could win as many as thirty-five votes and escape conviction, he said, thinking aloud, although the day before he had been informed that his support had all but vanished.

He would not mind continuing to fight even now, he told his friends, but the country could not stand it. His family unanimously opposed his stepping down, but the national interest came first. "I hope you don't feel I am letting you down," he said as he left, his eyes welling with tears.

Kissinger visits Nixon twice that evening, the second time from 10:00 P.M. until the early hours of the morning. Earlier in the day David Eisenhower and Edward Cox, Nixon's sons-in-law, had been seen making rounds of White House offices saying good-bye. It is apparent that this is the day. The decision has been made.

Thursday, August 8

At 11:00 A.M. Nixon summons Ford to the White House. In an hour-and-ten-minute briefing session he notifies him privately that Ford is about to succeed him to the presidency.

At 12:23 P.M. a pale and somber Ronald Ziegler announces to the press that the president will speak to the nation from the Oval Office at 9:00 P.M. that evening.

Following his meeting with Ford, Nixon goes alone to his hideaway in the executive office building to edit Price's last draft of his resignation speech. A few hours before he was to address the nation, Nixon calls in two groups from the Hill. The first was a formal delegation of the leaders of Congress to whom he spoke an official and controlled good-bye. The second, at 8:00 P.M., one hour before air time, was a last nostalgic reunion of forty-six of his closest friends in the House and Senate. Here his composure finally gave way as he wept openly and profusely in the presence of his friends. At the end he had to be helped out of his chair by others who wept unashamedly with him.

At 9:00 P.M. Nixon was on the air for the last and most difficult speech of his life. His typical control returned once more. In a dramatic and tense fifteen-minute address, Nixon made the historic announcement: he would resign the following noon as president of the United States.

The plight of the man was heart-rending and tapped deep emotions in the listening world. The content of his resignation address, however, was in keeping with his history. Although the speech had been written by Price, the ideas were his own. Nixon went out as he came in. His valedictory is composed of the same half-truths which have been his stamp from the start. Loudest and most eloquent are the avoidances and the disappointing omissions. It is still a cover-up. And it pours forth with the same earnestness he must have had as a debater in Whittier High, the same thrust and look of sincerity as Nixon demonstrated at his height.

Nixon is resigning because "I no longer have a strong enough political base in the Congress" to justify continuing to fight. Last year, Ford's congressional seat in Michigan was lost to a Democrat for the first time in sixty-four years not because of Watergate but because of the political situation! "If some of my judgments were wrong, and some were wrong, they were made in what I believed at the time to be the best interest of the nation." This was the closest he came to an admission of guilt; some judgments, nothing else, were wrong. "I have never been a quitter," he repeats from his Checkers speech in 1952.

Wearing an American flag in his lapel, Nixon cites his accomplishments toward peace and expresses his hopes for the continuation of the laudable goals of his administration.

Near the end of the speech, as the burden of the presidency is about to be lifted, an unusual spontaneity appears. In the most tender section of his farewell speech, Nixon begins to talk about Theodore Roosevelt to whom he has turned and whom he has been reading these past few days. This sudden identification, the full meaning of which is not apparent at once, gives an indication of Nixon's image of his "self" as he makes his tragic exit from political life:

> Sometimes I have succeeded and sometimes I have failed, but always I have taken heart from what Theodore Roosevelt once said about the man in the arena: "whose face is marred by dust and sweat and blood, who strives valiantly, who errs and comes short again and again because there is not effort without error and short-coming, but who does actually strive to do the deeds, who knows the great enthusiasms, the great devotions, who spends himself in a worthy cause, who at the best knows in the end the triumph of high achievements and who at the worst, if he fails, at least fails while daring greatly."

This is Richard Nixon's view of himself as he is forced from the political scene. He has maintained his self-esteem, enabling him, as he

had announced he would several times in advance, to go out if he had
to "with his head held high." Control has been with him to the end and
there has been no break, at least before the national audience to whom
he speaks. Only the perspiration, glistening most perceptibly on his
upper lip, attests to the strain and betrays the agony which must lie
within. In a psychoanalytic paper many years ago I described how the
snout, the area of the most direct human contact since the earliest days
of suckling as an infant, remains throughout life "the window to the
emotions." Nixon's usual tight smile, wan now and with an occasional
quiver but still manufactured at regular intervals, and the beads of
perspiration centering around his lips, give some indication of what is
being held back as well as the control which enables him to do so.

In a strange and unpremeditated way he has, with this very "success,"
made the task of the nation a bit easier. Just as the June 23 tape, with
its clear proof of guilt, finally made possible a separation of the people
from Nixon, so now does the absence of a "confession" and Nixon's
imperviousness to contrition aid the process of separation and healing.
His continuing control and failure to break down actually augur well for
the reparative process, sparing the people much anguish by lessening
their collective guilt both for the long cumulative collusion and the
present final break.

Another immediate result of Nixon's continued denial has been the
cessation of a plan for immunity, which had already been whispered
about by members of Congress. Taking their cue from a swell of public
sentiment against it, leaders in both the House and Senate have followed suit. While impeachment will not now be pressed, and few in
public life want their president to go to jail, there is an increasing desire,
House Speaker Carl Albert says, to avoid the ambiguities of "an Agnew-
type situation." Senator Edward Brooke, who the day before had spon-
sored a Senate immunity resolution, toughened his stand after Nixon's
speech. "I do not believe he should be given immunity from prosecution until the American people have received all the facts," Brooke now
states. Only after "a full confession" and "a full disclosure of his involvement in Watergate" should Congress express support for immunity.
Sen. Robert Byrd is thought to speak for many on the Hill when he says
that the "record ought to be complete" on Nixon's guilt.

However, even now there is a spectrum. On Tuesday, August 6, the day after what columnist George Will has aptly called "the smoking howitzer" was made public, a poll throughout California showed that while 66 percent now favored impeachment, 24 percent—the same one-quarter—still opposed it. This is a consistent and perhaps the most significant and instructive statistic of all. Again, could this one-quarter, which remains impervious to irrefutable evidence, represent the proportion of the average individual's intrapsychic forces which would condone any action on the part of that individual, no matter what? Is this, in the service of human survival, the limit of the superego's influence? In the same poll, while 54 percent reject immunity from criminal prosecution, 31 percent are for it. Republicans are more favorable to the president in all categories.

In Savannah, Georgia, the American Federation of Police today announces that it has awarded Nixon the group's highest award, calling him "the most outstanding American who has made the greatest contribution to world peace."

Friday, August 9

At 9:30 in the morning, with two and a half hours of his presidency remaining, Nixon appears in the East Room of the White House for his last public act as president. Bidding farewell to his Cabinet and personal staff, he speaks spontaneously, jokingly complains that the press will misconstrue this too as staged. Nixon seems more genuine at this last hour than at any time during his career. His emotions seem credible, he is personal in a way that few have seen before, and communication is more direct. Many feel that had he spoken this way earlier he might be continuing as president.

"You are here to say good-bye," he begins. "We don't have a good word for it in English; the best is au revoir. We'll see you again." Many who listen are overcome as he tells them to be proud of their record with his administration. Near the end he too fights for composure and chokes back tears as he tries to keep his voice from breaking.

But through the tears the same distortions and defenses persist. They are less noticeable at this sad moment, but are not without their effects. The same mechanisms can be felt, the devious twistings of the past coupled with the aggrandizement of the self, both antidotes necessary to prevent collapse.

"As I pointed out last night: sure, we've done some things wrong in this Administration, and the top man always takes the responsibility, and I've never ducked it." No, not true: he ducked it all along. "But I want to say one thing: no man or no woman came into this Administration and left it with more of this world's goods than when he came in. No man or woman ever profited at the public expense or the public till —mistakes, yes, for personal gain, never." Sorry, not true. He ignores his own taxes, his homes, the gains, financial and otherwise, of many. His vice-president had left his office because of financial kickbacks. For a president to have to resign is a first in our history. That his vice-president also had to go was so against the odds that it is beyond conceivability, has therefore almost been forgotten.

"People . . . say, 'What'll I tell my kids?' You know, they look at government . . . and get the impression that everybody is here for the purpose of feathering his nest. . . . Not in this Administration. Not one single man or woman." Nixon is humble as always. "I only wish that I were a wealthy man—ha! At the present time I've got to find a way to pay my taxes." Whatever the reality, the words ring an appeal, serve as a point around which many may identify. His knack for repetition is uncanny. In the Checkers speech at the other end of his career, he could not afford a mink coat but only a cloth one for Pat. And after disposing of the slush fund accusations in that speech, he seized on a statement of Eisenhower's, that Nixon was "as clean as a hound's-tooth," to found the "Order of the Hound's-Tooth."

His self-esteem continues to hold up. The White House—he clearly is identified with it—"isn't the biggest house, many and most, in even smaller countries, are much bigger. This isn't the finest house. Many in Europe, particularly in China, Asia have paintings of great, great value, things that we just don't have here. But this is the best house. . . . This house has a great heart and that heart comes from those who serve it."

Nixon conveys emotions now. The area around the lips is more open, shows the vulnerability more in keeping with the circumstances. There is not the usual gap between what he says and how he looks. The quiver of the chin, the perspiration around the mouth with less of a need to cover it with the produced smile, show the deep emotions he is going through and bring him in contact with his audience.

A glimpse into origins comes spontaneously. He speaks of his father. "I remember my old man, I think that they would have called him sort of a little man, a common man. He didn't consider himself that way—he was a streetcar motorman first and then he was a farmer—then a grocer, but he was a great man. Because he did his job, and every job counts up to the hilt regardless of what happens." His own ambivalence, his belittling of and disappointment in his father shines through.

And his mother: "Nobody'll ever write a book, probably, about my mother. . . . My mother was a saint. And I think of her, two boys dying of tuberculosis, nursing four others in order that she could take care of my older brother for three years in Arizona and seeing each of them die. And when they died it was like one of her own." He idealizes his mother and misses her at this moment of agony and need. His eyes are moist. With the burden of the presidency virtually lifted from his shoulders, Nixon can finally abandon a front and the need for control.

He returns to Theodore Roosevelt whom "I was reading last night in the White House" (his last night there; he had referred to Roosevelt in a speech the day before as well). "As you know, I kind of like to read books. I'm not educated, but I do read books." His insecurity behind his modesty and his attempt to deny it come out. Citing a moving section from the diary when, as a young man, Teddy had lost his first wife after childbirth, the meaning of this sudden identification becomes clear. The relevance of this reference for Nixon stems from two directions. One was the suffering of early death which he had just spoken of in connection with the stay of his mother and brothers in Arizona. The suffering was his as well as his mother's. "She was beautiful in face and form," he quoted from the Roosevelt diary, "And lovelier still in spirit. As a flower she grew. . . . When she had just become a mother. . . . and the years seemed so bright before her. . . . death came to her. . . . and the life went from my life forever." Nixon's mother had been lost to him too during those trying years when death separated her from him as well as from his brothers.

But then came the real and most poignant link. "That was T.R. in his twenties. He thought the life had gone from his life forever, but he went on. And he not only became President, but as an ex-President he served his country." Here the identification reaches a peak as Nixon allows himself his first glimpse into the future. "Always in the arena, tempestuous, strong, sometimes wrong, sometimes right, but he was a man and as I leave let me say, that's an example I think all of us should remember."

As he reads from the diary, Nixon puts on eyeglasses, the first time one can remember his having done this in public. He can at last be human, has nothing more to protect, no longer has to wear the cloak of invincibility.

Near the end of the speech he returns to self-depreciation, the underside of his real self-image. This is both an accurate portrayal of what he feels about himself and a defense against a view of his reactive omnipotence. He passed the bar exam the first time because "I was just lucky. I mean, my writing was so poor the bar examiner said, 'We just got to let the guy through.' " Then the fight, the comeback side of his character again: "We think that when we suffer a defeat, that all is ended. We think as T.R. said that life has left his life forever. Not true. . . . The greatness comes not when things go always good for you, but . . . when you're really touchy, when you take your knocks, some disappointment, when sadness comes, because only if you've been in the deepest valley can you ever know how magnificent it is to be on the highest mountain."

At the end comes a philosophical observation and piece of advice which, had he observed it himself, might have spared him this moment: "Never be petty," Richard Nixon advises, "Always remember: others may hate you. Those who hate you don't win unless you hate them. And then you destroy yourself."

Alice Roosevelt Longworth, now ninety, the daughter born when her mother died, felt that Richard Nixon's references to her father "were not particularly pertinent." What a young man did in his twenties "had little bearing on what a man in his sixties does in an altogether different situation," Mrs. Longworth said. "I don't know why my father's recovery from the loss of my mother gave President Nixon heart."

A few hours later, when Nixon was thirty-nine thousand feet over

Jefferson City, Missouri, in *The Spirit of '76*, he was succeeded as president of the United States by Gerald R. Ford. Upon arrival in California as a private citizen, Nixon lifted his arms to the group who awaited him: "I am going to continue to work for peace among all nations. I am going to work for opportunity and understanding among our people in America." To shouts of "We want Nixon" and the singing of "God Bless America" he spoke not of Watergate but of the founding fathers and the coming two hundredth anniversary of our country.

Gerald R. Ford, President

At noon on Friday, August 9, 1974, Gerald R. Ford was sworn in as the thirty-eighth president of the United States. In the ten-minute address which followed immediately, the new president, in what he described as "not an inaugural address . . . not a campaign speech, just a little straight talk among friends," spoke to the heart of what was troubling America.

"I believe that truth is the glue that holds the government together, not only our government, but civilization itself. That bond, though strained, is unbroken at home and abroad. In all my public and private acts as your President, I expect to follow my instincts of openness and candor with full confidence that honesty is always the best policy in the end." A rededication to these discarded values would, as nothing else, act as a balm and promote the process of healing.

"To the peoples and the governments of all friendly nations . . . I pledge an uninterrupted and sincere search for peace." "Sincere" is the word to underscore. Sincerity is never automatic even in the normal run of life. A letter signed "sincerely" is not taken as meaning what it says. But this trait has been in complete eclipse these past few years and needs to be lifted back at least to its normal place.

"My fellow Americans," the new president continued, "our long national nightmare is over." Here he unwittingly was already less than straight. We had been dreaming. It had not happened. We had been asleep. With this, Ford invited the people to regress again, to misperceive what they had just been through.

But we had not been asleep. And it had really happened. The painful events would be forgotten in any case. Unpleasant memories are obliterated in their natural course and we do not need extra encouragement to do so. The opposite of what Ford said would actually have been better advice. A traumatic experience is worked through with the greatest eventual efficacy not by denying that it existed but by facing its effects, in the short and long range, however long the reparative process. Nixon had left Washington, but Watergate has not. The nation needs to stay awake and alert. There are even some immediate posttraumatic sequelae to be contended with, not the least the fate of the now ex-president which is still to be determined.

Referring in his speech to the unique method by which he had come to office—without a platform or campaign and without having been elected—Ford derives from this a special advantage: "I am indebted to no man." Here too the new president encourages an immediate distortion. While this is not a moment for petty objections, rational listeners will have to keep the sequence of events straight and not yield to this example of what appears to be a continuous series of invitations to cover up facts. The new president was indeed indebted to one man, more than anyone ever elected by the people. He owed it all to one specific and particular man, the now deposed ex-president. This is another piece of reality which will always have to be taken into account.

Ford's eight months of apprenticeship as vice-president did not rest folicitously on the base of honesty, candor, and truth which he now espouses. His start was otherwise, and he will have to live that down. His stance as vice-president was, to be sure, due to mitigating circumstances. Now he is, by his own assessment, a "free" man. And the people are of a mind to give him a chance. There is nothing they wish for more at this moment than someone who is "straight."

Immediately after his inaugural address President Ford begins to confer with the leaders of Congress and to seek their advice on the vice-presidency. A new and fresh note of communication and cooperation has been sounded. The president announces that he will appear on Monday, August 12, before a joint session of Congress to share with all his views on the priorities of the nation. The people's hopes are with him.

Republican National Chairman George Bush, who only recently had warned the country not to overreact to Watergate, now declares, "It's a hell of a relief for everybody. [I feel] emotionally wrung out, yet I have a feeling almost of elation. The situation looks more encouraging." For the country or especially for the GOP? The Democrats, perhaps for the same reasons, are now beginning to worry.

Ford comes across as likable, natural, relaxed. The comments used to describe him reveal what the country has been hungry for. "Sincerity" is the word most often stressed—honesty, candor, devotion to duty, a plain sense of right and wrong. To quote an editorial in the *Los Angeles Times:* "He is relaxed . . . straightforward. . . . When he talks he sounds like a decent man. He talks in clichés, but they are believable clichés. . . . If his words were without polish, they were also without guile." And concerning his inner state, after the sensitization to which all have just been exposed, "his ambition . . . has had no darker sides. He has always seemed to be at ease with himself." There is no wide gulf between his self-estimate and his ego ideal, no canyon over which ambition drives him to his own destruction.

One result of the long polarization of the mass as well as the split within the individual is a general move toward the middle. Everything is now moderate, low key, middle of the road; nothing is wanted which is loud, raucous, or strident. Ford fits the new bill, both by nature and by his acquired temperament. He can take cues from Congress, from people, from the mood around him. "A ready conciliator and calm communicator" was his own job description of himself as a potential vice-president. In words that Richard Nixon might have used about himself, Ford told the Senate Rules Committee weighing his nomination for vice-president, "I consider myself a moderate, certainly on domestic affairs, a conservative on fiscal affairs, but a very dyed-in-the-wool internationalist on foreign policy." On another occasion he told the House Judiciary Committee, "Compromise is the oil that makes governments go." Described as a blend of middle American morality and pragmatism, Ford's every remark now is aimed toward the center. Politically a conservative, he has already turned toward the liberal. His first major decision was to name Nelson Rockefeller as vice-president. Rockefeller himself during the course of his career has also moved toward center, but from the opposite side, from liberal toward conservative. They meet at the center post.

A period of rest for the convalescent nation is in order during which natural healing and resolution can be allowed to occur. But that is not yet to take place.

September 8: The Pardon

Exactly one month to the day after acceding to the presidency, President Ford grants Richard Nixon "a full, free, and absolute pardon . . . for all offenses against the United States which he has committed or may have committed or taken part in during the period from January 20, 1969 through August 9, 1974." The announcement came without advance warning, on a Sunday morning while most Americans were relaxing or in church.

That same day, across the country in Idaho, Evel Knievel, attempting to leap across the Snake River Canyon with his Sky Cycle X-2, shoots off the rim, sputters, falls, and lands in his parachute at the bottom of the canyon. He comes up cut and bleeding from his nose and face, and his knees "a little busted up," but otherwise safe and appearing sound. If Ford had looked for dream symbolism again, he could not have done better. If anyone had such a dream the next morning, it would have been easy to interpret.

"From January 20th, 1969," a curious date, the day of the first inauguration, "for all offenses which he has committed or may have committed." Is this an insurance if more offenses surface? In case, for example, it turns out that Nixon's involvement began before the June 23 date which is now looked upon as the beginning—for example, before the June 17 break-in? Could it be that Ford knows something? Nothing is too cynical to be considered.

Whatever explanations Ford offers in rapid succession, the reasons are so many and come so fast that one feels that the real one remains unsaid: "Richard Nixon and his loved ones have suffered enough. . . . Serious allegations and accusations hang like a sword over our former President's head, and threaten his health as he tries to reshape his life. . . . Many months and perhaps more years will have to pass before Richard Nixon could hope to obtain a fair trial." Actually the opposite has been the case for years; the people have turned the other way, ignored all evidence, refused to pursue or face the inescapable facts. "During this long period of delay and potential litigation, ugly passions would again be aroused, our people would again be polarized in their opinions and the credibility of our free institutions of government would again be challenged at home and abroad." These are precisely the effects the pardon has produced, an immediate repolarization and an aching revival of the loss of credibility of the free institutions of the American government. "It is not the ultimate fate of Richard Nixon that most concerns me . . . but the immediate future of this great country." These might have been Nixon's words. "I cannot prolong the bad dreams that continue to reopen a chapter that is closed." They are not dreams but memories. And Ford's new action adds another, not to the dreams but to the series of traumatic events.

Reagan and Goldwater support Ford's move. Democrats are generally appalled. White House counsel Philip Buchen emphasizes that Ford's concern was for the country, not for Nixon. And Betty Ford says her husband acted "in good faith"; he had gone to church and taken communion before making the announcement. The foreign press is mixed in its reactions. The people register disbelief, all signs having pointed by now to a resolution by the law. A significant segment of the population, perhaps the same one-quarter as before, feels that this shock too can be justified and absorbed. To them this might even be preferable. An objective conclusion was never too welcome.

Without himself having officially committed a crime, Ford may have joined Nixon in the cover-up. This may turn out to have been a fatal mistake. In pardoning Nixon, Ford was out of phase with the psychic rhythm of the nation. His move, if it was to be acceptable, was premature; it might have received a more favorable response after some accounting had been forthcoming. The majority of the people were not yet ready to return to their normal accepting state. Their own psychic wounds were still too fresh and needed longer care and respect.

Sincerity, recently reestablished, has again declined. On November 5, 1973, at the Senate Rules Committee hearing on his confirmation as vice-president, when Ford was asked his views about pardoning a president who had resigned, he had responded, "I do not think the public would stand for it." In the opening days of the new administration, Ford's new press secretary, J. F. terHorst was asked the same question, and referred reporters to the position taken by the president in November. And on August 28, 1974, less than two weeks before the pardon, at his first press conference as president, Ford was questioned once more about whether a pardon for Nixon was possible. On that occasion he had said it would be "unwise and untimely" for him to comment until and unless formal charges had been lodged.

Ford had begun to draft the pardon on August 30, two days after his August 28 statement, according to his counsel, Philip Buchen. Confronted with the discrepancy, Ford was able to match Nixon's classic ploys on the subject of lying. Where Nixon had declared previous statements "inoperative," or present facts as being "at variance with" what he had said before, Ford, under the same pressure and in the same spirit, explains: "I must admit that many of these decisions do not look at all the same as the hypothetical questions that I have answered freely and perhaps too fast on previous occasions." Thinking and speaking, even promising, are hypothetical; they operate under a different set of guiding principles than when reality arrives.

The honeymoon with the people has come to an end, and a cynical depression has returned. Questions are asked which were suppressed and put aside or at least not articulated before. Was the fact that Ford was chosen by Nixon the bottom factor in Ford's final decision? Was it the reason he was chosen in the first place? Was a pardon inevitable from the moment Nixon announced Ford as his choice eleven months ago? There is much speculation about "a deal." One columnist asks whether Ford's quick advocacy of limited amnesty for draft dodgers was a prelude to making the later pardon of Nixon logical and palatable. Others wonder about political motives: Could this have been a gesture to the Republican right, to soothe their hurt feelings over Ford's appointment of Rockefeller? Disharmony between ego and superego has again been stirred up in the national unconscious. There are reasons which could well have been accepted for Ford's actions. Considerations of mercy, compassion, and human empathy cannot be denied, although justice tempered with mercy would have been preferred. That Ford could genuinely feel that the tranquility of the country would best be served by the pardon could have been envisaged and believed. And the reason he gave, to avoid a long legal process for the country, could also have been accepted by many. Even a feeling of personal obligation, a payment of a debt of such magnitude by an act of loyalty, could have been understood if it were openly acknowledged. It probably would have been better tolerated at this moment than Ford's denial of it.

The people want above all to believe, first in their leaders, and through them in themselves. And this is again what has been denied them. The issue was specific, but the reaction was general. Is this what one's word was always to mean? After having promised to listen to the viewpoints of others, in contrast to the decision-making process as practiced by Nixon, will the new president also make great decisions in the manner just demonstrated? Will he always announce the most momentous acts after intense secrecy, with no sounding or preparation, in the hope that they will be absorbed more easily during the state of shock? "My conscience says it is my duty, not merely to proclaim domestic tranquility, but to use every means I have to ensure it," he stated in his speech announcing the pardon. If this was an attempt at shock therapy, it was not only ill-conceived but administered without consent.

Whatever Ford says and whatever the reasons he offers, the inescapable suspicion exists that he has paid his debt to the man to whom he owes the presidency, a prompt sequel in action which contradicts his words "I am indebted to no man." Once it is admitted that Ford had to do this, the timing and the method fall into place. The longer he would wait, the more difficult his task would become. He had to take the big gamble.

Within a few hours after the announcement, J. F. terHorst, Ford's first White House appointee, whose advent to the national scene had been welcomed after the era of Ziegler, announced his resignation in protest at the pardon. Joining Cox, Richardson, and Ruckelshaus, terHorst explained, "The President acted in good conscience and I also found it necessary to resign in good conscience. . . . I knew my credibility would be difficult to sustain." Credibility has returned as the main question about the White House.

Nixon himself, who, it now turns out, had been consulted beforehand in a week of intense negotiations, promptly accepts the pardon, hoping that this "compassionate act will contribute to lifting the burden of Watergate from the country." Again he concedes mistakes but no legal guilt: "That the way I tried to deal with Watergate was the wrong way is a burden I shall bear for every day of the life that is left to me.

. . . I was wrong in not acting more decisively and forthrightly." Ford, in an effort to bolster his defense against criticism, states that Nixon's acceptance of the pardon can be construed as an admission of guilt, even though Nixon himself fails to admit it. Those who defend the new president join with those who still try to defend Nixon in this estimate of recent events.

Instead of having produced a feeling of fairness, the pardon has magnified its opposite. While the leader has been cleared, others have gone to jail. Maureen Dean calls for the president to demonstrate the same compassion for her husband that he has shown to Nixon: "I pray he will not overlook those who have fully cooperated with the government in getting out the truth of Watergate. These individuals are suffering because they told the truth . . . which is something we have yet to hear from Mr. Nixon." What effect will the pardon have on the prosecution of six major former aides, including Haldeman, Ehrlichman, and Mitchell, whose trial is scheduled to begin at the end of September? What will Nixon's relationship now be to the accused, and to the evidence which only he can provide toward ferreting out the truth?

An agreement is announced along with the pardon that Nixon, by an elaborate double lock-and-key system, will control access to all tapes and other materials and reserve the right to eventually destroy them, while they will also be available for use by the court. After five years, Nixon may order destruction of any of the tapes, and all of them will be automatically destroyed in ten years or upon his death, whichever comes first. This provision, Mr. Nixon explains in a letter spelling out the details, was made "to guard against the possibility of the tapes being used to injure, embarrass, or harass any person and properly to safeguard the interests of the United States." Through this arrangement between Nixon and the Ford administration, less publicized than the pardon, the assurance of a permanent and irreversible cover-up is reaching its final stage.

Ford tries to patch up the cracks which have suddenly shown up in his character and in his support. Two days after the pardon, in a move which may only add fuel to the controversy, Ford gingerly tests the nation by releasing an announcement that an exploratory study is under way for a possible pardon of all Watergate defendants. (There are now forty-eight of them, of whom thirty-eight have either pleaded guilty or been convicted.) As with his soundings about amnesty before the act, Ford now probes making amends after the fact.

At the same time that Deputy Press Secretary John W. Hushen makes this announcement, the White House releases two documents, one from the Watergate special prosecutor and one from Nixon's attorneys, to continue to explain and defend the motivations behind the pardon. The main thrust of these is to point to the complexity of the case against Nixon and to make a distinction between pardoning the former president and others involved in the Watergate scandals. In response to Elliott Richardson's call to make public "the full record of what the potential charges [against Nixon] might have been," Special Prosecutor Jaworski indicates that he "probably will" include Nixon's role in a comprehensive report at the completion of the forthcoming trial. In a nationally televised press conference on September 16, 1974, Ford faces the nation again to declare that there had been no deal, there was no secret reason, and his only motivation for the pardon had been to heal the wounds of the country.

In California, while the state bar convention is voting 347 to 169 to denounce Ford's pardon as undermining "the confidence of our citizens in the American system of justice," Nixon's personal attorney, Dean S. Butler, carries to the president of the bar association Nixon's intention to resign from the California State Bar. This was not motivated, Butler states, by any desire to escape possible disbarment but by the fact that Mr. Nixon had no desire to continue practicing law. He presumed that a resignation from the New York State Bar would be submitted as well. Both of these moves would end the likelihood of any disciplinary move from these two quarters.

On September 10, District Attorney Joseph Busch of Los Angeles had announced that Nixon can no longer be prosecuted for the break-in at the office of Daniel Ellsberg's psychiatrist because the three-year statute of limitations on that crime had elapsed eight days ago.

The other principals awaiting trial are watching developments with more than academic interest, some feeling that Nixon's testimony will be indispensable for their defense. And they cannot be sure of him. Nixon himself was tougher minded than Ford in a reverse situation. It is now reported by Bernstein and Woodward, the original information gatherers, that Haldeman and Ehrlichman fared less well at the hands of Nixon than he did under the mercy of Ford. Within the last forty-eight hours of the Nixon presidency, the report goes, both of them urgently requested presidential pardons which Nixon rejected with deep resentment. Haldeman's pressure was particularly strenuous and was regarded by Nixon and Haig as threatening and tantamount to blackmail. "He'd send Nixon to jail if he didn't get a pardon," said one source of Haldeman's message to Haig.

Art Buchwald, who had sensitively stepped aside during the grim period following Nixon's departure, finds the atmosphere ripe for his return. After the shock of the pardon has worn off, the misery can again be best treated by telling the truth in his way.

A column entitled "Just Like Any Other Tom, Dick, or Gerry" consists of a note left to "Dear Gerry" by his disillusioned young bride:

By the time you find this note I will be gone. I don't know how to tell you this, but the honeymoon is over. . . . What a glorious month we had. As far as I was concerned you could do no wrong. I hung onto every word you said. After my bitter breakup with "you-know-who," I thought you were different. He lied to me and cheated on me and treated me like a fool.

I said I would never fall in love again. And then you came along with your honest face and strong jaw and sincere smile and damned if my heart didn't go flip-flop.

I said to myself you were special. You knew right from wrong and you would never be swayed by a lot of rhetoric and double-talk. Gerry, you promised me you wouldn't do anything until justice took its course. You told me under the stars as we held hands that the long nightmare was over and we would love each other forever and ever.

Oh, Gerry, what made you change your mind? What happened to all those dreams you had for us?

I know you tried to explain it to me. You said you had to forgive "you-know-who" as an act of compassion because he had suffered enough. But he hasn't suffered half as much as we have, Gerry. We'll never know all the things he did to us. Even now he refuses to admit that he did anything wrong. He keeps talking about mistakes in judgment. They weren't mistakes in judgment and you know it. They were criminal acts and you had no right to forgive him before we knew what they were.

Sunday, after you told me what you were going to do, I decided to go see Evel Knievel jump over the Snake River in his steam rocket. I thought this would make me forget. But it did just the opposite. As I stared at the red, white, and blue Sky Cycle I thought of us going into space together.

I could see us flying across chasms and mountains, sharing the danger and thrills that had been so much a part of our honeymoon.

But then as the rocket filled with hot air and the steam built up and the vehicle started lifting off the ramp, something happened. Before it got off, a parachute opened and, instead of streaking out across the canyon, the rocket nose-dived and floated head first, crash-landing on the rocky bank of the Snake River.

At that moment, Gerry, I broke into tears. I wasn't crying for Evel—I was crying for us. The rocket more than anything symbolized our honeymoon. It looked so beautiful on the pad with all that steam coming out of its nozzles, its nose pointed toward the sky as if to say, "Here I come world, ready or not."

The only trouble, Gerry, with Evel's rocket and your rocket on Sunday about "you-know-who" is that neither one of them would ever fly. . . .

P.S. Don't try to find me.

Ford's Sunday morning sell-out will take its place in history alongside Nixon's Saturday night massacre. By perpetuating the cover-up, Ford has joined the tail end of Watergate, playing a part in shaping it and making himself an extension of it. He had had a similar brush with Watergate at its inception. Much earlier it had come out that he had helped marshal Republican support to head off an early inquiry into Watergate by the Patman House Banking Committee, but this had been respectfully overlooked. Giving Ford the benefit of every doubt could no longer be justified.

Reacting alternately with defense and pique, Ford's old conservatism shines through his newly donned liberal cloak. His ex-press secretary terHorst writes that the country is aching for a breath of fresh air. The nation hugged Ford to its bosom when he took over, hungering for a change from the past. But now the hopes for a break with the Nixon faces have suffered disappointment as Ford has locked himself in with most of Nixon's Cabinet and many of his aides and staff. More disappointing now, however, is a visible continuation of old traits, not the break-ins but the atmosphere, not dirty acts but a muddy background of events.

In his attempts to hold both ends together, Ford is leaning more and more on clichés, slogans, and semantic maneuvers. We are not in a recession but in "a very mixed situation," not in an inflation but a "stagflation." The WIN button, Whip Inflation Now, included by Ford in the antiinflation program he presents to Congress on October 8, does little to accomplish its purpose but provides for button manufacturers their second most popular button since the Smile face of a few years ago, which was the all-time bestseller. There are feeble attempts at humor. "I never promised you a rose garden," Ford tells reporters assembled in the White House Rose Garden for a press conference, "but I guess Ron Nessen did."

Having moved from the right toward the center—"I have not subscribed to any partisan platform," the president said when he was sworn in—Ford's recent acts have turned him back toward the end of the spectrum from which he had begun. The economic program he presented to a joint session of Congress is considered solidly conservative, rejecting most of the suggestions of the left and sticking with those adopted by the Nixon White House. Reminiscent also of his predecessor, Ford attacks two crucial decisions of the Supreme Court and has taken to blaming Congress for energy and other problems, not with the direct blame of Nixon, but a more oblique one: referring to the failure of his plans to end the nation's reliance on imported oil he adds, "Unfortunately in too many cases the Congress has not responded."

Foreign policy and domestic conditions cannot help but be interlocked. Moral problems at one end lead to doubtful actions at the other. For a long time, there have been ugly and persistent rumors about the CIA and its role in Chile. Again Kissinger stands among the accused, along with other top State Department officials, of possible perjury, this time regarding testimony he gave before Congress in 1973 during an investigation of possible CIA involvement in the coup which overthrew the government of Marxist President Salvador Allende. Two legislators,

Sen. Philip Hart of Michigan and Rep. Michael Harrington of Massachusetts, have called for a public explanation by Kissinger of his testimony that to the best of his knowledge "the CIA had nothing to do with the coup" which had resulted not only in Allende's overthrow, but in his death. Both noted that according to secret testimony by CIA director William Colby an eleven-million-dollar covert operation against Allende's regime was approved by the "40 Committee," a shadowy interdepartmental group chaired by Henry Kissinger. Referring to Kissinger as "the author of the policy toward Chile," Harrington declared that statements made to the Senate and House committees about this were "if not outright lies, at least evasions of the truth."

In an opening statement at an unprecedented two-day public conference in September 1974 on the activities of the CIA, Senator Hart says that there was an "apparent contradiction" between Kissinger's testimony that he knew of no CIA involvement and the fact that he "presumably chaired sessions of the '40 Committee' at which the ongoing Chilean intervention was approved." A number of former government officials and authors have also stated that the CIA, through its covert activities around the world, has sacrificed democracy in the interest of stability. Former CIA official Victor Marchetti, co-author with John Marks of a controversial new book about the agency, declared that its ostensible mission of "saving the world for democracy in fact is nothing more than propping up corrupt dictators who couldn't stay in power five days without the CIA." David Wise, in a book *The Politics of Lying,* points out the unprecedented degree to which deception has become part of the anatomy of government. Capping revelations he made in two previous books, he said that the CIA operates its own air force and conducts secret political operations, including attempted overthrows of governments in which leaders are sometimes killed.

Shades of President Ngo Dinh Diem and his brother Nhu, assassinated in Vietnam over a decade ago; the same talk about the role of the CIA existed at that time and was never disproven or put to rest. In one of the "White House horrors," it has been revealed that E. Howard Hunt, Jr., forged cables about the Diem assassination from Vietnam to smear and to lay blame more directly on the Kennedy administration. Now Hunt's wife has perished in a plane crash and the name of the CIA is again mentioned—this time by Colson.

At a September 1974 meeting of the Senate Foreign Relations Committee, Sen. Frank Church of Idaho points out, after raising the question of Chile, that a totally pragmatic foreign policy can become "utterly unprincipled." When he asks Kissinger how he could justify a policy of "unfettered intervention in Chile designed to [de]stabilize a government that had been freely elected," Kissinger observes that he can not be specific in public testimony. It is true, Kissinger now says, that the CIA operated covertly in Chile; but this was to head off "one-party government," not to "destroy or subvert" the Allende regime.

Just after the trial of the remaining Watergate defendants begins, Kissinger sets out on another trip to the Middle East. This one is not rooted on solid soil and the atmosphere shows it. Ford must now be doubted on all fronts, and Kissinger is suspected of having lost his influence or his wisdom. In Egypt the June bloom of cordiality has failed. While this is due mainly to Ford's calling for enlightened prices by oil-producing nations, there are other factors. The spur-of-the-moment gift to Sadat, the two-million-dollar White House executive helicopter left by Nixon during his triumphal visit in June, has never been flown since there are no Egyptian pilots or mechanics qualified for the elaborate aircraft. A training program to have been financed by the American Embassy was never started. A delay in the start of the American aid program to Egypt, which was to have been two hundred fifty million dollars for the fiscal year ending in June, was explained by Kissinger as now having to await congressional authorization which would probably not be forthcoming before February of 1975. The fates of past and future promises must now all be questioned.

Kissinger's reception in Israel is not any better. His meeting with Prime Minister Yitzhak Rabin at the latter's home is interrupted by hundreds of demonstrators smashing through police lines shouting "Kissinger, go home!" Earlier, eight thousand demonstrators had gathered outside Rabin's office after Kissinger arrived. His pose with an Arab headdress in Jordan when conferring with King Hussein, in spite of his joking when he did it, did not endear him to the Israelis. Kissinger must now travel in a bullet-proof limousine. His method of diplomacy, leaning heavily on secret messages which mean vastly different things to the parties involved, seemed at this moment to be in collapse. Neither side trusts what he said privately to the other.

Jurists such as Melville Nimmer, professor of constitutional law at UCLA, point out that it is still possible to obtain the full story of Nixon's involvement despite the precipitate pardon, if that is wished. Nimmer describes three legal methods presently available whereby the full facts can be exposed and weighed: Congress can still proceed with impeachment; a blue ribbon Warren-type commission can be established; and the validity of the pardon can be challenged. With little wish for this in Congress, however, and no public pressure, none of these is likely. Special Prosecutor Jaworski, who had previously held out hopes that his own investigations and the forthcoming trials would reveal the full extent of Nixon's involvement, now notifies members of Congress that he lacks the authority to issue such a report and invites Congress to enact legislation authorizing him to do so. Since Jaworski is also quoted as saying he accepts the pardon, it is unlikely that he will make any move to challenge it.

Returning from his seven-day tour of the Middle East, Kissinger, in an address in New York on October 16, to the annual dinner of the Alfred E. Smith Memorial Foundation, declares that there is no longer any reason for bitterness and warns that a continuing national attitude of distrust could spawn "dangerously erratic" behavior by the government.

Reviewing the first fifty days of the Ford administration, one reporter points out that in the month between Ford's accession and the pardon the press was too gentle and uncritical in its treatment of the new president, frequently imputing to him many virtues that, in the words of Peter Lisagor, White House correspondent for the Chicago *Daily News,* "he didn't possess, we knew he didn't possess, and he didn't even claim to possess." Again what was demonstrated was the strength of the wish. Honesty, moreover, should be a basic qualification, not an exceptional quality that deserves special praise.

Responding to the continuing pressure, Ford agrees to an action unprecedented in American history, a president's subjecting himself to examination by a congressional committee inquiring into his moral powers of leadership. Testifying before the House Judiciary Subcommittee on Criminal Justice, the president is treated with courtesy and restraint. Rep. Elizabeth Holtzman of New York, however, voices to him directly the "dark suspicions" which have been aroused by the early pardon. President Ford again declares that there has been no deal, or secret understanding, or any motive other than to get the Watergate scandal behind the country. During the hearings some further damaging testimony emerges when Ford acknowledges that the possibility of an executive pardon was mentioned to him eight days before he assumed the presidency, a fact which had been omitted from all previous accounts. Called by Haig on August 1 with private news of the "smoking gun" tape, this possibility, Ford says, had been mentioned to him as one of a half-dozen options. In response, he said, "I inquired as to what was the President's pardon power, and he [Haig] answered that it was his understanding from a White House lawyer that a President did have the authority to grant a pardon even before any criminal action had been taken." The next day, however, Ford told Haig that "nothing we had talked about the previous afternoon should be given any consideration in whatever decision the President might make."

In spite of Ford's emphatic denials, the committee was not unanimously persuaded that all of the facts had come out. "I am convinced," said Rep. William L. Hungate, chairman of the subcommittee, in opening the hearings, "that the issue of the pardon will not be behind us until the record of the pardon is complete." But, said Rep. John Conyers, Jr., of Michigan following the hearings, the committee would have to have access to nearly two hundred conversations between Nixon and Ford while the latter was vice-president before they could be sure. Although Ford now told the committee how stunned he was by the incriminating revelation on August 1, on a subsequent trip to Mississippi and Louisiana on August 3, 4, and 5, he had continued to tell reporters he did not believe Nixon would be found guilty of an impeachable offense.

To Alpheus Thomas Mason, professor of jurisprudence emeritus at Princeton, Ford's testimony before Congress is "a deed to remember," of far greater significance than the issue of whether his pardon breached the spirit if not the letter of the Constitution. Ford clearly acknowledges that a president's actions are subject to review, a process which Nixon had vehemently tried to deny and subvert.

While Ford repeats that he considers Nixon's acceptance of a pardon tantamount to an acknowledgment of guilt, Nixon himself continues to "tough it out." On the same day that Ford sits before the congressional committee to explain the pardon, Nixon sues White House Presidential Counsel Philip Buchen and two other White House officials to bar the Ford administration from turning over his tapes and documents to the Watergate special prosecutor. This, he charges, is a violation of the September 6 agreement made just before the pardon providing for a speedy transfer of the materials to a federal depository near San Clemente with Nixon having possession of a key for access.

The Final Trials—and Phlebitis

The trial of the remaining defendants, including Haldeman, Ehrlichman, and Mitchell, begins on October 1. High in responsibility but not enough so to have been pardoned directly, their trial is expected to run three to four months, which should bring us to the end of this memorable year and on into the next.

Meantime, Nixon's health is suddenly becoming more of an issue and reports of its decline are being sharply stepped up. On September 16, Nixon is described by his former White House physician, Dr. Walter R. Tkach, as "a ravaged man who has lost the will to fight." After examining Nixon at San Clemente for a reported flare-up of his chronic phlebitis, Tkach announces, "Mr. Nixon's condition has worsened in the past several weeks despite the pardon." Tkach had decided against hospitalizing the ex-president after Nixon had said, "If I go into the hospital, I'll never come out alive." Tkach added, however, that Nixon was rational and showed no signs of mental imbalance. In a thirty-minute interview with NBC News, back at his quarters at Andrews Air Force base near Washington, the military surgeon explained that a new blood clot had developed in Nixon's left leg, causing it to swell, and that he was fatigued and very tense. He was "mentally alert," however, despite the "severe strain and physical fatigue."

Reports about Nixon's health during this period have followed a varied course, particularly with reference to his emotional condition. While family members have described him as "in pain" and "not feeling well," others have reported him as appearing well and in good spirits. Contradictions such as this have followed Nixon since Ford's reference to his health in the pardon statement had raised questions about his physical and emotional state. Ford's longtime confidant, Melvin R. Laird, is now reported as having said that the pardon was granted as "an act of mercy and compassion" due to Nixon's being in "very bad shape" and "having lost contact with reality." Ford's counsel, Philip Buchen, who played a role in the pardon negotiations, declares that the pardon was given to spare the nation the pain of watching the ex-president "go step-by-step toward the brink."

Reports circulated among friends that Nixon occasionally would go all day without shaving, that he would wander the grounds of San Clemente, talk to the gardener, rummage through stacks of unanswered mail, and disconsolately play the piano. Others, however, who had also seen or talked to Nixon directly, reported no evidence of ill health. Robert H. Finch, fellow Californian and Nixon's former secretary of health, education and welfare, said he had heard that an effort was being made to point up Nixon's condition, lobbying, in effect, to help obtain legal concessions in the future. Nixon's brother Donald found him "in good health and good spirits" and said that he "looked very good, was tan, busy, and had a lot of things to wind up." A San Clemente neighbor, Paul Presley, reported after a visit, "He looked super. He looked more relaxed than when he was President. He definitely isn't sick." Presley added that Nixon told him he had been swimming, walking, and getting his work done.

A week later, despite his previous protestations, Nixon agrees with his physician's advice to enter the hospital for further tests. On September 22, nine days before the trial is scheduled to begin, Nixon is hospitalized at the Memorial Hospital in Long Beach, California, for a series of diagnostic studies and a trial of therapy with anticoagulant medication. On October 1, Nixon is in the hospital when the Watergate trial begins.

Haldeman and Ehrlichman, the stellar defendants, declare at once that Nixon's presence and testimony will be indispensable to their defense. Such an emphasis is not without good reason; it is increasingly apparent how problematic that possibility is becoming. Although the shadow of his deeds looms over the trial, the likelihood of Nixon's presence becomes less each day. There is a race in the making between the trial and his illness.

After twelve days in the hospital Nixon is discharged on October 4 more physically exhausted than when he went in. Dr. John C. Lungren, his personal physician and a friend of Nixon's since 1952, announces that Nixon will not be able to travel to Washington for one to three months, depending on how well he responds to anticoagulant therapy. And although Nixon has been summoned as a witness by both prosecution and defense, he will not be able to make a deposition for use by the court for two or three weeks. Alluding to speculations that he was helping Nixon avoid an appearance in court by providing medical justification, Lungren states, "I know there are lots of doubting Thomases. The place is full of them. I have been honest. I am trying to be completely unpolitical and to give you my professional attitude." One possible risk, Lungren explains, is that Nixon could develop stress ulcers and massive gastrointestinal hemorrhages stemming from the anticoagulant drugs he is taking to prevent clots. The day before Nixon leaves the hospital his attorneys request that Judge John Sirica excuse him completely from testifying at the trial. Among the options open to him, the judge can appoint a panel of doctors to examine Nixon and report to the court. Sirica takes the motions under study.

Two weeks later, on October 17, the same day that President Ford is testifying about the pardon before the congressional subcommittee, Nixon's attorney informs the judge that Nixon will probably be healthy enough to testify at the trial within several weeks. On the basis of this, Judge Sirica asks for a detailed report on Nixon's health in three weeks and states that Nixon will be needed in the courtroom by late November, unless he is gravely ill. There is still no unity, however, in the Nixon camp. On the same day, Ronald Ziegler issues a statement that Nixon is "not very well" and that his spirits are sagging as he waits to hear whether he will be called to testify.

Meanwhile at the trial itself, which in addition to Haldeman, Ehrlichman, and Mitchell includes as defendants former Assistant Attorney General Robert C. Mardian and Kenneth W. Parkinson, a private attorney for the Nixon campaign committee, new light on Nixon's activities will emerge from fifty-five White House tapes obtained by Jaworski which Nixon had not surrendered to the House Judiciary Committee. It is expected that more than thirty of these tapes will be played publicly at the trial; special earphones have been provided for the principals. These tapes, which may lead to a flare-up of antagonisms among the defendants and a new freedom for Haldeman and Ehrlichman to speak more openly about Nixon's role, may also provide new insights and material evidence.

But before any of this can come to pass, an unexpected shift in personnel has quietly occurred. On October 12, Watergate Special Prosecutor Leon Jaworski resigns suddenly saying that "the bulk" of his job has been done. His action, he explains, rests entirely on his desire to return to Texas and private life; he is sixty-nine and tired. Jaworski's departure, it is considered, will deprive the prosecution of significant power and prestige. After succeeding Archibald Cox, he had amassed a record of strength and respect. His pursuit of the evidence and truth had been as firm and resolute as that of his predecessor. President Ford immediately expresses "very deep gratitude to Mr. Jaworski for his devoted service."

"The evidence will show [that Nixon is] guilty just as much as a guilty plea," Jaworski says as he resigns. Earlier, following the pardon, when he had been pressed to come forth with a full report on Nixon's involvement based on his own long and complete investigation, Jaworski had notified members of Congress that he lacked authority to issue such a report and invited Congress to enact legislation to authorize him to do so. Urged also to challenge the legal basis of the pardon, Jaworski had stated he was convinced that Ford had acted within his constitutional authority and therefore it would be against his conscience and "tantamount to unprofessional conduct" for him to issue such a challenge. Following his resignation, the prosecution has been taken over by Jaworski's assistant, James F. Neal.

The trial proceeds. New tapes, never before heard, reinforce the centrality of Nixon's role. In a tape of March 17, 1973, four days before Nixon had long insisted he first learned about a cover-up from Dean, Nixon is heard telling Dean that Watergate should be "cut off at the pass" and that White House officials should "make self-serving goddamn statements" at Senate Watergate committee hearings. Later that same day, (October 18) the jury, in the first public playing of the famous tape of March 21, listened to Nixon telling Dean and Haldeman to get a million dollars "hush money" to meet the demands of Watergate burglar E. Howard Hunt: "And you could get it in cash. I, I know where it could be gotten." In the same tape everyone in the courtroom, through padded earphones, heard Nixon refer to Sirica as "a hard-liner

judge" and heard Dean reply that Sirica was "a peculiar animal," adding, "He can be a, just a son-of-a-bitch." Beneath his earphones the
judge is reported to have blushed and chuckled.

While only Nixon himself can now fill in the gaps and round out the
picture not on the tapes, Nixon's condition takes a turn for the worse.
On October 23, he is readmitted to the hospital in Long Beach, California. His phlebitis has not done well, drug treatment at home has not
succeeded, and "if anticoagulant treatment cannot be adequately established and controlled," surgical intervention will be considered.

The tests fail. The treatments do not hold. The phlebitis, which began
ten years ago in Japan and has dogged Nixon from the time of his trip
to Egypt as president in June to his self-exile in San Clemente, has
spread through the veins of his left leg, almost totally blocking circula-
tion in the femoral vein and causing blockages throughout the calf. On
Tuesday, October 29, Nixon undergoes "urgent" surgery at 5:30 in the
morning. Six hours after the operation he goes into a state of surgical
shock, after which his condition stabilizes.

Nixon's mental state is variously reported. Some depict him as cheerful, others as "glum, deeply depressed, emotionally exhausted, and pes-
simistic about his future." On Friday, November 1, President Ford visits
him and the pair discuss foreign policy. Ford describes the ex-president:
"He was very alert. He was very interested, but it was very obvious to
me that he had been very very ill. But he showed a great deal of
strength mentally and physically." On November 3, Nixon is removed
from the critical list. His doctor is now unusually optimistic.

Nixon is in the hospital on Election Day, November 5, the first election after Watergate. Three weeks before the election, the Fair Campaign Practices Committee had believed that candidates were running
cleaner campaigns than usual "because they realize voters will react
against anything that smells of Watergate smear tactics." As Election
Day approached, however, there was an upsurge in the number of
complaints received, comparable to the year of Watergate. Two days
before the election, Dr. Samuel J. Archibald, the executive director of
the committee, reported that the 1974 campaign was as dirty as ever.
"In 1972," said Archibald, "there was the big drop into the political
sewer. [Today] We're climbing back into the sludge. All candidates
learned from Watergate is how to play dirty politics." Watergate never-

theless had its effects: the Republicans suffered the expected defeat.

Ford's attitude toward Congress has become more complaining, and the reactions in return have been less restrained. Buchwald writes another column: "Can This Marriage Be Saved?" President Ford had said earlier that he did not want a honeymoon but a marriage with Congress. Now, three months later, the couple sees a marriage counselor, with rather hopeless prospects ahead.

Settling down after the election, Ford lets it be known that he will definitely be a candidate to succeed himself in 1976; he "enjoys" the job. In assessing the first one hundred days of his presidency, the press comments on the amount of traveling he has done to get himself known. Ford's thinking about issues is still to be developed. His tenure has been marked by drift, uncertainty, and absence of policy. The only decisiveness he has displayed was in his abrupt pardoning of Nixon. This seemed to come from within and to be accompanied by worry but not by doubt.

At the trial, new material continues to link Nixon directly with the crime of cover-up. In a tape of January 8, 1973, Nixon discusses with Colson the strategy for granting executive clemency to Hunt because of the latter's "sensitive" knowledge of improper White House activities. This corroborates Dean's Senate testimony of last year which Nixon had denied. Again and again Nixon discusses with his top aides "payoff," "hush money," and "pardons" for the Watergate break-in burglars.

In one plan Nixon discusses how Ehrlichman will call Mitchell in to tell him he must admit guilt and take the blame. (When Martha Mitchell had long ago made this claim, she was regarded as mentally unbalanced and never questioned.) "But John Mitchell . . . will never go to prison," Nixon adds. "I think what will happen is that he will put on the goddamnedest defense. . . ." Mitchell flushes with anger as he listens to this in court. "They won't give him immunity anyway . . . unless they figure they could get you," Haldeman states, "He is as high up as they've been." "He's the big enchilada," Ehrlichman adds. "The obstruction of justice," Nixon admits, "is our main problem at this time." The cover-up, he fears, involves "the king of the mountain." Nixon's language is also made more presentable in the transcript. A remark that Colson was "up to his ass" in the scandal was changed to "up to his navel."

In strange contrast to his lack of awareness of the potential danger of his own collection of tapes, Nixon expresses concern to Haldeman that Dean may have taped him during the March 21 conversation in which the two had discussed raising a million dollars in hush money for the burglary defendants. "I just wonder if the son-of-a-bitch had a recorder on him," says Nixon. "That's what may be his bomb." "It's so remote as to be almost beyond possibility," Haldeman assures him.

There then follows a musing piece of insight in which Nixon comes close to understanding the thesis I am presenting here. Nixon becomes philosophical: "You know, in a strange kind of way that's life, isn't it? We'll survive and you'll even find in Mississippi a half-dozen people that will be for the President. Who knows?" "Be a lot more than that," Haldeman replies, laughing. "Yeah, yeah, that's right," Nixon says. "Despite all the polls and all the rest, I think there's still a hell of a lot of people out there, and from what I've seen, they're—you know, they want to believe, that's the point, isn't it?" They do, and at that point they very much did.

In mid-November Sirica receives a report from Nixon's attorney, Herbert J. Miller, about Nixon's health. The former president has agreed (!) to be examined by a court-appointed panel of doctors "if they really feel it is necessary." The physician-patient privilege must apply, Miller says, and the court will have to bear the expense. Sirica assures the attorney that the court will bear all the expenses. The judge then suggests that the panel, besides examining the medical records, might "want to get someone else in, a psychologist or whatever."

There is a peculiar imprecision or lack of professionalism in this offhand suggestion about both the need for and type of mental examination indicated. Both of these questions might well have reached a more definitive stage at a much earlier point. It has always been ambiguous whether protective activities on Nixon's behalf were related more to physical or mental grounds. Reports coming out on Nixon's mental state have always been elusive and contradictory, alluded to whenever it was to Nixon's advantage to stress his limitations and denied whenever emotional factors could be construed as reflecting on his character. The judge's advice was never reported as having been taken; no record of a psychiatric examination was ever announced. All in all, a rather anachronistic attitude was displayed toward modern professionalism in this area and a primitive stance toward mental illness at the nation's top level where such involvement is or should be of great concern.

On November 29 the three-member panel concludes that Nixon is too ill to testify at the trial, and that he will not be well enough to appear in court before February of 1975. He could answer lawyers' questions at his home in San Clemente at an earlier date, but not before January 6! The report is unanimous; only the conclusions are given, no back-up medical data. "This would involve specific information," the chairman explains, "which we have been instructed is confidential." One cannot help but compare this with the Nixon administration's attitude toward confidentiality between the patient Ellsberg and his physician-psychiatrist. The material in this instance is hardly as delicate, not the content of a man's mind.

The case, it is generally thought, is to reach the jury about Christmas and to come to a finish at about the end of the year. In one of the most exquisitely timed medical histories on record, Nixon's long-festering illness comes to a head and makes him too ill to comply just before the culmination of the trial which happens to be the last chance to extract the testimony which it is to his deepest interest to avoid.

The findings of the medical team must be regarded as accurately reflecting the medical condition. Certainly the organic illness, the vascular constriction, the venous clotting and infection, and the finding of a small embolus in the lung were demonstrably visible and constituted a pathological condition with a distinct present and future danger. None of these can be considered as having been consciously brought about or maneuvered. One cannot overlook, however, the psychosomatic unity which determines the functioning of the human body. There is also the matter of unconscious timing, as well as the use to which organic symptoms are put for unconscious purposes of secondary gain.

The autonomic nervous system radiates out to every system in the body, including the vascular, and is finely tuned to react to psychically threatening events. By a process of somatic compliance, an organ which is the most vulnerable serves as a locus of least resistance and thus is the first to react to psychic pressures and needs. For Nixon, his vascular system was the complying organ. This propensity has been with Nixon for many years, in active and inactive form, chronic and acute. Flare-ups, when they occurred, were variously used in relation to crises and survival needs. When decisive action, including mental as well as physical exertion, was necessary for his defense and survival, the illness was relegated to a secondary position and activity, even dangerous to the physical health, was carried on in spite of it. Nixon, we remember, went to Egypt and then to the Soviet Union against medical advice. In the present circumstances, the opposite obtains; his interests are better served by inactivity and avoidance than by action and confrontation. What can be said as fact, from what is publicly known, is that the timing of the flare-ups of Nixon's thrombophlebitic illness, which included his refusal of medical prescription at one time and his ready compliance with the limitations imposed at another, in both instances dovetailed with his emotional and, in this case, legal requirements.

It is now neck and neck whether Nixon's vascular system will permit him to testify before the end of the trial, or whether the trial will end first, or whether, if nothing else, the trial will be slowed to wait for the man. The issue is no less than the alternatives between final success of the cover-up or a last-minute exposure of the truth.

One week later, on December 5, Judge Sirica provides the answer. The trial "will proceed without interruption"; the ailing ex-president "is simply unavailable." There is no time for the former president to testify; questioning him before January 6 "could seriously jeopardize his health." Moreover, decides Sirica, after all the medical studies which have been gone through and considered, there is *no need* for Nixon's testimony! It would not materially affect the case of the defendants. But for whatever light it might shed on the case of Nixon, the finality has come from an unexpected direction; the last avenue is closed.

Without impugning motives, it must be seriously questioned whether a medical or psychiatric or psychosomatic prediction, without psychiatrists present or even if they were to have been part of the team, could be made with such precision about a patient's future ability to withstand psychic stress, the possibility of hemorrhages, stress ulcers, or emboli notwithstanding. There is no day in which danger disappears, no day when one can say it would have been that much worse the week before. Danger does indeed exist and can never be vouchsafed as gone. But so it does in every case, and there is always stress at a trial. And the guiltier or more tense the witness, and the greater the fear of uncovering, the more the stress. January 6 would not have changed any of these factors.

There are cases every day, even among those who play lesser roles in this very Nixon story, where a propensity for a serious physical occurrence as testified to by medical specialists is ignored and the trial pursued. Armand Hammer, for example, who was accused of illegal contributions to the Nixon fund, is hospitalized with arteriosclerosis, abnormal heart rhythm, angina pectoris, and a possible need for the implantation of a cardiac pacer. Although a cardiologist testifies that Hammer could suffer a fatal heart attack, the judge in that case denies his attorney's plea, and the seventy-seven-year-old industrialist is brought from his hospital room to the court. Arriving in a wheelchair, the defendant proceeds with his trial hooked to a cardiac monitoring device, with portable resuscitative equipment nearby for "any untoward event."

The best of men continue to be affected by the Nixon influence, whether originally by Nixon the man or as now by the power of and respect for the office of the presidency. Not only did this affect those involved at the beginning; it continues to touch those drawn in from any direction. There was Gerald Ford; and Jaworski, who incurred criticism for leaving his post before the job had been done; the doctors, needing to render objective statements about a clinical condition of which one could never be sure; and now Sirica himself in this final decision. All unwittingly play their successive roles in assuring the cover-up its final success. With a few notable exceptions—an Ervin, Cox, Richardson, or Rodino, who were able to stick it out—most reach a point of maximum tolerance and show an inability to remain clear to the end.

In one of the last tapes to be played at the trial, that of April 25, 1973, Nixon overtly showed his imperviousness to the seriousness of the tapes. When all was said and done, he thought, they would even work to his advantage. Reminiscing with Haldeman about what the tapes might reveal, Nixon saw more good than bad, more indications in them that he had hesitated to go along than incriminating evidence that he did. "Incidentally," says the president to Haldeman, "I always wondered about the taping equipment, but I'm damn glad we have it, aren't you?" "Yes, sir," answers Haldeman, "just one thing I went through today, it was very helpful."

Haldeman, Ehrlichman, and Mitchell, whose attorneys have stated that Nixon's testimony was indispensable for their defense, have to go on without it. Coming closer to decision day, the heretofore sturdy and stolid Ehrlichman reaches a point similar to that reached by Nixon and finally chokes with emotion. Speaking of his concern for his children on the eve of his resignation, Ehrlichman's voice breaks for the first time, and his eyes fill with tears as he tells the jurors of a farewell conversation with Nixon a day before his forced departure. His apology to Sirica is met with understanding, and the trial is recessed for ten minutes. A touch of humanness hitherto suppressed finally emerges, as had been the case with Nixon himself. Nixon too, Ehrlichman says, had broken down at one point and cried. "He said he felt I had tried to be his conscience," Ehrlichman says.

There is now a general wish to claim the long-neglected superego. Ehrlichman reaches for it probably both as an inner support and as an aid to his defense. Following this release of pent-up emotion, the next day Ehrlichman breaks ranks with the others and accuses Nixon directly for the first time. Bristling at having been kept from knowledge of the tapes, he complains, "I was in fact deceived" on at least four occasions after the break-in and knew "pitifully little" about the scope of the cover-up.

In summing up the defense for Haldeman, his attorney John J. Wilson makes an astonishing final statement. The tapes, Wilson declares, disclose "normal human conduct" but no evidence of criminal wrongdoing. The discussions were like family members "gathered around the dining room table to discuss a brother, sister, or husband who's in trouble. . . . This is just human nature. You are hearing things sometimes quite inelegant, but these things go on." If one can get past the initial offense and Wilson's sweeping of the official crime under the rug, one can see how such a statement could be made without eliciting total disbelief from the court and the press. Many have said all along that their revulsion toward what was on the tapes was due not to the content so much as to the high level from which they emanated. This was recognizable talk, but embarrassing and shocking from the table of the president of the United States.

Whatever sympathy Wilson was able to elicit with his statement was negated soon thereafter. The full blast of his scorn was leveled at Dean and Magruder, the confessed conspirators whom he termed "professional liars." It was Dean, Wilson declared, sparing any wrath against Nixon or Haldeman, who "has a kaleidoscope of criminal activity which seems to be almost beyond the pale of an ordinary human being." Such reasoning brings to mind the hierarchy of values often seen among prisoners. The informer, the "rat-fink," is the most scorned.

In testimony given by another defendant, lesser in stature than the big three, an arresting statement is made. Former Assistant Attorney General Robert C. Mardian said that he believed that Nixon was running the Committee for Re-Election *at the time* of the Watergate break-in itself. Mitchell, he said, who was supposed to be at the head of the committee, "was overruled on several occasions. I don't know of anyone in government who could overrule John Mitchell but the President." This statement of such major import received little or no attention from the public, the press, or the prosecutors at the trial. This was another example of the operation of the screen phenomenon. Nixon was free of anything not recorded on the tapes. And just as the tapes were a screen which covered what was *not* on them, the attention to the cover-up covered the original crime itself.

In his final rebuttal, Chief Prosecutor James F. Neal, in an impassioned summation to the jury, compared statements made by Abraham Lincoln and Franklin Roosevelt with those of Nixon. "With malice toward none and charity for all" or "We have nothing to fear but fear itself" could be contrasted with Nixon's "Give 'em an hors d'oeuvre and maybe they won't come back for the main course."

On New Year's Day 1975, Haldeman, Ehrlichman, and Mitchell, along with Mardian, were found guilty of all charges against them. Kenneth Parkinson, Mardian's associate, was found innocent. The decision was reached on January 1, just five days before the medical team, whose interest was to protect the ailing Nixon, had judged that he would be well enough to answer questions.

Judge Sirica had read the collective mind well; his sudden decision had caused no public shock. The inner struggles of the public are not gone, but the craving now is to be left in peace. But what was prevented from happening directly became evident indirectly. The man who was not there and who was not officially on trial appeared thoroughly convicted just as Jaworski had said he would be. Everything revealed on previous tapes was minor compared to the torrent of evidence in tape after tape heard for the first time during this three-month trial, which established Nixon's complicity at every step of the cover-up from June 23, 1972, on. The evidence forced into the open by the prosecution of others established Nixon's guilt in the last court left, the court of history, in the words of one editor, "beyond all reasonable doubt." This was important, the same editor pointed out, because Nixon had left office admitting nothing and because there are still those who believe him.

"Was Nixon Sick of Mind?"

The question has come up repeatedly during the long ordeal, but has never been satisfactorily answered. Professionals have been reluctant or unable to apply a definite diagnostic label, and have differed in the interpretation of the words "sick" or "neurotic," in the same way that the word "criminal" was unclear for a long period of time. Terms used have been mostly descriptive or pejorative, such as "cynical," "amoral," or "chaotic."

Whatever private neurosis Nixon may have been subject to—whether hysterical, obsessive, depressive, or paranoid, all of which have been mentioned at various times—no label explains the consistent and astonishing characteristics which have guided his behavior during his entire political life, and from the fragments available, his earlier life as well. There is no evidence in any statistically contolled study that neurotics or psychotics are less honest than subjects who do not suffer from such psychiatric syndromes. Any of the neuroses or psychoses conventionally known on the scale of psychiatric pathology can exist without psychopathic, antisocial, or immoral behavior. Conversely, opportunistic, self-seeking, rule-breaking behavior, from the mildest to the most severe, takes place every day with none of the typical neuroses necessarily accompanying them. Of course, the two may coincide. But even when they do, they need not be causally linked.

The fact is that Nixon was sick in the realm of integrity. This is an area in which the mental sciences have lagged. The central thrust of the behavioral characteristic which was pathognomonic of the Nixon syndrome was his predictable preference, whenever a life situation presented the necessity to choose, for the alternative which led to self-advancement at the expense of truth, principles, or the well-being of others. This is, to be sure, not an uncommon trait. But Nixon, because of the supreme level at which he demonstrated it and the unfailing degree to which he was shown to have practiced it, has come to epitomize for our age what I have called the syndrome of the compromise of integrity.

The forty or so men under Nixon, who almost to a man went along and who participated with all that Nixon did, link the syndrome from the individual to the group. Not having initiated the behavior but for the most part followed makes the difference only a matter of degree. With respect to the primary crime, the break-in itself, they were, according to the record at least, thus far the actual leaders and doers rather than followers. And in the secondary crime of the cover-up, which was the one for which they were punished, they were as fully participating as Nixon himself.

The mind of Watergate was more a collective property than due to an accidental series of individual quirks. All shared a common conflict, each with his own individual stamp. To some extent an interest in one individual is a defense against knowing the role of the group. And if our concern is for the future as well as for the past, the former is of less importance than the latter.

In quantitative terms, the syndrome of the compromise of integrity is no small category, but a large generic one on the level of neuroses and of the same ubiquity. From the nosologic standpoint, just as there is hysteria or obsession under neurosis and paranoia or depression under psychosis, so can subdivisions be classified under the rubric of compromise of integrity. Nixon's own activities, as well as the manifold types of psychopathology of those who followed and allowed him to lead, demonstrated the variety of paths and manifestations these subdivisions could take.

To indicate its place in a quantitative sense, compromise of integrity constitutes perhaps a quarter of the length on a linear scale of psychopathological behavior. If in the center we have normal, going toward the psychic interior we have neuroses first, and then psychoses. Moving in

the opposite direction, toward the outside environment which sur-
rounds the individual, we have always had psychopathy and crime as
the ultimate acting-out. I now add compromise of integrity as the lesser
and milder type of behavior within this genre. Figure 1 illustrates these
relationships

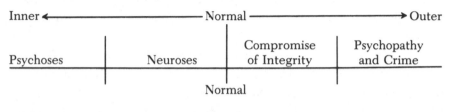

Figure 1

As neuroses are to psychoses, so is compromise of integrity to psychopathy and crime. Although the Watergate activities finally crossed
the line into crime, the substrate and background during the months
and years before the overt crime was actually entered into stood firmly
rooted in the milder compromises on the legal side of crime. As neuroses are the larger field within the psychic interior, so is compromise
of integrity the more common condition at the externally directed end
of the behavioral spectrum. And just as neurosis does not incapacitate
the subject, so does compromise of integrity not destroy the object.
Each nibbles at and takes it out on its object, the self in one case and
the outer object in the other, while in each case permitting its target-
victim to survive.

The sickness exposed in "the sick society" was also not hysteria or a
depression or an obsession, but a sensitivity and weakness of the moral
fiber, an absence of resistance against the effects of these and a resulting
deficiency in the realm of integrity. That the outbreak of a national
crisis in this area occurred in the early seventies was consonant with a
common diagnosis of the sixties as the "me" generation. The self, narcissism, "the I" were paramount; by a convergent diagnosis of psycholo-
gists and sociologists, the era has been called narcissistic.

The inclusion of the compromise of integrity as a pathological syndrome in no way implies a lessening of responsibility. In fact, I would
expand the applicability of responsibility to other areas of psychopa-

thology as well. To the extent that unconscious factors operate, responsibility for one's actions wanes. The celebrated Leopold and Loeb case
of the 1920s, with its landmark influence on the field of social justice,
added knowledge of unconscious motivations, but also led to a misinterpretation which I believe needs rectification.

Freud used a metaphor of the ego as the rider on the horse. While
the rider is dependent on the force of the animal beneath him, he plays
a part in guiding it to where he wants to go. With unconscious drives
representing one source of direction and power, the ego, taking into
consideration all forces, internal and external, decides and guides the
outcome. Decisions, we have learned in recent years, are actively made
unconsciously as well as consciously. Focusing again on Nixon, he can
no more derive freedom from responsibility from a deeper understanding of his superego deficiencies than he would by being diagnosed as
hysterical, depressed, or having paranoid trends. He knew the right and
the wrong, although his drives and character were such that he had a
problem doing right.

What others show in attenuated forms, Nixon presents in pure culture. A desperate pressure to serve the self with a reciprocal callousness
to the welfare of others was layered over by a two-tiered defense. First,
the priority of the self was covered and obscured by a constant emphasis
on how much he cares for others. Recall his loudly proclaimed patriotism; everything he did was for the good of the nation. The insincerity
intrinsic to the existence of this gap was then itself covered over by an
increasingly exaggerated look (and probably feel) of sincerity.

There were layers of cover-up, chronic and built-in, long before the
specific one which finally destroyed him. It is likely, in my opinion, that
Nixon continued to believe in his total motives more than he was disturbed by the final lie. In an insider's account of Watergate, Raymond
Price, who advised Nixon to resign and wrote his resignation speech,
surveys Nixon's political life and comes out with a strong defense. Writing from a position generally regarded as one of conscience and integrity, Price concludes that Nixon was guilty mainly of inattention and of
an admirable if excessive loyalty to subordinates. There is no doubt that
in the sum total of his conscious mind Nixon himself shares this view and
evaluation of his life.

Such a self-concept was behind Nixon's "paranoid" stance. Increasing pressure and mounting criticism could only result in a lengthening of his list of "enemies." To have confronted himself with the content of the complaints would have threatened to undo his system of defense and was hardly a way for insight to be gained. As the gap widened between the facts and his claims (or, as Price would have it, as "the psychology of the chase [took over] with the pack in full cry") and Nixon's weakened defenses had to be bolstered by more of the same, his "sincere" look became more intense and increasingly pained. One wondered how long the spiral could go on. But it did to the end; he resigned before he broke.

Even the "smoking gun" which separated him from his supporters in July did not rout his internal structure: "Yes, there is a tape which will show things that may look like lying. But it can all be explained." A combination of enemies, dupes, and disloyal friends, and yes, also some good people who misinterpreted facts, made it look that way. Here was Nixon's internal as well as external defense. Mostly, I believe, he believed this. Only partly, and probably slightly—we will never know quite how much—do I feel Nixon allowed himself to know "the truth." The space between unconscious defense and conscious lying—Nixon had lived there most of his life—is not a line but a gray area separating and connecting the two.

In the treatment of the "sickness" we are discussing—and we should speak of treatment if we are describing a syndrome of pathology—it is considered an advance when a patient moves from psychopathy to neurosis. When anxiety can be experienced and located in inner sources, rather than projected into the outer environment, although suffering increases, the patient is on his way to improvement.

To the extent that Nixon was said to have suffered from depression or even suicidal tendencies, which were mentioned as having existed near the end, these would tend to bring him closer toward the normal end of the spectrum. To have been *without* depression at the experience he had just suffered actually raises more questions than the reverse.

"Integrity" is a word close to "integration," and the two are related not only etymologically but in principle. Nixon was not integrated but fragmented. His avowed values did not fit with his actions, reality with what he said were facts, his emotions with the revelations which poured out, his productions with his promises, his instincts with what he gave as his goals. There was no consistency or unity of outer with inner, nor within the latter of its individual parts. Nixon was a splintered personality. The opposite of integration is disintegration. This was demonstrated by the path which he took and upon which he led all who worked with or for him.

To date, there has been no surface evidence of guilt. He can still play golf, wear the presidential seal on his jacket, greet neighbors on the beach with a smile, and shake hands energetically with people who accost him much as they would a normal ex-president. Perhaps he even feels he is special, having been hounded and mistreated more than any other leader. If there is a flicker of deeper insight, this is withheld from public view. Neither repentance nor the search for insight have been prominent Nixon traits at any time during his succession of crises.

In 1962, Nixon wrote in *Six Crises,* "Leaders are subject to all the human frailties: they lose their tempers, become depressed, experience the other symptoms of tension. Sometimes even strong men will cry." We can believe that he felt those emotions then—we hope so for the sake of his not suppressing the fact that he is human—but, knowing Nixon, these words could have been written for the sake of expediency. Nixon became more and more the automatic man, saying not what he felt but what seemed best. It is also possible, however, that behind the automatic mask, genuine feeling was being held back, then and now.

A combination of inborn traits and early life experiences caused Nixon to develop a drive to achieve which became malignant and a guiltlessness about methods which would leave a trail of victims in his wake. Whatever specific traumatic experiences determined this direction, a general dynamic mechanism can be said to be at work: the smaller the man in relation to his ambition, the greater the insecurity and more panicky the reach. Failure and frustration increase the insatiability which in turn increases the anxiety in an ever-spiraling effect.

Other presidents, or aspirants to that top position, have had equally high ambition but not as low a self-esteem, and not as wide a gulf between the two. Whether from birth, as with a Roosevelt or Rockefeller, or by achievement, as with an Eisenhower, or from a series of experiences from within and without, as appears perhaps in a Truman, the distances between drive and the possibilities of life were bridgea-

ble, or at least potentially so. With Nixon, in contrast, a chasm existed
between insatiable wish and the always shaky feeling about its fulfillment. Thus, even when success occurred, it was never sufficient. The
always-expected gap spurred Nixon's risky and pathetic moves. In a
story on young Nixon by Donald Jackson that appeared in the November 6, 1970, issue of *Life*, a classmate remembered seeing Nixon cheat
during a college debate. He had been citing facts and figures from a
piece of paper that was actually blank. From there to cheating on an
exam in law school at Duke, to Watergate where his actions went out
of control, he was his own victim.

There is another important character trait to consider in assessing
both the causes and effects of the Watergate mentality. This is the
quality of courage, a trait or capacity not usually considered in a "scientific" study of a mental state. More specifically, to focus on the problem
faced by the men under Nixon, I refer to courage within the group
situation: this is the retention of the capacity to think and act as a
separate individual while under the influence of the surrounding group.

Here is another area in which the medical meets the societal model.
It is an area in which objective clinical descriptions may be thought to
give way to pejorative labels and value-laden concepts. But it is precisely in the field of values that the Nixon "sickness" as well as the
softness of character of his co-conspirators have their roots. Only one of
forty men retained this individuality under the pressure of the group
atmosphere in which they worked. I have offered the opinion repeatedly that this is not a fortuitous observation but one which points to a
ratio of profound significance.

It may appear simple and routine to think, feel, and act as an individual under conditions that psychoanalyst Heinz Hartmann calls "the
average expectable environment," but in common practice few succeed. Aside from the repeated findings in the present study, from
decades of clinical work, from social living as a psychoanalyst with its
inevitable observations of self and others, and especially from leadership positions in national and then international organizations, I consider the question of ordinary courage in group situations to be the most
pressing problem of human character in civilized man.

Nixon himself was aggressive but not courageous, no more at the end
than during the course of his career. He did not have the courage to

trust the people, never feeling that they would like him if they came to know him. While his actions presented him with an increasingly difficult task, who could say but that a final earnest display of personal courage—a decision for once to come clean with a sincerity which could not be doubted—might not have won him approval which could have saved his political career as well as his mental life? Yet the character limitation which hemmed him in was necessitated by another related mental characteristic, his sense of narcissistic invincibility. All tied together, and tied him up.

The men under Nixon, with less to lose, had a less difficult time. Before the exposure of Watergate, almost to a man they went along with him; after the fall they achieved their freedom to variable degrees and in different ways. None chose Nixon's path to the end, to their salvation and relative peace of mind. As much as they were all solidly with their chief during the early days of planning and execution, they eventually left him at various speeds during and after the ordeal of crisis.

In a capsule formulation of a theoretical summary, the oedipal and Watergate complexes which I have been placing in apposition demonstrate two aspects of the father figure with which the children-subjects have to relate, with two consequent methods of "solution." In the Oedipus complex there is the killing of the father who is envied but who has been seen as strong and essentially good, therefore the guilt. In the Watergate complex (which without this designation has existed as long as the history of man) the subject-child sees the corrupt side of the father. Through a combination of fascination and awe, and by the common mechanism of identification with the aggressor, there is a mutual pact to join his strength. There is no destruction of the father, hence no guilt. A more "normal" resolution in keeping with social goals would be to identify with the good aspects of the father figure, and to have both join in alliance against the bad in each.

These are parallel processes, always in tension. While the Oedipus complex, even with its patricide, fashions the superego, the Watergate complex affords it a holiday for years at a time. In the best of times, narcissistic aggression is not obliterated but controlled, in action if not in thought, and partially, if not with perfection.

There is a delicate piece of history that bears a relationship, a contrasting one, to this subject of integrity. Once upon a time a man named Thomas Eagleton was nominated to run for vice-president with Senator McGovern on the national Democratic ticket. He was young, appealing, energetic, and had accomplished much. His future seemed bright.

It was suddenly discovered that Thomas Eagleton had been depressed—and that he had received professional help! He was disqualified from running at once, with little or no debate. The embarrassment was automatic and deep.

Eagleton's counterpart on the Republican ticket had no trouble; he was now as much, perhaps more, of a shoe-in than was Nixon over McGovern; no questions about him were asked. Questioned on the "Today" show as to why he had not informed McGovern of his full medical history, Eagleton replied that when asked whether he had "any skeletons rattling around," he had automatically answered no because "a skeleton is something that's dirty, filthy, corrupt . . . and there's nothing about having been fatigued and exhausted and in a state of mild depression that I found sinister, dirty or ugly."

Depression is caused by an opposite intrapsychic situation than that which exists in problems of integrity. Depression is brought about by a superego which is harsh, vigilant, a taskmaster, but in compromises of integrity the superego is lenient and seducible. Where the conscience is strict, guilt or then depression result. Where it is lax or corrupt, anything goes, and usually does.

Abraham Lincoln was a depressive. He could not do something merely because it was for his own good. Other considerations impinged. He worried, felt badly, had conflicts, and would become depressed. People who can be inconsistent with impunity, even with righteousness, avoid self-doubt and also depression. One who has a need to be consistent, or who requires this of himself, is more often troubled than one who does not. Adlai Stevenson was severely criticized as a candidate for president as being indecisive. One cannot say that this is why he was defeated each time he ran, but this was an opinion widely held and much used against him during his campaigns. Nixon did not have this problem, either with the trait or with the criticism, and the traits he was known to have were not held against him. Nixon was decisive; there was no guilt to hold him back. His motivations were firm and unequivocal, all on one side, on either side, of any question, uncontested by doubt about the other. An indecisiveness would have gone along with a greater honesty, with a proclivity to facing all the facts.

A serious question arises from these considerations. Is a severe superego, which may go with guilt, doubt, indecision, or depression, more of a danger in the political arena than a too-permissive one? Although this problem has never been directly faced or articulated, the presence of the former in our political and governmental life has been regarded with suspicion, while the latter is scarcely subjected to questioning.

Depression and doubt, of course, are not desirable qualities in leaders of state. But while their dangers when excessive are not to be minimized or overlooked, their absence can point to equally significant problems. Signals of caution and restraint are needed in a world where sudden and impulsive actions, especially in high places, can trigger untold catastrophe. Too much inhibition or action can be equally destructive. If candidates for political office are to be questioned regarding mental traits, or indeed even disqualified for them as was Eagleton, the criteria of evaluation should be considerably broadened. The acting-out end of the behavioral spectrum needs to be as carefully considered as the tendency to inhibit.

As an interesting postscript, in the fall of 1974 the same Sen. Thomas Eagleton, running for reelection, enjoyed a popularity greater than ever before in his home state of Missouri. The old "charge" of two years before was never referred to, and he won a victory larger than at any previous time in his career. Depression, which eliminated him from the vice-presidential race, was never brought up as a deterrent for a senator. Perhaps there was more than a small degree of guilt and embarrassment, a sense of injustice done, of something not having been quite right. Eagleton now received a large bipartisan support, and according to one reporter, "continues to receive an avalanche of supporting mail, is in great demand as a speaker, and is even mentioned as a possible Presidential candidate." Eagleton, however, said he would never again seek national office.

V

The Sequel

The end of the trial is the bridge to 1975. The collective superego, ordinarily dormant, is now alert. Scandals, past and present, are being flushed out with less resistance, even an eagerness to expose them.

If there was any illusion that corruption and politics are synonymous, big business has joined the ranks openly and in full force. The two, however, freely intermingle. The list of companies involved is illustrious: Gulf, Northrop, Lockheed, I.T.T., Rockwell International, United Brands—national and international. In an ingenious fusion of the political and the corporate, Bob R. Dorsey, chairman of Gulf Oil Corporation, admits to having paid four million dollars in illegal contributions to the ruling political party of South Korea. Kissinger's response to the disclosure: although "we oppose illegal actions of American corporations abroad," the disclosure of the Korean payoffs would not affect the United States security commitment to that Asian nation.

Northrop, in a Senate investigation of thirty million dollars in overseas fees, acknowledges that it paid four hundred fifty thousand dollars to two Saudi Arabian generals. Lockheed paid seven million dollars to an ultra-right-wing militarist who served as its agent in Tokyo. The Japanese government is shaken at its highest level. Former Prime Minister Tanaka is jailed and indicted, and his successor and his government are besieged: "Our Watergate is more complicated than yours. We have lots of Nixons to force out," a Japanese bureaucrat in national security

affairs explains to an American reporter. The royal house of the Nether-
lands joins the ranks of those affected. Prince Bernhard, alleged to have
received 1.1 million dollars in payment by Lockheed, resigns his defense
post, the presidency of the World Wildlife Fund, and the chairmanship
of the Bilderberg Conference, the prestigious international think tank
which he had launched twenty-two years earlier to promote transatlan-
tic cooperation.

United Brands—whose president not long ago leaped from the window of a skyscraper—is revealed to have paid millions of dollars to
officials of the Honduran government. And closer to Nixon politics at
home, the chairman of Phillips Petroleum is reported to have delivered
fifty thousand dollars personally to Mr. Nixon as a campaign contribution in 1968, a year before the period covered in Ford's pardon.

In a "South Koreagate," embarrassing payoffs are discovered to have
been made by President Park Chung Hee to a wide sampling of American congressmen. As though to underscore the fact that the phenomenon under observation is not entirely an American phenomenon, similar incidents occur in rapid succession in other countries. France suffers
its own "Winegate." Willy Brandt resigns as chancellor of West Germany following a sex-spy scandal. Prime Minister Indira Gandhi of
India is convicted of corrupt practices in winning her 1971 landslide
election victory to Parliament. And in Israel, the discovery of an illegal
foreign bank account in Washington by the highly respected prime
minister results in the collapse of the labor government which had been
in power since the inception of the state of Israel in 1948.

From politics to money to sex: the latest revelations center in the
sexual sphere. Rep. Wilbur Mills and Fanny Foxe, Elizabeth Ray and
Rep. Wayne Hayes strike across party lines. Shady women suddenly in
the limelight include on their lists of friends a bipartisan representation
of government and Congress. A congressman from one party is arrested
for soliciting a prostitute on the West Coast, and another has two fami-
lies, one in his constituency at home and another during his work week
in Washington.

No age group or profession or ethnic group is exempt. A massive
practice of cheating is discovered at West Point in the worst scandal in
the history of the United States Military Academy. A two-million-dollar
fraud in Medicaid payments to doctors is uncovered in New York.

Charles Evers, the mayor of Fayette, Mississippi, is charged with having evaded income tax payments of fifty thousand dollars and of having embezzled nineteen thousand five hundred dollars from the emergency fund collected to aid his city's economic development. Probably the only reason there was such a small representation of minority groups in the Watergate scandals—so few blacks, women, Jews, and other ethnic groups—was because they had been discriminated against by Nixon in his original appointments.

The headlines involve figures in the multimillions, not the smaller corruptions which characterize the "sick society." The present larger exposures make it easier for people to dissociate themselves from such events. It is more clearly the "they," not "I." Each can now join the general condemnation, rerepress his own exposed interior, and in doing so speed the work of reparation.

Is all this worse than ever before in history or are these "normal" activities which are being flushed out at this time? Opinions are varied and the truth probably is on both sides. The chairman of the board of Rockwell International, whose company was criticized for entertaining government and Pentagon officials at company-owned recreational facilities, told a prayer breakfast that American corporations overall are "purer than Ivory soap." And a majority of business managers polled, while admitting the widespread presence of the moral decay of business, feel that today's ethics in general are far superior to those of any earlier period. President Ford, reacting in the name of what the country wants, calls such payoffs "a source of deep concern" and condemns "in the strongest terms" the bribery of foreign officials by United States firms doing business abroad. Press Secretary Ron Nessen announces that the president is "leaning toward the idea of establishing a Cabinet level committee to review the practices of American corporations in this area and to review the applicable American laws."

Washington politicians need especially to be cautious. "Corrupt" and "immoral" are catchwords which alert the reacting public. "Honesty" and "integrity" are words which are claimed by all. In a recent national public opinion survey Walter Cronkite was rated the most trusted and objective newscaster on television. Dan Rather, "commonly cast in the role of the President's arch foe," and called by the New Yorker magazine "the reporter the White House hates," has scored the greatest advance in public trust. Yet William Saxbe, after citing historic scandals from the Whiskey Ring in the Grant administration to the Teapot Dome under Warren Harding, takes note of how things are going after this one. "What is astounding is not only the amount of corruption the nation has tolerated," he remarks, "but how quickly it seems to forget what happened and to allow evil ways to reassert themselves."

Historians, political scientists, and commentators across the country present unequivocal opinions about Nixon's place in history. The Watergate scandal, in their estimate, does not merge with moral laxities of the past; it was one-of-a-kind in our nation's history. "It is absolutely unique," says Arthur M. Schlesinger, Jr. To Henry Steele Commager, "We haven't had a bad President before now. Mr. Nixon is the first dangerous and wicked President." And Richard H. Rovere refers to "Nixon, the first President who has really been a crook." In an article in *Esquire* in March 1975, Alden Whitman of the *New York Times*, who had come to know the late Chief Justice Earl Warren during the last year of his life, discloses that Warren "detested Richard M. Nixon with a most unjudicial choler." Warren had died two weeks before the House Judiciary Committee voted for Nixon's impeachment and a month before the ex-president, his old California political rival, resigned. "Tricky," said Warren, "is perhaps the most despicable President this nation has ever had. He was a cheat, a liar, and a crook, and he brought my country, which I love, into disrepute. Even worse than abusing his office, he abused the American people."

Most historians are skeptical now even about the truthfulness or the lasting effects of Nixon's self-proclaimed and also widely acclaimed diplomatic triumphs. On his achievements in foreign affairs Schlesinger writes, "I find this a mystifying judgment. I doubt whether history will sustain the current self-serving myth propagated by the Nixon people that he was great in foreign affairs. It really doesn't stand up." And Commager; "I don't know what the achievements are yet. It is by no means clear we have had a détente with Russia."

Among the people, attitudes toward Nixon vary across the spectrum from those who want to see him punished, up to and including jail or worse, to those who feel that he has had enough and resent those who cry for revenge. Those who are currently against the pardon are not necessarily those who were against Nixon all along, and those who feel that he has suffered enough are not all those who kept believing in him in the past.

Nixon himself has settled into seclusion and is only occasionally glimpsed. Periodically there are reports of his mental instability in the days before resignation, of how he drank, talked of suicide, and behaved in a bizarre manner that worried his aides. Theodore White describes him during his last days in office as "a time-bomb which, if not defused in just the right way, might blow the course of all American history apart." A number of senators and congressmen report a remark made by Nixon at a White House meeting called in an attempt to dissuade House members from impeaching him: "I can go in my office and pick up the telephone and in twenty-five minutes millions of people will be dead." One congressman, reported Peter W. Rodino, Jr., to whom this had been told, "was so upset that he went directly home from the White House and almost puked."

But from what can be gleaned publicly, Nixon's defenses have been restored and his energies are focused on building his case. He is working on his memoirs and the announced future television interviews with David Frost. In his first public appearance since he resigned, in a deposition seeking control of documents and tapes, Nixon argues that the final release of presidential materials will be his decision alone and that the time for full disclosure has not yet arrived. In doing so he will consider "the national security problem, the embarrassment, the private issue. By 'embarrassment' I am speaking of personal embarrassment and not speaking of embarrassment with illegality of course." There is a stubborn reinstitution of a strong self-defense.

In a new foreword Nixon has just written to his public papers, only errors of judgment are admitted, not guilt. "Each attempt on my part to deal with it [Watergate]," he writes, "led me and my administration deeper and deeper into a tangled web of suspicion and confusion." Occasionally there is a slight degree of critical introspection and with it a more appropriate response of remorse. There has even been an indirect indication of a normal anguish. In a telephone call which made him feel sad, Rep. Dan Kuykendall reports that Nixon asked him, "Do you think the people are going to want to pick the carcass?" The congressman reassured him that people "don't seem to want any part of this revenge thing."

Ronald Ziegler, loyal to the end, decries the "vindictiveness of some in Congress and some in the Ford White House" toward the former president. Ziegler's own vindictiveness is not against the man who dehumanized him but against those who brought this grotesque charade to an end. When asked by reporters about an offhand remark, "contrition is bullshit," that he made at the time of the pardon, Ziegler resented only the fact that a private statement had been so widely quoted. He is about to leave his post as chief of staff at San Clemente, and will embark on a nationwide speaking tour of colleges, universities, and business groups. What he has to say is still of interest to large numbers.

The tapes continue to make legal news; Nixon's claim to ownership of the tapes is scheduled to reach the Supreme Court. In a hundred-page brief filed in the United States district court, attorneys for the Justice Department and the General Services Administration have stated that Congress, in declaring the Nixon materials to be public property, "had a rational basis for perceiving that his Presidential materials might not pass intact into the custody of the United States if he were permitted to have custody of them—even temporarily. The suggestion by Mr. Nixon that he, his wife and daughter can perform the segregating out of the private material from the official is, to put it kindly, unrealistic."

The enormity of this governmental argument is not generally recognized. A criminal, such as any one of the president's men sentenced to prison, is judged to have committed a crime, not to have a bad character. After serving his sentence he is free and officially eligible for further trust. Mr. Nixon, not convicted of a crime, is declared officially to be of such character that he cannot be trusted with government material, his own included. Such an accusation, publicly recorded, is more globally incriminating than conviction for an act. This official affirmation of the likely effects of Nixon's character on his deeds can indeed be relevant in judging Nixon's good deeds as well as bad, and his previous quarter century of dubious behavior.

Prior to closing his office and winding up its work, Watergate Special Prosecutor Henry Ruth expressed the fear that Watergate may occupy only a handful of pages in the future texts of American history and that the banishment of Nixon from his presidential office may already have lost its impact and effect. The lust for more facts is a cop-out, he feels, against having to remedy the evils already well documented. Thirty-five recommendations had been prepared by the Ervin committee and today, two years later, virtually none have been passed or even seriously debated by Congress. Individual scholars and historians, to be sure, are seeking access to the materials, but Ruth is struck by the lack of institutional response to the enormous abuse of power which has occurred.

On November 5, 1974, in the first election after Nixon's resignation, the four Republicans of the House Judiciary Committee who voted against impeachment, including Rep. Charles Sandman, Nixon's staunchist defender, were all defeated in their bids for reelection. Sandman, however, still garnered 45 percent of the vote! Both figures, the 55 percent by which he lost and the 45 percent still for him, say something about what goes on in the mind. Committee Chairman Peter Rodino, however, was reelected overwhelmingly against two opponents by 85 percent of the vote. Earlier supporters of impeachment were considered to be the ones most vulnerable to negative public reactions, despite overwhelming evidence that impeachable offenses had been committed. But that was before the turning point had been reached.

March 1975

As the military fortunes of the South Vietnamese deteriorate rapidly, Kissinger makes an impassioned plea to Congress for more military aid to that beleaguered country. With a stridency displayed in the past only in private, Kissinger now reveals that Thieu had received a "moral commitment" that United States aid would continue if he accepted the Paris agreement under which American forces withdrew in 1973! No contradiction is seen or embarrassment is felt for what was said at that time as to how the peace negotiations had come about. Hanoi, it will be remembered, was said to have initiated the peace moves and to have provided the pressure which led to the end of American participation in the war.

When members of Congress express suspicion that a more formal promise may have been given in secret, Kissinger, the architect and negotiator of the peace accords, denies that there were any such obligations "of which Congress is not aware." However, after repeated pressure from Senator Henry Jackson, secret agreements previously suspected but always denied from above gradually come to light. The existence of "confidential exchanges" between Nixon and Thieu are admitted by the White House through Press Secretary Nessen. Jackson hints that the commitment extended beyond a promise of aid to an actual pledge of military intervention if Hanoi were to invade on a large scale.

Kissinger is still active on behalf of the war which, without us, is slowly winding to an end. A refusal on the part of Congress to send more military aid to South Vietnam would "destroy an ally," he declares. Our role in this continuing war will indicate whether the United States is willing "to help those countries . . . prepared to help themselves"; failure to help will reflect unfavorably upon recent reverses in the Middle East, Portugal, and Cyprus, in addition to Indochina. With an interpretation of history as astonishing as it is revealing, Kissinger rebukes the American public for the erosion of "central authority" during the Vietnam War and Watergate: "The central authority of a major country cannot be under persistent attack without ultimately paying a price in foreign policy." It was not the actions of the administration but criticism of it which was at fault. Without so labeling it and without the public allowing themselves to openly "know" it, Kissinger joins Nixon in his central attitude and his basic assessment of the history of the decade.

On April 21 Thieu resigns, paving the way for his government's collapse. In a final display of corkscrew reasoning which rivals that of Kissinger himself, the South Vietnamese president demonstrates his version of gratitude. In a desperate and dramatic resignation speech, Thieu's ire is leveled mainly at Nixon and Kissinger whom he blames for his country's plight. Never does he acknowledge his own inept political and military rule over the past seven and a half years. Perhaps there is poetic justice in such an inevitable consequence of this long and twisted series of events.

May 1975

An incident takes place in the far Pacific which shows that critical faculties and a vigilant conscience are not yet automatic in the American people as a result of their experiences of the past few years. The *Mayaguez,* an American freighter, is reported illegally seized and occupied in international waters by Cambodian forces. Ford strikes back swiftly and hard, recovering the American crew from the Cambodians, at a cost of forty-one American lives. The public response is immediate and overwhelming: twelve to one in support of the president. Ford's stock rises dramatically; he is, for the moment, a hero.

The Cambodians' version is that the vessel was a spy ship, or one with military cargo, real or suspected, within Cambodian territorial waters, boarded and held for inspection and interrogation.

Whose report was accurate? Our country's reasons may well be good ones. Even so, now that we have lived through recent history from the Gulf of Tonkin through the U-2, the Bay of Pigs, and the *Pueblo,* crossing the administrations of Eisenhower, Kennedy, Johnson, and Nixon, would it be irrational or disloyal to receive our official explanations with a degree of skepticism? Need no questions be asked? Such as: What was our ship doing there in the first place? And was it within Cambodian territorial waters? Why would Cambodia seize a merchant vessel in a proper international position and expose itself to charges of international piracy? The Cambodians accuse us of systematic spying on the month-old regime. "Every day American planes have flown over Cambodia and especially over Phnom Penh, Sihanoukville, and our maritime region," says Minister Hou Nim. And United States agents have been left in the country to carry out espionage and economic sabotage. The only reason the Cambodians capitulated, they explain, was because they were too weak for a confrontation with the United States. The *Mayaguez* was intercepted in the Gulf of Thailand two and a half or three miles east of Vay Island, well within their administrative area. Several other spy boats in addition to the *Mayaguez* had been seized in those same waters, they point out.

Only one out of twelve readers of the news doubted the usual immediate reports of denial. The press, to be fair, did include the facts of both sides within its total coverage. But those who compose the headlines and lay out the stories, as well as the editorial writers and commentators who give them their meaning, were of the same mind as the people, in the same direction and in the same proportion.

It is again the usual minority fringe, the small percentage of press and people who remain independent of the general trend, who resist the group swell. As an example I can again point to the cool and rational analysis in the *New Yorker,* in which an objective distance is properly maintained and incisive and penetrating questions raised. To ask these questions is not disloyal but dispassionate. The one in twelve who resisted the tide in this current national test take their place on a long line of predecessors: the "Nixon haters" of the most recent past; before that the same small group, of about the same proportion, who in the sixties opposed the Vietnam War from the beginning; still before that, in the fifties, the lonely minority who stood aside from the mass and were upset at what Senator Joseph McCarthy was up to; and even long before that, the same isolated, small, and atypical group who were the "premature anti-Fascists" back in the thirties.

This group is typically always unpopular. Its feelings and opinions are against the current grain. And history, with rare exceptions, does not reverse its judgments. Errors of public opinion remain undetected more often than not, and even in the exceptions when they do come to life, people resent those who predicted or "knew."

Public indignation, which had to be suppressed for years, can now be expressed where it is accepted and safe. Congress joins in the outpouring of praise for Ford. Those who were the most critical of our past policy in Indochina can unite on this issue with their conservative counterparts. "President Ford is to be commended for the way he managed the crisis," says Senator Frank Church. "From the beginning to the end he had my full support." Our Western allies back the actions taken. China and North Vietnam accuse the United States of "an outright act of piracy."

Disturbing reports appear. In launching the attacks into Cambodia, American troops violated agreements on the use of our bases in Thailand. Kissinger apologizes and regrets the action but states that it was necessary. Thailand recalls its ambassador from Washington and orders a full-scale review of all treaties with the United States. Charges comes from many sources that the United States acted with undue haste and failed to make sufficient inquiries along diplomatic lines. Pentagon officials are embarrassed by the disclosure of an American bombing raid on a fuel depot and railroad yard half an hour after the American crew was safely abroad the rescuing destroyer *Wilson*. No explanation is offered.

Did Ford need such an incident for his own rescue? In treating this occurrence as an emergency, did Ford see an opportunity to "tough" it and act like a hero? Questions such as these press just below the level of consciousness. The *Mayaguez* incident could not go on now to another Vietnam. The people would not permit this again so soon. But group reactions have returned to "normal" and are again based on emotional, identificatory, and nonideational modes rather than on rational and cognitive methods of response. The public reacted too little to Watergate, too much to *Mayaguez*, and inappropriately to both.

In May, immediately following the *Mayaguez* drama, a Polish fishing vessel, the *Kalmar*, is spotted off Monterey, California, two miles within the United States twelve-mile limit. The ship is immediately boarded, seized, and escorted by the Coast Guard into San Francisco Harbor, where the crew of seventy is interned and questioned. In contrast to the *Mayaguez*, the article reporting this event appears on the back pages of our newspapers, as did the Watergate story originally. The mood of the reporting is casual and amused, referring to the manner and appearance of the Russian crew. No juxtaposition occurs between this incident and the United States ship held at Koh Tang or about the differences between the subsequent actions which ensued.

To highlight the contrast further, in the same month, on May 29, a high-flying United States Air Force U-2 plane crashed in West Germany about sixty miles from the East German border. Although French and West German news agencies report that the plane was coming from an easterly direction when it crashed, Pentagon sources announce that these American planes do not fly over Eastern Europe.

Spying is obviously an accepted and probably a necessary international activity. But the stances taken with respect to it in the cases cited do not enhance the credibility of our government. Since credibility comes up in analyzing "the mind of Watergate," it cannot be dealt with lightly. Are there not ways in which respect and trust can be maintained even in the performance of sensitive tasks, rather than an escalation of distrust by a compounding of error?

The Ground to the Figure—the CIA

The CIA is increasingly the subject of investigation. Both the Senate Intelligence Committee and the Rockefeller Commission, the latter appointed by the president directly, report a degree of unlawful activity which boggles the mind. Illegal break-ins and the invasion of constitutional rights, a mass surveillance of citizens unprecedented in our history, have been routinely practiced far beyond anything disclosed publicly before. Break-ins, wiretaps, and the opening of mail of hundreds of thousands of Americans—activities banned by the 1947 law that created the CIA—were commonly practiced, known to its directors, and condoned, even ordered, by presidents.

Both Johnson and Nixon had pressured the CIA to mount a domestic spying operation that director Richard Helms knew violated the agency's charter. Operation Chaos, designed to cover foreign influence behind domestic unrest, lasted from 1967 to 1974 despite repeated findings that antiwar and racial demonstrations at home were not directed from abroad. Both Johnson and Nixon had ordered the CIA to go back and try harder when it reported that protests against the Vietnam War were not being orchestrated in foreign capitals. Chaos's gathering of information on domestic political activity, according to a report by the Senate Intelligence Committee staff, constituted "a step toward the dangers of a domestic secret police." Helms, now in 1975 the United States ambassador to Iran, had denied knowledge of such illegal activities in previous congressional testimony.

Illegal data collection, as offensive and repulsive as such violations are to citizens of the United States, is not the lowest depth to which such practices have plunged. Assassinations, suggestions of which had appeared from time to time in timid and apologetic headlines, have now become factual history. What had been "known" unconsciously for a long time has now been raised to the level of conscious awareness. The possibility that high government officials could have authorized not only break-ins but government-condoned murder "is a matter of such gravity that it goes to the roots of our morality as a nation," said Frank Church, chairman of the Senate Intelligence Committee, when the first evidence began to appear. (Church's new role has already elevated him to a position alongside Cox, Richardson, Ruckleshaus, and Rodino, the group of investigatory heroes who emerged out of the muck and mire, and his name begins to be mentioned as a candidate for the presidency.) Assassinations and coups against foreign leaders had been plotted by the CIA under four American presidents, the committee reports. These included plots against Lumumba, Castro, Trujillo, President Ngo Dinh Diem of South Vietnam, Allende of Chile, and Duvalier of Haiti. Lumumba, Trujillo, Diem, and Duvalier had actually died, as did the Chilean chief of staff, General René Schneider, during the coup against Allende.

The assassination of Castro had been planned by the CIA, organized in collaboration with the Mafia, and actual attempts were made on a number of occasions in the early 1960s. A discussion of the possible assassination of Castro recorded in minutes in the hands of the Rockefeller Commission had taken place at a 1962 meeting of a "Special Group" called "Operation Mongoose," which included high officials of the Kennedy administration. A few years later top FBI officials who knew of this CIA plotting withheld the data from the Warren Commission investigating the subsequent assassination of President Kennedy.

If the break-in at the Watergate was the political crime of the century, the first to result in the resignation of a president, here was the soil from which it sprang. And if the break-in resulted from "the mind of Watergate," here is the substructure which shows the normal and chronic operations of that mentality over a longer period of time. Is the extent of a crime to be judged only by its result or by the quality of the offense itself, regardless of the outcome? Is a governmental burglary which had such momentous effects to go down in history as a higher crime than government-condoned multiple murder which was more quietly absorbed, based pragmatically on the consequences of each? Such seems to be the psychology of large groups, in this case of the American public under its recent governments.

Any invasion of the privacy of one's declared enemy, up to and including his liquidation if necessary, can be condoned in the interests of national security, the existence of which can be decided upon by the perpetrator of the act. Does it not make one wonder how far we have come from the Borgias or the Medicis or beheadings by rival royal houses? Except that democracy has since become known and added as a conceptual guideline to man's aspirations. On the last page of *Portnoy's Complaint,* the analyst says to the hapless Alex, "Now vee may perhaps to begin. Yes?" This is how I feel at this late point in this story. Perhaps we have come to the beginning.

Here was the hidden part of the iceberg of which Watergate was the tip, the ground to the figure of "the mind of Watergate." In a chilling 396-page report, the Senate Intelligence Committee documents a forty-year pattern of official lawlessness by internal agencies during both Democratic and Republican administrations from Roosevelt to Nixon. Accompanying the deeds was the institutionalization of lying and other deceptive practices by government agencies to cover up the official and routine breaking of the law.

Yet even as these revelations unfold, aside from a shift of personnel and the replacement of directors, no prosecutions are considered. Cover-up, the only punishable crime of Watergate, was always built into these activities and was routinely operative—and still is. Even as the proportion between openness and cover-up is altered for the moment during the actual time that the revelations are taking place, cover-up is still being maintained, and the more common ratio between the two will come back to normal.

Declaring that there will be no cover-up, Ford makes public the domestic activities uncovered by the Rockefeller Commission; but he will withhold the material on assassination. These he will send to the Justice Department and to House and Senate congressional committees. The credibility of the Ford administration again comes to the test and the bitterness of Watergate can be felt to return. Pressed about his decision, Ford states that while he is "totally opposed" to political assassinations, "In fairness, none of us should jump to conclusions as to events that may have occurred in the past fifteen or twenty years." "I'm not passing judgment," Ford tells a press conference, "I'm simply saying that for us fifteen or twenty years later to put ourselves in the position of people who had the responsibility in the highest echelons of our government, we shouldn't be Monday morning quarterbacks."

Attorney General Edward Levi is shocked by the material he receives. But after having had time to recover, Levi joins Ford's conclusion that alleged illegalities should be judged in the context of "how things may have looked at a prior time." No one can remain pure as soon as he himself is involved or entrusted with the moral course of the nation. Senator Church, to whose committee the assassination issue will next be turned over, and who can at this moment still be relatively detached, is more openly and unequivocally disturbed. "Clearly the Rockefeller Commission had a choice," he states. "It could deal with the assassination issue or duck it. Evidently it has decided to duck it." Press Secretary Ron Nessen, questioned by reporters about cover-up and evasion, reacts with sudden anger and with a bitterness reminiscent of the Watergate era, abruptly terminates a session with reporters, and marches out of a press conference.

The Senate committee makes ninety-six recommendations for reform. These and the findings of the Rockefeller Commission, President Ford says, assure us "that we [will] end up with a C.I.A. and an intelligence community that will do an excellent job for the future of this country." And Nessen, returning to his duties, solemnly announces that President Ford will not permit United States participation in political assassinations.

A series of public statements can now be grouped together which makes for an eerie sequence. "I am not a crook" has advanced to "I do not believe in murder." For those who will remember related history, "I am not a Communist" became, to the man who had insisted that this needed to be said, "I am not a crook." The man who pardoned Nixon now felt it necessary to say, for himself and future heads of state, "We do not believe in murder"! Actions and attitudes at the highest levels have indeed made a twisted maze of our values.

The role of the CIA in the assassination of John Kennedy becomes increasingly obscure and tangled. Evidence continues to mount that the CIA had prior knowledge about Lee Harvey Oswald and knew of his movements before the assassination took place. The CIA had taped a conversation which Oswald had had with the Soviet Embassy in Mexico City eight weeks before the assassination. This knowledge had not been turned over to the FBI and was later withheld from the Warren Commission. No explanation is offered.

The acquisition and collection of intelligence data is defended as necessary by many sober appraisers and can hardly be dispensed with in the interest of survival in spite of the outrage its abuse may produce. There are many, like Ronald Reagan and William Buckley, who selectively point out this aspect of the problem and who decry any attacks on the CIA on that account. Such attacks must cease, they declare, to preserve the good which the agency must do.

There is an equal number who emphasize the converse position, opposing any and all surveillance of "enemies" on the ground that the abuses this invariably engenders never justify the advantages gained. The problem remains of whether any such data collection can be achieved without boomeranging against the citizens themselves and offending the very roots and goals of a democratic life. Can the aims which are necessary be achieved while safeguarding against the natural dangers? Or does the end justify any means, as terrorists on the left and tyrants on the right, or more accurately, terrorists and tyrants on the left or right, would have us believe? In the interests of national security, and in the bureaucracy characteristic of present-day governments, can things be moral? Or rather, how moral can they be? How much will lessons of the past few years advance us toward a balanced goal?

In an interesting rationalization which has acquired an institutionalized status, FBI agents accused of illegal break-ins, wiretappings, and intrusions of citizens' rights have testified that the documents they acquire by these illegal means are not "stolen" but "borrowed"! Here is another variant of the "inoperative" of the Nixon years to take its place in the list of linguistic ploys used to allay anxiety and responsibility both for the perpetrators of actions and the audience who receives them.

Loose ends are supposedly being tied up. In April 1975, a judge ruled that there was no proof that sabotage was involved in the crash of the United Airlines plane that killed Mrs. Dorothy Hunt and forty-five others. Ruling on damage suits filed against the company, the judge declared that the airline "violated its duty as a common carrier" and that no material fact had been advanced which could "relieve defendant airline of its legal responsibility to innocent passengers by reason of loss of control of the aircraft." The case was officially closed.

As from the beginning, with all the suspicions which Watergate engendered, it has always been harsh to suggest the worst. But with domestic invasion and foreign murder having been established as operative principles, who can vouchsafe against an extension of these in an "accident" involving this particular "case." In the state of desperation which existed at the moment, who can guarantee it automatically, with ten thousand dollars in hundred-dollar bills of the Watergate hush money having been found in Dorothy Hunt's pocketbook in the ruins of the crash?

Nixon himself now asserts that Kissinger selected the names of persons to be wiretapped without court order in the first Nixon administration, directly contradicting previous testimony given by Kissinger that it was J. Edgar Hoover who had selected the names. The grandest of alliances are not immune to decline. In a sworn statement filed in a damage suit brought against him and others by Morton Halperin, a former aide to Kissinger, Nixon states, "I of course did not select the names myself because I did not know the individuals. . . . It was his [Kissinger's] responsibility . . . to furnish the information to Mr. Hoover." Visibly annoyed, Kissinger, whose previous explanations often had been inconsistent with the role he played in the wiretap program, declares, "I believe that there is substantial agreement in all of the statements that have been made on the essentials of the issue." A House Intelligence Committee report on covert activities from 1965 to 1975 is critical of both Nixon and Kissinger, stating that the CIA "has been utterly responsive to the instructions of the President and the assistant to the President for national security affairs."

Dean and Magruder, released from prison after having served relatively short sentences, felt "cleansed" for having told the truth. "The feelings of guilt have been washed away," said Jeb Magruder, released on January 8, 1975, after serving a seven-month term. John Dean, emerging from prison after four months, recommended that Nixon do what he did and tell all. If he does, Dean advised, "In a relatively few years the ugly side of the Nixon Administration will begin to roll back. If he does not, the good will be obscured. The feeling of retribution will linger. Telling the truth is an extremely cleansing, happy way to live."

Rabbi Baruch Korff resigns in May 1975 as Nixon's chief legal fund-raiser. Fighting back tears, he tells a news conference, "I am not stepping down in my friendship for him. I spent . . . my own funds both in contributions and expenses. I have reached the very bottom of my ability to sustain myself. I can no longer afford it."

In the most casual way, further remarks come out by insiders about when Nixon first "knew." Nixon probably was aware of the June 17, 1972, Watergate break-in almost immediately, Magruder now states. Alexander Butterfield, whose revelation catapulted the case to a new level of exposure, now declares that he believes Nixon had knowledge of the break-in prior to its occurrence: "To have done something that big, he had to have given the okay." In Butterfield's opinion, Nixon knew about a first break-in into Democratic headquarters in May 1972 when electronic eavesdropping devices were installed in the office. "Once they had permission to do what they first did, then that was considered tacit approval to go back again," said Butterfield. "That is strictly a personal opinion based on a damn clear knowledge of the system—the way Nixon operated. . . . There's little question in my mind . . . that Nixon knew about it. I don't think it is a unique point of view." Two days later, after the flurry which followed this statement, Butterfield publicly apologizes to the Nixon family. He does not retract his statement but regrets having reopened the subject when it came up in a magazine interview about his present job and plans.

On May 20, 1975, one week after this news item appears, the Senate, by a vote of forty-seven to forty-two, defeats a bill to reinstate Butterfield to his status as a retired air force colonel, thus denying him eligibility for military retirement pay and other benefits. Butterfield had resigned his commission in 1973 when he was appointed head of the Federal Aviation Administration, which is reserved by law for a civilian. Exceptions had been made for two other retired air force officers who served as FAA administrators. How much can this have been due to resentment against Butterfield, not only for this latest expression of opinion but because he had opened up the can of worms in the first place? Squeezing Butterfield from the opposite direction, a retired air force colonel, Fletcher Prouty, identifies Butterfield as a CIA "contact officer" at the Nixon White House, an accusation Butterfield vehemently denies. Prouty says he himself had served in a similar capacity at the Pentagon.

Two years to the day after his famous letter which forced Dean and the procession of others into becoming cooperative witnesses, James McCord, who along with Butterfield did more than anyone else to move history into the path of justice, goes to prison to serve a one- to five-year term. The other principals at the moment are mostly free, either on bail or awaiting appeal, or out of jail after parole. Or, like Nixon, entirely free in a system of criminal justice "corrupted," McCord feels, by Ford's pardon.

Cooperation, a willingness to inform, and the game of plea bargaining has paid off well for the most prominent of the defendants, not only in their original sentences but in their subsequent early releases. Dean has bought for himself a position of celebrity status. He has become a model of sorts, now to be envied and emulated by the ambitious on a different level than when he was the president's counsel. Four months later McCord achieves a similarly purchased freedom and quietly leaves through a side gate of the federal prison following an early parole.

It was "Hanging John" Sirica whose tough, no-nonsense approach brought home to the Watergate group the message to cooperate or else. Generally, after hard original sentences, those who cooperated were released early. Hunt and Liddy were treated the most severely. Gordon Liddy, who stonewalled from the beginning—the only one who did—received the longest sentence, six years and eight months to twenty years in prison, with an added eighteen-month sentence for contempt. To date, Judge Sirica has turned down petitions to reduce Liddy's sentence. "This defendant's obstinate disregard for the processes of law is difficult for the court to comprehend," Sirica says of Liddy. "He has not given the court even a hint of contrition or sorrow."

It might just be that Liddy's persistent silence, and his willingness to suffer his fate as he does, means that he alone of all the defendants genuinely believed that what he did was right. Perhaps to him, and him alone, the national security was truly at stake. With this ego judgment, the superego value of protecting the nation's security could have taken precedence over laws of the land conceived, in Liddy's scale of values, for situations of lesser scope.

Ford, in the meantime, has long since lost automatic acceptance. In June 1975, after several weeks of sharp exchanges in which reporters call Ford a liar, accuse him of covering up news and of lacking credibility, Press Secretary Ron Nessen becomes impatient and angry. Interrupting a regular press briefing, Nessen charges the reporters with "blind and irrational mistrust" and "cynical thinking habits." Ford has been in office for ten months, he states, and that is time enough "for this blind, mindless, irrational suspicion and cynicism and distrust to evaporate." Threatening to discontinue the briefings in their present form, Nessen states that he has to lance this "festering wound" and hopes his criticisms will end what he called the poisoned atmosphere that he regards as a heritage of Watergate.

Ron Nessen's behavior is a pale version of that of the first harassed Ron, Ron Ziegler. Both brought to mind a statement of Truman's that "If you can't stand the heat, get out of the kitchen." In each case it was not the reporters' questions which were the noxiae, but what was being questioned.

Before the year's end another small trial was held and another verdict entered the books. In November 1975, Ralph G. Newman, president of the Chicago Library Board and a nationally known Lincoln scholar, who put a value on the prepresidential papers for which Nixon qualified for a tax deduction, was found guilty on two counts of lying to the IRS on Nixon's behalf. Nixon's tax lawyer, Frank DeMarco, and White House counsel Edward Morgan had conceived a way to backdate the deed for the papers, but Newman's corroboration had been needed for the plan to work. The case against DeMarco had been dismissed by a federal judge and Morgan, who had pleaded guilty, had spent four months in jail.

When the jury's verdict of guilty was announced, Patricia Newman, wife of the defendant, gasped and burst into tears. The government contended that Newman, facing five years in prison on one count and three years on the other, had "intentionally and deliberately" lied to federal agents "to please the President of the United States." Newman's lawyers said he had made a human mistake. Both statements deserve more careful consideration in that each was right and each incomplete. In answer to Newman's lawyers, his action was a mistake but it was also a crime. As to the matter of lying to please a president of the United States—when there is a president whose pleasure can be bought by lying!—here is the core of the abuse of power. How many in a position to do so would forfeit the opportunity to incur the president's pleasure and instead elect to incur his wrath—even if telling the truth was what had to go? Especially when the lie could be rationalized without much effort or the truth stretched only slightly? An otherwise-respected scholar lied to please the president of the United States! So did all the others, to please the president but also to enhance themselves; both, they thought, could be accomplished simultaneously.

The People Get Ready to Choose—Finally

As 1976 looms into view, the people will have a chance for the first time to pass judgment on Nixon's choice of successor. Hats begin to appear in the ring, and the men who own them gradually step up to be counted and fitted for size.

For Ford the watchword from the beginning has been expediency, a middle-of-the-road caution. "Expediency" as a word has a positive ring, connoting a practical, useful, and constructive bent. But since the political life of Richard Nixon, expediency has acquired a new meaning and now stirs up a suspicious if not negative reaction. Instead of a moderate approach based on a principle of good, it has come to mean opportunism with an absence of principle. Both liberal and conservative views must now be espoused and fused. For Ford, inheriting and falling into this game, this has meant a conservative position in a liberal package. His support of proposals that are anathema to the political right and previously to himself, particularly necessary after the pardon, have included his stands for national health insurance, leniency for Vietnam deserters and draft evaders—leniency but not amnesty, a difficult position but successfully in the middle—a ban on imports of chrome from Rhodesia in protest against that country's racial policies. In concession for these and to make up for his appointment of Nelson Rockefeller as vice-president, Rockefeller has slowly been disengaged and finally has been definitely dropped as a vice-presidential candidate for the next time around.

To further appease the conservative wing, the word "détente" has been dropped—not the action but the word. Whereas for Nixon it was expedient to introduce the act of détente, by Ford's time expediency meant dropping the word. This, incidentally, gives the Soviet Union the opportunity to appear—or even to be—more consistent and logical than the American administration. An official Kremlin magazine points out that Ford has pledged to continue efforts to ease tensions and that his present semantic course is a matter of packaging, not a change of policy. "If the content raises no doubt, why should the packaging arouse concern?" asks the official news agency Tass. "Renunciation of a word is not renunciation of a policy course."

When Ford, interviewed by Barbara Walters, claims that he advocates an understanding with the Soviet Union, she teasingly but good-naturedly reminds him of his having dropped the word "détente." "Come, Barbara," Ford replies, "you know it isn't the word which counts." But words can be changed, he implies, to camouflage meanings where necessary.

While some may feel critical, others identify. There are as always two streams of motivations in fused coexistence. Ford's dilemma is received sadly but not angrily. The wish for a leader above the common man is there, but not wholly. It is wanted, but ambivalently.

"In two weeks President Ford made us forget Representative Ford," wrote a columnist shortly after Ford assumed the presidency. To change in office is not automatically bad, can also be a sign of flexibility and growth. After becoming president, Harry Truman said, "Don't judge me by what I did as Senator." It is questionable whether future history will continue to support the idealization of Truman, brought about by the present need for a hero and by Truman's happening to have the particular traits so sorely missing on our recent political scene. Alongside the feisty, outspoken, and liberal Truman portrayed by James Whitmore in a current play, and the courage and idealism with which he "gives 'em hell," other commentators looking back at the Truman era are beginning to contribute another view of that period. Lillian Hellman, for example, as well as a number of revisionist historians, are pointing out that not only was it Truman who ushered in the cold war but that he directly paved the way for the McCarthy years and was single-handedly responsible for the history of the next two decades. There were two sides to the man, and while history chooses now one and now the other, it takes both to make up the whole.

After the glow of Ford's start as president, which existed simply because he was not Nixon, the image of "Mr. Nice Guy" is being rapidly eroded under the impact of past revelations and present lacks. A number of references now surface about the pardon, which Henry Ruth, resigning as special prosecutor, terms "atrocious," referring to matters that Ford had not disclosed or had even denied in previous testimony. Ten days before the pardon, on the day of his first press conference, Ford gave private assurance to General Haig, Nixon's chief of staff, that a pardon would be granted. A memo is revealed from former Nixon counsel Leonard Garment in which a pardon is urged on the basis of Nixon's mental and physical condition with the implication that unless Nixon is pardoned he might take his own life. In addition, a statement was prepared by former Nixon speechwriter Raymond Price to be read by Ford at that first press conference announcing the pardon. His statement was not subsequently used. These revelations contradict a number of public statements made previously by Ford, including testimony before the House Judiciary Subcommittee in October 1974 to the effect that "at no time after I became President on August 9, 1974, was the subject of a pardon for Richard M. Nixon raised by the former President or by anyone representing him." During that same questioning, in a maneuver to retain truthfulness, Ford had reworded a question asked by a reporter, "Did Haig discuss a pardon *for* Nixon?" to "Did Haig discuss a pardon *with* Nixon?" before answering, "Not to my knowledge."

Ford continues to lose his reputation for candor and honesty. Forced to dismiss James Schlesinger as secretary of defense, he first denies any tension, as is rumored, between Schlesinger and Kissinger or that this was the reason for the dismissal. At about the same time, however, in an interview on "Meet the Press," he admits that "growing tensions" within his Cabinet had indeed contributed to his decision. The feeling of the people that they have a president who levels with them is gradually and steadily wearing off. One of the main efforts of his political campaign consultants is to get Ford "to look presidential." From time

to time Ford himself summons a handful of special friends for conferences at the White House for a private critique toward effecting this
image.

Nor does Ford appear completely disengaged or clean of the Watergate stain itself. There are questions as to whether or not he had per-
jured himself at his vice-presidential confirmation hearings in denying
that he had acted on White House instruction in helping to halt the
Patman congressional investigation into Watergate in 1972. "Is the President a Perjurer" was a featured article by Marjorie Boyd in the October 1975 issue of *The Washington Monthly.* When Ford was a ranking
Republican member in Congress he "moved heaven and earth" to
prevent an investigation of the break-in before the 1972 elections, says
former Senator Sam Ervin; Ford had persuaded "every Republican on
the House Banking and Currency Committee to vote against sub-
poenaing witnesses. . . ."

In February 1976, Judge Sirica, while lecturing at the George Washington University School of Law on the obligations of lawyers to professional ethics, falls over the speaker's lectern and suffers a massive coronary occlusion with cardiac arrest. He is treated on the spot with
mouth-to-mouth resuscitation, then in an emergency room with an
electric shock to the heart and fortunately and thankfully emerges from
a critical condition to recovery.

Cardiovascular pathology, especially coronary heart disease, is a
chronic and complex pathological process. Emotional conflicts are acknowledged to play a prominent part and certainly contribute their
adverse role. For two years Judge Sirica had been almost totally occupied with the affairs of Watergate and virtually embodied the great
conflict of the law. While he was the one who put pressure on the
burglars to testify before a grand jury, and ordered Nixon to turn over
the tapes, a ruling that eventually was upheld in the Supreme Court and
was instrumental in Nixon's resignation, he also had to deal with the
agonizing dilemmas which beset the judicial mind at each step of the
way. While he walked this tortuous path with strength and determination, his task was a superhuman one, and his decisions could not have
been taken without their severe toll.

As the candidates begin to jockey for position, Ford's main critic during the early stages is not any one strong Democratic contender but his fellow Republican, Ronald Reagan. Reagan seizes the opportunity to do what he does best. Taking the stump in the conservative cause and constantly gaining momentum, he calls for a fulfillment of the electoral mandate of 1972. "America voted to be conservative, not liberal," he declares in a personal interpretation of the landslide victory given to Richard Nixon. It is not Humphrey, Jackson, or Carter who chides Ford at this stage, but Reagan. Later, closer to the wire, he will put on the brakes.

Bellicose and aggressive, Reagan assails Ford's foreign policy. The United States should have originally met North Vietnam's final thrust into South Vietnam with B-52 bombers, he declares. We also should have acted "in any way to prevent or discourage" what Reagan saw as a Communist takeover of Portugal, and should now defend South Korea with military force if necessary: "B-52's should make a moonscape out of North Korea if South Korea is attacked." One can see the sheriff in the movies in action again. To those Americans who have been criticizing the extremism and repressiveness of President Park Chung Hee, Reagan explains that Seoul's proximity to the North Korean border "makes for less democracy in South Korea than we are inclined to agree with." However, he goes on to explain, with a complete somersault of principles and logic, if Americans dictate standards of democracy in South Korea as a price for our military support, we would be "involving ourselves in the internal affairs of another country."

The spirit if not the acts of the Nixon years is with us again. An inconsistency which is elemental exerts no internal restraint; any statement which will further one's course will do. The use of the military, even bombing, would not intrude into another nation's affairs but the advocacy of democracy would. And yet our involvement in Vietnam elicited Reagan's support and there was never this objection of interference with another country. The low regard for the American people's power of logical thinking is striking.

However cynical and callous this approach, Reagan is constantly gaining strength and support. The country is polarized as it always has been toward this type of extremist and illogical thought. While many cringe, many others share Reagan's tactical views. The inner drive to discharge aggression is universal and the permission to express it does not fail to appeal to a significant number of people.

Another basic Nixon trait, although not articulated, is exerting a distinct effect. This is the dependence on the visual rather than the auditory, on what is seen rather than what is heard. A highlighting of this perceptual avenue to the mind, so prominently used in the movies, directs its appeal to the emotions rather than to thought processes, to the unconscious and instinctual more than to the conscious and rational. Its effects are produced through gut-like reactions rather than cerebral activity.

Reagan's trademark has always been a look, the stamp of the good guy, the sheriff's tough but likable face. This visual image may be used to convey an opinion of rough idealism or a call to violent action. Reagan's look may be consonant with or at complete variance with what he says. His acting face has, first by training and now in a real-life role, the look of being sincere. It is the effect that Nixon always tried to achieve but at which Reagan is better. Nixon had to work at it, and in the end it failed him. With Reagan the look was professional; he had spent years as an actor perfecting it. It has now been transferred from the make-believe to the real. But in the political arena into which he has moved, the real and the make-believe mix.

More, however, than training and profession, Reagan's talents are grafted upon a natural endowment. Reagan's face is the opposite of the face with which Nixon was endowed. What looked put-on with Nixon seems the real thing with Reagan. Perhaps this is the basis of the charisma which is so much a part of Reagan and which Nixon always lacked. The appeal of each as a consequence, however, is different. With Nixon it is an identification of the people with the weak; with Reagan, with the strong. Each can bring its own type and degree of success.

Reagan is the first and only actor to come close to the presidency of the United States. This background, however, also carries with it some drawbacks. He may have spent too many years as an actor, and on that score his credibility is diminished. But those who disbelieve are probably fewer than those who identify with, follow, and even adore him as movie fans do.

Reagan does not overlook any weak spots in Ford's armor. Henry Kissinger will have to go if Reagan is elected, he says. With the twistings and turnings in Kissinger's political life it is difficult to be sure whether he can be more easily attacked by the left or the right. While he was a popular target for the liberals during the Vietnam War, he has become equally unsympathetic to conservatives since then, when he changed his orientation from a nationalistic to a world view. To Reagan's continuous barrage that he is selling out America's interests, Kissinger answers with a speech in Goldwater country. Speaking to the Downtown Rotary Club of Phoenix, Kissinger urges Americans "not [to] delude ourselves with fairy tales of America being second best," an idea Reagan has accused him of promoting. Aiming his remarks at Reagan without mentioning his name, Kissinger declares, "To oversimplify, to substitute brittle rhetoric for hard thinking, is not confidence in America. To offer slogans instead of answers is to show little faith in America."

Kissinger, in action, continues his own unique style. At the end of May 1976, with no external events to explain why now, he announces that "the time is approaching when new impetus must be given to movement toward an overall peace" in the Middle East. Addressing a meeting of the Central Treaty Organization in London, Kissinger states that the United States "looks to all parties to show dedication and willingness to take risks for peace" and that possibilities for renewing negotiations between Israel and the Arab states are being "actively explored." The time has come to move from step-by-step negotiations to a more generalized search for an overall peace agreement. The aura is being established and the timing suggested. Soon Ford could be presented as the indispensable man.

As convention time draws nearer, Reagan, as could be predicted, turns to persuade the opposite side as well. True to one who has been affected by the political bug, concern for consistency is again conspicuous by its absence. When pressed by those who are concerned about his belligerent views, and who can smell another war in Africa similar to Vietnam, Reagan retracts certain remarks he made about sending troops to Rhodesia and denies what he said about military aid. Trying to gain some advantage from the gloom of Watergate, Reagan states, "If I'm a candidate they [the Democrats] will have to change their strategy [about Watergate] because I wasn't there." It had suddenly become so simple. To be separated from Watergate, one had now only to have been out of Washington at the time.

While Reagan had always felt that Watergate should not be used as an issue between the two parties, he is not above using it himself now against Ford. Actually Reagan's connections to the Watergate problem were all along no more and no less than Ford's, and always on the same side. He was one of those who had jumped to Ford's side immediately after the pardon. A year and a half before the pardon, however, he had been against the push to investigate Watergate at every step of the way. Watergate spies should not be considered criminals, Reagan had said, because they "are not criminals at heart." It was "sort of ignored" that the burglars were "well-meaning individuals," committed to the reelection of the president: "I doubt if any of them would even intentionally double park." This was the arena to which Reagan had relegated the Watergate crimes. Both before and after the pardon he did not believe that Nixon should be prosecuted. "Enough is enough" was his tolerant and sympathetic attitude.

Reagan is not the only person whose activities haunt and disturb Ford. On the eve of the important New Hampshire primary, Nixon returns to the news and headlines by accepting an invitation to visit China and his old friend Chairman Mao. With complete disregard for the impact this trip could have on his appointed successor Gerald Ford, Nixon, now in the role of a private citizen, discusses foreign policy in Peking, repudiating the Helsinki agreement and the policy of détente that he himself had willed to Ford. Even Goldwater by this time has had enough of Nixon. "If he wants to do this country a favor," Goldwater says in an interview on a television show, "he might stay over there. He is violating the law. . . . The Logan Act says no one but the President and the Secretary of State can discuss foreign policy."

Some coincidences of timing provide ironic twists. On June 1, 1976, Martha Mitchell dies of multiple myeloma, alone and destitute, in a New York hospital. A small band of mourners carries "Martha Was Right" signs at her quiet funeral. Martha's ex-husband John is not present. There are no notables, no retrospective look at or correction of the record: another example to be added to the file of history-never-catches-up items. The process of rerepression has as much power as any force which pushes to set the record straight. In a recent book, UPI correspondent Helen Thomas says that Martha Mitchell was "perhaps the only heroine of the Watergate tidal wave. . . . I consistently took her seriously. Indeed, I found at times that her credibility has stacked up higher than that of Presidents."

On the same day that Martha dies, the White House announces that an economic summit meeting with governmental leaders of seven nations will be held in the Caribbean in early August. In view of its timing, just before the Republican convention to be held in Kansas City from August 16 to 19, Kissinger is asked whether the conference could possibly reflect political opportunism on behalf of Ford. "It can't be a political ploy," Kissinger replies, "because they're not involved in our politics. . . . It has nothing to do with politics." One cannot help but compare this with Kissinger's statement when his peace mission to Vietnam happened to bring him home to Washington in October of 1972, just prior to the coming election. His answer today is received in the same way as it was then, with quiet respect. Again it is brought home: a good memory is not one of the characteristics of a group.

The Summer of '76

The summer of our bicentennial year is the summer of the conventions. Both parties make an effort to keep Watergate at a distance. But below the surface it exerts a powerful effect, and neither side will let it get too far out of sight.

For the Democrats, the presence of Archibald Cox at their convention symbolizes the phenomenon of Watergate. His appearance on the platform, not centrally but as one of many, is a clear reminder of the claim his party can make. At the Republican convention the name of Elliott Richardson serves that purpose, in a paler but equally definite way. His name is rumored to be on the list of candidates for vice-president, but not among the top names. Richardson does not appear on the platform, as do Cary Grant and others, and is not even seen, but his name and presence are felt.

Senator Robert Dole is the person who refers to Watergate by name most directly. Offense is the best defense, and perhaps mentioning it first will defuse it and disarm the opposition. Although integrity is the trait of the moment, the assembled delegates of both parties are cautious about reaching too high to claim it. There are demonstrations at each convention, loud and lusty, but not for Cox or Richardson or under the banner of morality. It is as though there is a general pact not to come too close to this. Too aggressive a stance can boomerang.

At the Democratic convention in New York City, the first of the two to be held, with Ted Kennedy out, Humphrey tired and sick, Henry Jackson fighting a hawkish image, and others lacking in money or support, Jimmy Carter, determined and organized, and sufficiently unknown to have avoided a large negative charge, walks away with the prize. His campaign has been cool, deliberate, and steady. Only Jerry Brown, too young and inexperienced, and also too late, had matched him in spirit and given him a scare, actually defeating him not in one but in the four presidential primaries he entered. By convention time, however, the acceptance of Carter had become a foregone conclusion and its execution went exactly as planned.

The emotional discharge in this political hall—to have such an outlet has become a tradition in nominating conventions—came from the superego side of the intrapsychic spectrum. Both in the collective and the individual, the need felt by the Democrats stemmed from the side of conscience, of human rights, of the redress of wrongs, and the drive for social justice. It was Mo Udall, by convention time, in whom these hopes had become embodied, who came to represent the concentrated projection of the lofty goals present in all but submerged by practical needs and the routine of life.

Apart from the expected demonstration for the chosen candidate, which was sufficient but routine, it was the presentation of Udall's name to this convention which excited the wildest enthusiasm. Planned but spontaneous, the demonstration was reminiscent of the ovation given to Adlai Stevenson in 1960 when John Kennedy had the nomination sewed up, as Carter had now. The fact that Udall's support was in name only and that from a practical standpoint he could not be the one nominated simply increased the outpouring of love. There is always a special affection for the one who should have made it but could not. Mo Udall did not have enough money, support, organization, and impetus. A symbolic emotional discharge was all that was asked, and needed.

For his part, Carter has been cool and calculating. His first decision after the nomination tests his capacity to think under pressure and shows him coming through his first crisis well. Feeling out the reactions to the vice-presidential list, he takes his time, resists being inundated, and names Sen. Walter Mondale of Minnesota. His decision and leaning was to the left of center from where the emotional discharge and pressure had come. However, there is no reason to doubt that he made the decision for Mondale because he believed in it. That would be a comforting change. He took a calculated risk with his own constituency and will have to sell his vice-presidential choice to his southern colleagues from whom opposition can be expected to come.

One month later, the Republican convention takes place. After a close heat and agonizing finish, Ford makes it in Kansas City. This time the emotional discharge—the hysteria, the shouting and clapping and screaming—came from the right, for Ronald Reagan. In these preliminary outbursts, one could see the definitive differences between the two nominating conclaves. Here we had not an impassioned plea for idealism, but an angry wish to return to what had existed before. The platform adopted is Reagan's. It could well have been Nixon's. More than a few observers feel that Nixon could have been renominated at this convention by this wing of this party, perhaps even by acclamation.

In the end the two candidates who were rejected tell more about the differences between the parties this summer than the two who were finally chosen. The two who were nominated are close together and hug the center. Reagan and Udall would have stood apart. Unless they too, had they been chosen, would have come together!

Another decision is made after Ford's victory. In the heat of the hysteria and without time to cool off, Ford announces his choice for vice-president, Senator Robert Dole of Kansas. To Ford at this emotional moment, the reassurance of immediate acclaim was the overriding need. It was the short run and not the long term which exerted the main pull. His challenge had come from the right, and those were the people whom he had to appease and win back at once. The fact is, he did not properly evaluate the price. The nature of the long run, including his own fate within it, was certainly not carefully and accurately assessed.

This type of thinking cannot be reassuring in a leader who must conduct international affairs, not when an eyeball-to-eyeball confrontation can suddenly present itself. Ford's decision for Dole may have shown his loyalty to the party but also demonstrated his inability to think as an individual under the pressure of a group. Was this not also the major deficiency of "all the president's men"? Ford goes along now with Reagan and his supporters as he is said to have gone along with Nixon earlier, regarding obstacles to the Patman committee—and perhaps regarding the pardon as well!

There was another factor, however, in Ford's choice of a running mate. We have heard of an old and new Nixon; have we not also had for some time an old and new Ford? While Ford's politics had to move toward the center when he reached the highest office, his heart under pressure is tugged back to the right. Although he has been forced to run against Reagan and his principles, it is with them that Ford would wish most to be. There is an emotional show of unity on the platform, not without its irony and conflict, as Ford, responding to the excitement on the floor, beckons Ronald and Nancy Reagan to the rostrum where Ford, Dole, and Reagan embrace and wave to the wildly cheering crowd.

The composite arrived at after this hectic week's work was a patchwork to face the Democratic pair. This included the liberal face of Ford, the conservative platform of Reagan, and a vice-presidential nominee who was not only a longtime conservative but a supporter of Nixon to the end. None of these images could be wholly given up. The only recourse was to combine them. Carter must have been watching and feeling good.

In his acceptance speech, prepared in advance and when he was under less pressure, a strong Ford makes one of the finest speeches of his career, a temporary reassurance to the convention which had to choose him. "Two years ago, on August 9, 1974, I placed my hand on the Bible which Betty held," he said and reminds the country of the initial statement he made when he assumed his presidential office. " 'My fellow Americans,' I said, 'our long national nightmare is over.' " Again he wishes he could deny the past and repeats the same call to distortion as before. Ford then tries to establish his claim to trust, at least with words. "On a marble fireplace in the White House," he goes on, "is carved a prayer which John Adams wrote. It concludes: 'May none but honest and wise men ever rule under this roof.' Since I have resided in that historic house, I have tried to live by that prayer."

Perhaps all political candidates from now on, from whichever side of the psychological spectrum they come, will have to approach the political center. Whether from the side of instincts, impulses, and the id, in favor of more direct and uninhibited expression, or incorporating the demands of the conscience and the superego, speaking more for restriction and socialization, in each case the shift will be for the sake of expediency, and the end results presented to the people for their choice will inevitably be operationally close together. The task of the electorate will be to separate the fine points of difference.

Campaign 1976

Carter comes in clean. "Southern" and "Baptist" cause some concern, but there is no tangible or known stain which can rationally hurt him. Ford, on the other hand, who has come to this point through the mire of Nixon, enters with the greater problem. The result is an eighteen-point advantage for Carter at the start.

Even so, there are intangibles which make Carter's edge less sure. Ford is still a nice guy and a good man; history and performance and individual mistakes do little to change his image. People can understand and sympathize with his problems. And the platform of the Democrats is not essentially different from the one Nixon had beaten by a landslide. There are many unknown leftover emotions to be dealt with and watched.

In its early stages the campaign is singularly lackluster. Issues are avoided and kept vague, and confrontations are slow to develop. The candidates are low-key, Carter because he is confident and instinctively knows the danger of overdoing it; Ford because he is insecure, has just been battered by Reagan, and the polls and predictions do not give him heart. Carter keeps up a patter, mostly on issues which are safe. He is passive on Watergate, intuitively sensing that the reactions can be unpredictable on this touchy issue.

Even after Carter picks up speed, Ford remains conspicuously quiet. However, for Watergate watchers, who are very few now, and for those whose ears are open to resonances from the past, another interesting event is taking place. Kissinger is on the move again. Shortly after Labor Day, the traditional beginning of the election campaign, word comes out that Kissinger has been ordered by Ford to start a personal shuttle diplomacy in Africa. Kissinger will visit six or eight African capitals in a personal effort to spur negotiations toward a future transfer of power to the black majorities of white-ruled Rhodesia and South West Africa (Namibia). The idea originated, correspondents are told, when a message arrived in Paris, while Kissinger was visiting there, from Tanzanian President Nyerere inviting the visit to the African states. "I'll do almost anything to stay out of the United States during election time," quips Kissinger as he leaves the Élysée Palace after a meeting with Giscard D'Estaing.

If one wants to follow the subtle unfolding of masterplans, one has but to watch the movements of Henry Kissinger—and listen to his humor. The goals announced are certainly not unwelcome and would not arouse suspicions on their own. But simultaneous statements from other sources and a willingness to read between the lines offer more likely clues for motivations. Winding up a summit meeting of African leaders in Tanzania, the presidents of five African states deny the report issued by Kissinger on a plane between Paris and Hamburg that they had initiated this projected visit. "He is not coming at our invitation. He asked to come, and we said, 'Come on.' " Had the African heads of state initiated any communication with Kissinger? Their answer was "There was absolutely none."

Some of the delegates to the summit meeting felt that the move was to win votes for Ford, especially among liberals and American blacks. Kissinger had stated flatly that the trip "should have no impact whatsoever" on United States politics. The Ford administration was willing to risk failure in this diplomatic effort, Kissinger said, because there was no alternative if a Soviet-dominated "radicalization of all Southern Africa" was to be avoided. And "I would not expect that this can be achieved . . . on one trip"! Anyone open to history could feel a sense of *déjà vu* recalling his similar statements in Indochina.

But the monumental problems in South Africa were not as malleable at this political moment as was the long and unpopular war in Vietnam exactly one national election ago. Kissinger's move for foreign achievements by Ford did not permit magical results. The issues on the home front could not be covered this time, and remained for each candidate to face.

Political debates may yet become routine and expected, but at this stage of election practices they are typically pressed for by the underdog challenger and resisted by the incumbent who feels he has it made. The fact that Ford has agreed to engage Carter in debate shows in what a defensive position he feels himself to be. In this instance it is clearly Ford who needs to come from behind. And new accusations arise to put him under further pressure.

In September 1976 John Dean, in his long-awaited book *Blind Ambition,* revives and confirms the suspicion of Ford's interference with the original Patman investigation of Watergate. Coming at this crucial time, just before the first debate between the two candidates, Dean's assertion is a direct contradiction of Ford's testimony at his vice-presidential confirmation hearings in which he had denied any contact with White House officials about blocking the Patman investigation.

Dean meticulously and dryly documents what he says, source, content, time, and place. As he did with Nixon, so with Ford: Dean's statement is confirmed by a White House tape of September 15, 1972, in which Nixon wants Ford to block the Patman subpoenae. Nixon's transcript of this tape had shown a deletion of Ford's role. "Gerry has really got to lead on this," Nixon is heard to tell Dean and Haldeman. "Ehrlichman could talk to him. Ehrlichman understands the law and the rest, and should say, 'Now goddamn it, get the hell over with this. . . . He's got to know that it comes from the top. . . . That's what he's got to know.' "

Dean names names. It was a White House aide, William E. Timmons, and an aide to him and White House lobbyist Richard K. Cook, he adds on the "Today" show, who talked to Ford after contacts with Dean and others in the White House. Both men vehemently deny the charge but take no action. Ford himself refuses to reply to Dean's specific charges, saying, "I am not going to pass judgment on what Mr. Dean now alleges." But meanwhile an actual letter of Ford's surfaces in which he urged Republicans to attend the Patman committee hearing in order to withhold the committee's subpoena powers.

In another backward look, this one in fact way back, Dean refers to the time of Nixon and Hiss. Colson told him, Dean now reports, that

Nixon had said to him about the Hiss case, "The typewriters are always the key. We built one in the Hiss case." To this Colson, now in a religious retreat, sends an indirect reply through an aide that he has no recollection of such a conversation. But not everything that Dean says is pursued as vigorously as what he said about Watergate. The Justice Department states that the suggestion about a bogus typewriter was an old one.

As to what Dean was now saying about Ford, Leon Jaworski, in Atlanta promoting his own newly published book on Watergate *The Right and the Power,* expresses irritation that Dean had withheld this information in earlier testimony to the prosecutor and his staff. As to who was more guilty, the informer or the accused, Jaworski complains about Dean, "What bothers me is, why hold a matter of this kind for several years? . . . And then here, shortly before the election, it comes out . . . in connection with the sale of a book, as a matter of fact." Dean denies that he withheld anything about which he had been asked, and on a KABC news interview, states that he would be willing to testify under oath, take a lie detector test, or appear before any congressional committee if subpoenaed, but that no official body had asked him to do so.

Reps. Elizabeth Holtzman and John Conyers, Jr., of the old House Judiciary Committee demand an immediate investigation into these new charges from the present special prosecutor Charles Ruff. Otherwise, declares Representative Holtzman, "The American people may be confronted with a repetition of 1972—the potential re-election of a President who may face criminal charges." Ruff, after considering the request, rules against such an investigation, stating that the recently added information does not warrant a renewed inquiry. Any further questions about the accuracy of Ford's previous confirmation testimony, says Ruff, would fall within the province of the Justice Department. In thus ruling against a Senate investigation, Ruff eliminates any chance that the 1972 tapes could be heard before the November 2 election.

Declaring Ruff's decision "inexcusable," the two congresspersons write to Attorney General Edward Levi requesting an investigation of the question of perjury. The department, states Levi, has "carefully studied" the matter and finds "no credible evidence, new or old, making appropriate the initiation of a further investigation." Levi's decision is "irresponsible and smacks of a cover-up," states Representative Holtzman. "If the Attorney General believes the President who appointed him is innocent, why is he afraid to investigate the allegation?"

The matter cannot be put to rest with an easy conscience and difficult allegations continue to exist. To Levi's claim that the department had "carefully studied" the matter, Justice Department officials admit that only one potential witness, Richard Cook, had been interviewed, that he had not been placed under oath, and that neither Dean nor Cook's superior Timmons had been summoned by the department before the request of the two congresspersons had been rejected. Just as before, it is not an original crime which is under question but a cover-up, by now a cover-up of a cover-up.

The middlemen involved in the succession of testimony are disturbed about Ford's continuing explanations. When Ford, referring to the issue in his debate with Carter, states that both the House Judiciary Committee and the Senate Rules Committee had given him "a clean bill of health" on his previous testimony, the chairmen of both committees, Rep. Peter Rodino and Sen. Howard Cannon, state that Ford "misled the public" by overlooking the fact that additional information had become available since their committees questioned him. Both were disappointed that Ford did not urge a release of the tapes "to make it absolutely clear one way or another," in the words of Senator Cannon. "I have no doubt," the senator said, "that at some time the tapes will come out, and if it turns out that Mr. Ford was involved at the direction of the White House, it would give us another Watergate cover-up."

The Nixon dragnet and its peripheral effects continue to scoop up more good men among the bad. To the agonizing dilemmas suffered by such men as Jaworski and Sirica can be added the difficult conflicts encountered by Ruff, a distinguished and conscientious attorney and public servant, and now by the impeccable Edward Levi, previously the dean of the School of Law and then chancellor of the University of Chicago of which it is a part. Facing the unimaginable situation of a second possible impeachment of a president, the law can hardly be interpreted purely and unequivocally without risking the moral matrix of a government falling apart. During a campaign stop in Atlantic City, New Jersey, Ford supports Levi's thinking and decision. "I have full faith in the total integrity of the Attorney General, Mr. Edward Levi, and his decision. I think that fully and completely ends the matter."

Ford's trials are not easy and do not cease. Accused of the personal use of union political contributions to his election campaigns over a ten-year period, Ford is cleared of the allegation by the same Special Prosecutor Ruff three weeks before the election. Rocked by this series of exposures and accusations, Ford states to the press, "if there is anything more important or dear to me than serving as President, it is to preserve my integrity."

The net of Nixoniana extends to gather in more and more of those who were on the scene. Even men who built up sudden reputations or who were made into quasi-heroes are revealed as having had a touch of the other side as well. Samuel Dash, former chief counsel of the Senate Watergate committee, writes in his new book entitled *Chief Counsel: Inside the Ervin Committee* that Senator Baker of that same committee worked behind the scenes to curtail the investigation and to undercut the testimony of Dean. Such behavior was at variance with Baker's public position of total support for the investigation. His incisive questioning had won him a national reputation, and it was on the basis of his integrity and his opposition to the Watergate that he was included on Ford's vice-presidential list. In a closed session a month before Dean's testimony came out, Baker, writes Dash, made "a wild attack on Dean," calling him the "principal culprit in this Watergate affair." Baker had met earlier with Nixon "to obtain guidance" on how to conduct himself on the committee and after meeting secretly with him had joined Senator Edward Gurney in voting against immunity for Dean. Baker's strategy behind the scenes, states Dash, was to minimize the impact of Dean's testimony by producing first the principal witnesses who were the targets of the investigation—Mitchell, Colson, Ehrlichman, and Haldeman—and leaving for last the potentially most powerful accuser, Dean. "It was topsy-turvy. The accused would testify before the accuser was heard." Baker denies Dash's statements but declines to make a point-by-point rebuttal. "I didn't pay much attention to Sam during the hearings, and I don't intend to worry about him now," Baker says through a spokesman.

While Ford is fighting off these steady attacks, Carter bears a lighter burden. His Southern Baptist religion is a worry to some, but for many others it adds to the impression of morality. When it was "discovered" that Carter had stayed and golfed at a vacation resort owned by lobby-ists seeking his favor when he was governor of Georgia, Carter re-nounced this behavior. In his direct way, and smiling broadly, he said that what he did was wrong and that he would never do this again as president. His *Playboy* magazine interview and the discussion of his lust, also seized upon and wrung for all it was worth by the opposition, is similarly played down. The impression he gives is of frankness and of being straightforward.

Ford's external and past troubles are not the only burdens he must carry around; in fact, were they the only ones, he might yet prevail. He also puts his own foot into it, again and again. Ford comes through the first debate surprisingly well, better than anyone had expected, simply by being steady and honest and making no mistakes. In spite of all that has plagued him, his stock shoots up. He leaps forward in the race and assumes a new confidence. Carter appears worried. In the second de-bate, on foreign policy, where as the incumbent Ford has the chance for a knockout blow, he slips effortlessly into his famous "ethnic goof," the biggest and most incredible gaffe of the campaign. In an unre-hearsed comment, he shocks the "ethnic" clusters in every urban popu-lation in America by his spontaneous estimate of the comfortable posi-tion of the East European countries under Soviet rule. Carter, who had been slipping and knew it, now goes on the offensive—in fact a little too much so, and then pulls back. He has to refrain from pouncing on a defenseless Ford; sympathy can be too easily aroused. Unlike Carter, however, Ford does not know how to apologize and recoup. It takes him several precious weeks and a number of faltering statements to rescind and clarify what he said and get back to where he was.

Putting together Ford's blunder and Carter's *Playboy* misstep, Art Buchwald notes the goofs on both sides and suggests that each candi-date wants to give the election to the other. This is funny, but this time not true. Each wants the election badly, or perhaps, contrary to what this euphemism implies, we should say "well." There is nothing bad about wanting to be elected but only about what this desire can do—and in recent history has done—to character and behavior.

The campaign picks up speed. The goofs and evidence of humanness do not hurt, seem even to help. Ford's helplessness and absorption of blows not only do not knock him out, but actually seem to gain him

strength and support. As the voters sense that the gap is closing between the two candidates, their apparent apathy seems to lift.

Meantime, Ford's troubles do not end. Dean, in whose presence it is
becoming increasingly dangerous to speak, continues the role of informer and announces that a racial slur was made to him on an airplane
by an unnamed member of Ford's Cabinet. An investigaton of airplane
flight lists shows the offender to have been Secretary of Agriculture Earl
Butz. After a public round of accusation and defense, Butz is forced to
resign from the Cabinet and another member of the government de-
parts. President Ford, upset and in conflict as Butz goes, calls him an
excellent Cabinet member who paid dearly for a minor mistake.

In a report released by the chairman of the House International
Political and Military Affairs Subcommittee on October 5, the day before Ford's foreign policy debate with Carter, the General Accounting
Office concludes that the Ford administration acted with undue haste
and unnecessary military force in the rescue of the *Mayaguez* a year
before. It also noted that Ford's national security adviser Brent Scows-
croft had urged that this report be classified as secret.

The newly installed Communist government of Cambodia, the report states, had decided to release the *Mayaguez* crew before the onset
of the bombing raids in Cambodia and the bloody storming of Koh Tang
Island which resulted in the loss of forty-one United States servicemen.
Sightings by American fighter pilots of thirty or forty people who appeared to be Caucasians on a fishing boat headed for Kompong Som
were inadequately reported to decision makers in Washington, and
several possibilities for communication which could have been used
were not attempted. The Chinese government had informed the
United States State Department fourteen hours before the rescue that
it expected the ship and crew to be released soon. But the State Department had not followed up this advice.

The report was also critical of the dropping of a fifteen-thousand-
pound bomb, the largest nonnuclear weapon in the United States arse-
nal, on Koh Tang while the last contingent of marines was still being
pulled back. Although the mission was performed "with valor and
prowess," the report concluded, "Little weight appears to have been
given to indications that the Cambodians might be working out a political solution. . . ." Both the method and the extent of the rescue opera-

tion were deemed unnecessary. The president, it was felt, had reacted prematurely and excessively. It would seem, in retrospect, that the opportunity to bomb was seized.

At the United Nations, Ieng Sary, the Cambodian deputy premier in charge of foreign affairs, expresses complete agreement with the United States congressional report. "That's what we were trying to say last year," he states. In San Francisco, the scene of the presidential debate the next day, Ron Nessen disagrees with the negative conclusions of the report, and Ford states that its release was politically motivated. Kissinger, asked about the report in New York, believes that it was based on "an inaccurate assessment and insufficient knowledge." In an answer reminiscent of his explanations about Vietnam, "I know what happened and I know what the government knew. The channels through which we were dealing revealed no such information."

In the waning days of the election campaign, Henry Kissinger does what he can to shore up the sagging Ford defenses. Speaking before the Synagogue Council of America in New York, while declaring himself "detached from partisan debate," Kissinger decries the call for a moralistic approach in the conduct of foreign affairs and argues instead for a morality limited by reality. Reverting to a central philosophic underpinning of the Nixon-Ford era that "policy is the art of the possible," Kissinger enunciates an accurate limiting factor. The example he then proceeds to give, however, is less defensible than the principle and demonstrates that it is in its application that the dividing line occurs between protagonists. "We must always keep in mind," Kissinger warns, "that it was precisely under the banners of universal moralistic slogans that a decade and a half ago we launched into adventures that divided our country and undermined our international position." In this interpretation of the motives for the beginning of the long Vietnam period, Kissinger illustrates why he evinces such a polar opposition.

A funny thing now happens on the way to November. The campaign becomes more lively, but in an astonishing and seemingly paradoxical direction. In spite of—or who knows, perhaps because of—the continuous series of embarrassing events, Ford steadily catches up. Notwithstanding intermediate rises and falls, he gradually pulls up from eighteen points behind until he is running neck and neck with his opponent. The troubles he has endured, from the pardon to Patman, have been fully absorbed and may be working for rather than against him. His "nice guy" image has not abated, and there is an identification with the problems which beset every good and decent man. In the final poll in California before the election, Ford actually leads 46 to 40 percent, although the Democrats in that state are the majority party by 57 to 36 percent!

November 2: Election Day

The winner, Jimmy Carter, by a split decision. The turnout was sizable. The issues, the personalities, the emotional strings which were plucked, finally engaged the electorate. The margin they gave Carter was a bare hair's breadth. Only two other presidents in this century received fewer than the 297 electoral votes by which Carter won. Any one state could have reversed the decision, and just a few votes in one of many states could have given the presidency to Ford.

The final outcome, like the removal of Nixon, could easily have gone the other way. If Ford had not made one of a series of errors, such as the ethnic slip or certainly, most would agree, the choice of Dole as his running mate—to be dragged into the Nixon net was one thing, but to have chosen a running mate who was aggressively defensive of Nixon to the end, was another—he might have remained comfortably in the White House.

"Carter won barely an election he should have won handily," Dan Rather observed. The outcome, almost exactly down the middle, after the most traumatic experience in our national political history, is a remarkable statistic. A multitude of explanatory facts must be taken into account, but the exquisite ambivalence which this result demonstrates should not escape notice. While no judgment can be applied automatically to the individual voter, a general overall characteristic did hold: Ford represented the continuation of the Nixon line and Carter a fresh start. The people collectively were almost ready to accept as president the man appointed by Nixon, the same one who had pardoned him. In the last analysis, a mere 1 percent majority turned down Nixon's version of moral behavior and were persuaded to reject the Nixon line of succession.

VI

The Trail

By this time, many feel that Watergate is behind us, that its effects are past history and can best be forgotten. In a more accurate sense its most important sequel and derivative has just begun. As the new president takes over and faces the problems ahead, it is Watergate which has determined the history of the next four or eight years. Carter would not be that president today without it.

It is now up to Carter to show what he is. Whether a president is elected by a landslide or by 51 percent, he then acts according to what is within him to do. The mandate of the electors and the mind of the elected combine to produce the political reality under which both then live. From the time that Carter walked in the inaugural parade, through his folksy style and "depomping of the presidency," there was a new personality to relate to, and the possibility of a new alliance ahead.

One subtle and felicitous change on the psychological scene has already taken place. Ambition has become a positive value rather than an automatic cause for concern. There was nothing wrong with Jimmy Carter's coming from nowhere and openly announcing, "I am running for president." Pride is restored and the adage revived that "anyone can become president in America." The young can again be encouraged to seek and take full advantage of opportunities. And power is not something automatically suspect, but is expected and needed and only to be used properly.

Another result is that the question of the president's sincerity and purpose is no longer getting in the way between the public and the facts. In dealing with the economy, energy, or foreign affairs, actions are not automatically filtered through the question of the integrity of the president. What he says may lead to agreement or disagreement, but not to a question about him.

From Carter's human rights policy which he promptly asserts, to the decisions he makes on the vital issues of our age, ambivalent public attitudes toward morality play a part in their reception. There is a hypermnesia, or excessive remembering, interlocked with an amnesia, which result in skewed reactions in either direction. Watergate has had some strange immediate effects. After the election, the Carters take their first vacation at the home of their friend Smith Bagley, heir to the R. J. Reynolds Tobacco fortune at the latter's Musgrove Plantation on St. Simons Island, Georgia. Press Secretary Jody Powell promptly announces that the Bagleys will be reimbursed for the time the Carter family spends at their home!

From this point on, I will no longer follow the diffuse effects of the Watergate years but pursue only the more immediate trail.

January 1977

In a valedictory address to the capital's press corps on January 11, assessing the last eight years in which he was the principal architect of American foreign policy, Kissinger states that his largest achievement was helping the nation steer past "the trauma of Vietnam" and "the nightmare of Watergate." As a result of this and Ford's honesty and strength, the Carter administration, Kissinger avers, would inherit "a nation recovered."

Joking again about his duels with reporters over the credibility issue, Kissinger acknowledges that he had "duped" reporters at least once when he had denied in 1975 that he had set out for the Middle East. He had been carrying a list of Israeli prisoners, he explained, to be released by Syria, and was guided by "humanitarian considerations." He appealed for an end to "a state of perpetual inquest" which he attributed to cynicism brought about by Vietnam and Watergate.

A few weeks earlier Kissinger had been made an honorary member of the Harlem Globe Trotters. Already quite a globe trotter himself, Kissinger said he liked the free-style team because "I too make the rules as I go along."

On January 14, President Ford surprises Kissinger at a farewell reception by awarding him the Presidential Medal of Freedom, the country's highest civilian award. In bestowing the medal, Ford, referring to Kissinger as "this superior person" states that in his opinion Kissinger was the greatest secretary of state in the history of the republic.

Ex-President Ford makes a sad and graceful exit. His farewell speech to Congress is delivered through tears to a standing ovation. Nixon and Agnew resigned in disgrace, he says. This is the most open he has been about his predecessors. He is now a freer man. In declaring that since he took office the people can "once again believe in themselves," Ford gives voice to my own thesis about the Watergate depression: it was *themselves* the people could not believe in. Ford goes out the decent man that he is, however much his tie-up with his predecessor eroded his credibility. He takes off for California on a wave of good feeling, the final victim of Nixon's Watergate.

As the new Ninety-fifth Congress convenes, Sen. Howard Baker is elected Republican leader in an upset victory over Sen. Robert Griffin. The vote for the new Senate minority leader was nineteen to eighteen, again just above 50 percent. The repetition of this ratio is astonishing whenever the issue of Nixon and morality reappears, although there are of course other factors involved. Baker's original firmness on the Watergate committee compared to Griffin's loyal although scrupulously clean support of Nixon for a very long time was a major difference between the two. However, the shadow over Baker cast by Sam Dash must have had an effect in mitigating the purity of the image.

February

Secretary of State Cyrus Vance states that the administration is checking whether "we have all the papers" outlining Nixon's and Kissinger's promises to China. According to a report by columnist Joseph Kraft, such a search was initiated after a meeting between Carter and Huang Chen, head of the China mission in Washington. At a meeting between Kissinger and the late Chairman Mao a promise was "evidently made" to Peking by Nixon and Kissinger that the United States would end its connection with the Nationalist Chinese government on Taiwan in a few years.

March

Brady Tyson, a United States delegate to the United Nations, expresses regret in the U.N. Human Rights Commission over what he called United States involvement in undermining the government of Salvador Allende in Chile. The administration promptly disavows the remarks of its envoy as "not an expression of the administration's view." Former CIA Director William Colby had denied any such governmental role, and this view had been repeated a few days later by President Ford.

In a book which appears a few days after this apology in the United Nations, David Phillips, former CIA chief for the Western Hemisphere, states that Nixon himself had ordered agency officials to take any action necessary, including a military coup, to prevent the election of Allende in 1970. Only Kissinger and Haig were let in on the plan, and Richard Helms, then director of covert intelligence, was put in charge of a small group of agents, including Phillips, to run the project codenamed Track II.

April

Carter cuts twelve years off the prison sentence of Gordon Liddy to make him eligible for parole on July 9. A White House spokesman explains that Carter commuted Liddy's twenty-year sentence "in the interests of equity and fairness based on a comparison of Liddy's sentence with those of all the others convicted in Watergate-related proceedings." Liddy has already served nearly four years.

When Liddy petitioned for presidential intervention last September, Ford, who had given Nixon a pardon in the interest of fairness and because "he had had enough," did not, or could not, act. While in the case of Nixon he was supposed to prefer aiding the victim to his popularity, empirically he could do so only to the man who happened to have handed him the presidency. By what he did for one, Ford had lost his freedom to do for others. The draft evaders, for example, also had to wait. Carter, however, was free to do what he thought was right, and did.

May

This month marks the return of Nixon, courtesy of David Frost. His face on the television screen again brings it all back. Seeing him with Frost those four painful weeks is in every respect a déjà vu. To millions who had harbored a secret wish that after the three years he has had to think things over, their harassed ex-leader might emerge cleansed and refreshed, it is the last disillusionment. In spite of their lack of interest and avowed disgust, forty-five million people turned on their TV sets to see and hear him for his first appearance in the series. Half that number tuned in for the second act.

It is the familiar Nixon performance, the noble, self-serving exaltation and tugging at heart strings in areas where he can talk freely and cannot be checked up on, and the same dodging, twisting, evasive double-talk where the people have had experience and can now judge for themselves. Nixon has simply become an older version of what he always was.

With regard to Watergate, with which Frost opened the series to assure an audience, Nixon demonstrates a type of thought process to which he has treated the American people for some thirty years. As Frost repeatedly cites chapter and verse, able to serve as prosecutor as no one has before, Nixon ducks and weaves in the familiar pattern, showing only a little more discomfiture than he has in the past. Yes, he went "right to the edge of the law in trying to advise Ehrlichman and Haldeman how best to present their cases." And, yes, "I would have to say that a reasonable person could call that a cover-up," but he did not commit any crime.

With chin jutting forward, in the active rather than the passive approach whenever he can manage it, Nixon aggressively splits hairs and tries to differentiate between responsibility and guilt, motive and act, guilt over generalities or for an impeachable offense. Adding a new phrase of justification to the old "national security," his motivation now was "political containment," to prevent "any slipover or should I say slopover . . . that would damage innocent people." Making up laws as he goes along, "Political containment is not a corrupt motive," Nixon states, and a cover-up for a motive that is not criminal is not illegal. Yes, he is guilty, he admits, raising people's expectations for a moment; here might come the moment of truth: "As the one with the chief responsibility for seeing that the laws of the United States are enforced, I did not meet that responsibility." But then he slides away: he is guilty of having "screwed up" and "botched up," and "of having let the American people down." Frost, he explains, places him in a position where one might want to rationalize, which he does not want to do *(sic!)*. He is guilty of having been too soft: "I made so many bad judgments . . . the worst ones mistakes of the heart rather than the head."

He is guilty, he goes on, of not having fulfilled Gladstone's dictum that "the first requirement for a Prime Minister is to be a good butcher." He could not be a butcher to his loyal staff, to Bob Haldeman and John Ehrlichman, "splendid men." He waited long and tried every way he could to stave off having to fire his two trusted aides—actually Ehrlichman told Nixon that Haldeman could not be trusted and wanted him fired: "Maybe I defended them too long." But, finally, "I cut off one arm and then the other." Nixon is tender; he cannot see people cry. When not on the defense, Nixon can talk about emotions, even produce them, especially when they can have an effect. When the time came to tell Ehrlichman he had to go, "there were tears in our eyes, both of us." He told Ray Price, who was to write the announcement speech, that if he wanted to he could write in Nixon's resignation as well, but Ray would not do it. From a federal prison camp in Arizona, Ehrlichman, with all ties severed and no holds barred, finds this latest account "a swarmy, maudlin, rationalization that will be tested and found false." Just before Nixon fired him, Ehrlichman adds now, he "offered me a huge sum of money. I declined it."

If anything, Nixon must receive credit for sticking to his guns and to his distorted convictions. His broken-field running is as deft as ever, even if he never travels a straight line and never really goes over the goal for a score.

There is no look or act or behavior that denotes psychosis, if such a diagnosis, even in the negative, can be made from this arm's-length view. Alternately irritating and pathetic, he is pugnacious when attacked or when he needs to explain; sentimental, philosophic, and sadly unctuous when he can turn the talk to generalities. Never is he without that mixture of control and pathos with which he has characteristically faced the public in his times of stress.

But his paranoid way of thinking, if not actual paranoia, shines through. Statements he made about Watergate which were not true were due to "that enormous political attack I was under. . . . It was a five-front war with a fifth column," he goes on, reminiscent of his talk during his anti-Communist days. But he stops himself short of going over the edge: "It was my fault. I'm not blaming anybody else. . . . I don't go with the idea that what brought me down was a coup, a conspiracy." But the way is left open: "There are some friends who say, 'There is a conspiracy to get you.' " And he is not sure: "There may have been. I don't know what the C.I.A. had to do. Some of their shenanigans have yet to be told. . . . I don't know what was going on in some Republican and Democratic circles, as far as the so-called impeachment lobby was concerned. . . . I had a partisan Senate Committee staff. We had a partisan special prosecutor staff; we had a partisan media; we had a partisan Judiciary Committee staff in the fifth column. . . . I gave 'em a sword, and they stuck it in and then twisted it with relish." And then again with some trace of compensatory insight: "And I guess if I'd been in their position I'd have done the same thing."

Insight and defenses, confessions and denials alternate and are fused, every hint of beginning to come clean followed immediately by a justification of his acts. This is what keeps the audience, eager for a solution, so glued to what he says. Anticipating a question Frost was putting to him, Nixon interrupts, "Paranoia? Am I paranoiac about hating people and trying to do them in: The answer is at times yes. I get angry at people . . . but in human terms." He dislikes others for being hypocritical and sanctimonious but "an individual must never let hatred rule him." (*Sic* again: insight and introspection are also abysmally absent.

Hatred, arising from insecurity, ruled his life.) Discussing his feelings about the antiwar protesters, Nixon says, "Call it paranoia, but paranoia for peace isn't that bad."

The "cascade of candor" promised by Frost turns out to be the same dry and sterile trickle as of old. It is the same Nixon, seeming to let go but always holding on. He does not remember whether Ehrlichman told him in advance of the plan to break into the psychiatrist's office: "He may have and if he had I would have said, 'Go right ahead.' " A potential confession, but a protection against it in advance. At the end of a long and incriminating summary by Frost enumerating in detail what the evidence showed, Nixon puts up his routine stone wall. "That's your opinion. And I have my opinion. . . . You could state your conclusion, and I've stated my view. So now we go on to the rest of it."

Although the general reaction, if one could read it, was against the ex-president after his first appearance, Nixon had not lost the quality of dividing and troubling the listening audience. The *New Yorker* referred to this general uneasiness perceptively and intuitively: "One reason is that Richard Nixon still has the power to provoke a deep anxiety in us. There is something unresolved in our attitude toward him. A major source of this anxiety is that we have never been able to answer the question of the extent to which Nixon, elected by us, is made in our image."

A good number of people feel satisfaction and relief that Nixon confessed as much as he did. To these his marginal admissions that he had failed his responsibilities, lied to the public, failed to enforce the law, and let the American people down were the equivalents of an apology and admission of guilt. Nixon showed "a contriteness that I had not expected," said Howard Callaway, Ford's former campaign manger. Rep. Charles Wiggins felt that he had "told the truth" on the essential points. This reaction was not purely along partisan lines. Former Gov. Tom McCall of Oregon, one of the first to call for Nixon's resignation, now feels Nixon is "a warm human being. If he'd just come out like this early, it probably wouldn't have been half as bad." And to James Neal, who had prosecuted Nixon's top aides in the Watergate trial, "He admitted that he had to resign because of his own faults."

Judging by a flood of telephone calls to TV stations after the first broadcast, while many felt that Nixon "is a liar," a new sympathy was created among others who felt that he was impressive and "came off looking very well." We will never know what the public reaction would have been had Nixon come clean at the beginning, if indeed he was ever capable of doing so. In an ABC News/Harris poll, 45 percent felt "sorry for him" now, although a decisive 71 percent felt that Nixon should not return to public life.

For most who were scornful and felt that nothing new had come to light, this evaluation too had a beneficial result. If there had been a deep hope that their ex-president might redeem himself, at least by being contrite, this was their final opportunity to let him return to his isolation with no need for them to feel further guilt. Says Rep. Peter Rodino, "It made me sad to see a President of the United States trying one way or the other to explain away the facts. You can't rewrite history." Senator Sam Ervin echoes the views of many: "I think it's good for the people to see it because he's still covering up." Charles Sandman, Nixon's staunchest supporter on the House Judiciary Committee, who later lost his congressional seat for his trouble, states, "He was humble, but does that change his guilt? I say no." Senator Goldwater feels no pity for Nixon now: "He's as dead as he can be. I have no sympathy for him at all."

Former Watergate Special Prosecutor Jaworski, in a modification of his former views written for *Newsweek*, feels that Nixon's admissions and contentions are not enough to right his wrongs. Whereas Jaworski had previously demurred in pursuing the Watergate trial, and in 1975 had said that nowhere in the final Watergate report was there any criminal evidence against Nixon, he now denounces Nixon's contention that "technically I did not commit a crime." "Why," he asks, "if Mr. Nixon only made mistakes and was not criminally culpable, did he seek a pardon and embrace it? This is not the course of innocent people. . . . I sympathize with his lot. But I cannot concur in his efforts to distort historical facts."

It is now clear why Nixon subjected himself to Frost's merciless probing: he did so for a half to a million dollars. However, another motivation emphasized by Frost may also have been present. Nixon could have seen the interviews as an opportunity to set the record straight, and it could be that the account he gives is what he considers the straight record to be.

In comparing himself with other presidents, Nixon leans on them indirectly for support. What if Truman had also used "political containment" as a motive? he asks. Kennedy and Johnson—Nixon calls up the names of predecessors in their problems as well as strengths—furthered the Vietnam War, and were right in doing so, he adds. John Kennedy bugged the hotel room of Martin Luther King as well as the rooms of people in the sugar lobby. Robert Kennedy ordered IRS investigations against seventeen right-wing organizations. Johnson, when president, deducted millions of dollars from his taxes as donations and had told Nixon he would be a damn fool not to do the same. Lincoln and Jefferson are quoted more than once. In a Civil War statement, Lincoln had declared, "Actions which otherwise would be unconstitutional could become lawful if undertaken for the purpose of preserving the Constitution and the nation." Fighting the same kinds of wars, Nixon is saying, linked him to Lincoln. In wartime a president has extraordinary powers: "The nation was torn apart in an ideological way by the war in Vietnam as much as the Civil War tore apart the nation when Lincoln was President." Here the usual guilt by association used by Nixon against others is converted by Nixon to acquire for himself stature by association.

Seeking strong company by reminding us of the encounters of others with corruption, Nixon reminisces that Eisenhower had his Sherman Adams. As he meanders on in long answers to questions, in ramblings which can serve as free associations, Nixon's mode of distortion is demonstrated on the television screen and comes out in statu nascendi. By way of underscoring his courage in doing what had to be done with Haldeman and Ehrlichman (if not with himself we might add!), Nixon free-associates about the role he remembers having played in the firing of Adams. Who was it who handled this problem for Eisenhower, who was the only one strong enough to do what had to be done, Nixon asks rhetorically. It was he, he points out, who in 1958 first pleaded with Eisenhower, who wanted Adams out, for mercy and compassion because of his natural sympathy for anyone caught in a trap. Later, however, when Eisenhower decided that Adams must leave but could not personally bring himself to tell Adams, it was Nixon, says Nixon now, who performed the task for Eisenhower by going in alone and telling Adams he had to go.

Stephen E. Ambrose, the editor of Eisenhower's official papers, immediately declares that Nixon's version of his role in the resignation of Adams is incorrect. Not only did Nixon not oppose the action against Adams, but Ambrose's research showed that Adams had been forced to step down in 1958 primarily because of pressure from Nixon and other Republican leaders. After a reluctant Eisenhower finally agreed, Nixon was not ordered by Eisenhower to fire Adams nor did he by any means go in alone as he claimed. Nixon, says Ambrose, was asked by Eisenhower to meet with Adams along with Meade Alcorn, chairman of the Republican National Committee, in an attempt to persuade Adams to resign. According to a further account given by *Time* senior correspondent John Steele, about an hour before the difficult session actually took place Nixon excused himself, telling Alcorn on the phone there were too many newspapermen around. Alcorn confirms that Nixon's recollection was in error. Speaking in Hartford, Connecticut, Alcorn states, "Mr. Nixon's statement last night is not accurate and it does not conform with my knowledge of the incident."

President Carter, demurring at first, finally comments on Nixon's performance. Carter feels that Nixon was guilty of an impeachable offense but also feels that it is likely Nixon believes what he said. "It is easy," says the president, "for people to rationalize what they do. Although I think he was mistaken."

In the interviews with Frost that concern post-Watergate topics, Nixon seems more comfortable and less under pressure. Here his memories and fantasies are applied to events with the same combination of qualities as in the past. There is that look of earnestness and sincerity which one would like to believe but which one feels forced to doubt, and there is the once-over-lightly attitude toward historical facts which one always has to question.

As Nixon's recollections are probed about the cold war, détente, Vietnam, the Middle East, his role in the history of our times becomes exalted, noble, lofty. He is a man of decision and boldness, resolute and in command, altruistic and peace loving in his motives and goals. With a delivery that appears to be modest he recounts his every move in self-serving terms. His was the firm steady hand in Washington through crises and troubled times. His role in admitting China to the family of nations and in initiating the SALT talks with the Soviet Union speaks for itself. The version he now gives of the nuclear alert he ordered during the Israel-Arab war in October 1973, which was met at the time with the widest skepticism, shows him to have been the architect of action with the purest motives. It was he who was a friend of Israel all along, who supported and protected it against its adversaries, and who stood firmly against Khrushchev and Brezhnev over the entire Middle East. In previous accounts of this same period, Kissinger and Schlesinger each had blamed the other for foot-dragging in the matter of ordering the airlift of weapons to Israel, with Nixon in each case as a more distant participant.

To elevate himself, Nixon is not above putting others down. Kissinger, whose role in his administration Nixon keeps trying to deemphasize, was emotional and hesitant where Nixon was forthright and decisive; in general Kissinger played less of a part than was thought. But when it comes to sharing the guilt for events for which Nixon had to pay, Kissinger is stated to have played a stronger role. Kissinger favored the invasion of Cambodia in April 1970, just as he did the Christmas bombing of Hanoi in 1972, contrary to the report of some of his liberal friends and columnists. When Kissinger had misgivings, however, about the invasion of Cambodia, upset at the adverse domestic reactions after the shootings at Kent State in Ohio, Nixon, in an expansive mood again, tells how he bolstered Kissinger's resolve when the latter had told him that Cambodia "could have been a mistake." "Henry, we've done it," Nixon says he told Kissinger. "Remember Lot's wife. Never look back. He got the point." To make himself appear strong, he lets his thinking become fuzzy. Nixon can hardly distinguish whether his present version makes him strong and a hero or just obstinate or vindictive.

While such a lack of dignity in a past or present president puts many people off, to others such a weakness continues to make him endearing. Were it not for all that was now known, some would still give strong weight to Nixon's present views of history. "If he keeps talking like that, I may vote for him," one technician on the set was quoted as saying. The same may be true when Nixon slips into gutter talk. "I couldn't care less about the punk," was the ex-president's way of speaking of Daniel Ellsberg for reporting to the public as he did about the Vietnam War. On the subject of criticisms of public officials by reporters, Nixon counseled his fellow sufferers to "come back and crack 'em right in the puss."

Woodward and Bernstein are "trashy people who wrote a trashy book." His wife suffered a stroke three days after she read it, he points out in a bitter and angry mood. He has only "utter contempt" for them "and I will never forgive them. Never."

It is difficult to say whether such colloquialisms make him more pathetic or more appealing. Such street-talk expressions of bravado and anger work to make him one of the people. While many are saddened and repelled, others feel not a separation but an emotional link.

Alternating with his tough talk, attacks, and aggressive defenses, Nixon still acts human and soft and pleads for understanding and compassion among men. Personal tidbits are offered about world leaders he has known, new friends from afar about whom he can inform the country. Brezhnev was easier to get along with, more cautious than Khrushchev, and "a much safer man to have sitting there with his finger on the button than Khrushchev." He is also evidence that "the new class is doin' pretty good" in the Soviet Union. He is "something of a fashion plate. He liked beautiful cars. He liked beautiful women." Khrushchev, on the other hand, was "boorish, crude, brilliant, ruthless, potentially rash, with a terrible inferiority complex." He would put on a "big macho act [with the] air of being just a common peasant-like person ... with a sloppy hat and a collar that wouldn't be too clean." Mao had "very fine, exquisite hands ... devilish sense of humor" and was helped around by "these rather pretty Chinese girl aides."

Nixon's comments about his own associates are less flattering than his reminiscences about his erstwhile opponents. Khrushchev and Brezhnev, in spite of criticism, are both treated with judicious and complimentary remarks. Mao and Chou En-lai emerge as more appealing than do some of Nixon's friends. Kissinger, considering his closeness to Nixon for years, comes off with a surprising amount of cumulative depreciation. He is egotistical and volatile, brilliant and immature, was an "associate," never a "personal friend." Kissinger is self-seeking and secretive, says Nixon, projecting his own characteristic traits. In another example of spontaneous projection, again to the same target who may well have deserved it, Nixon describes his discussion with Kissinger about the news leak of the bombing of Cambodia. "I'll never forget," Nixon says, "when the Cambodia leak occurred. . . . We said, 'Henry, it's possible it might be somebody on your staff.' " Then, scarcely hiding his aggressive if not sadistic pleasure, Nixon imitates Kissinger's heavy German accent as he goes on to quote him, "And Henry said, 'I vill destroy dem.' " Henry too, not only he, he says, had a streak of paranoia, "paranoia for peace," that is.

Kissinger disparaged Secretary of State William Rogers, says Nixon, and outmaneuvered him to take control of foreign policy. He looked upon John Connally as a "potential rival," which caused Nixon to drop Connally as his choice to succeed Rogers as secretary of state and to give Kissinger the job instead. "Henry likes to say outrageous things. . . . he was fascinated by the celebrity set and he liked being one himself." Nixon also used to go to Hollywood parties when he was vice-president, but came to disdain them. All they were interested in there was gossip, Nixon explains, after he has delivered his own morsels about those in high places.

His roots and origins, his perennial upward striving in the social hierarchy never lose their emotional impact. The Kennedys, he complains to the listening nation, never invited him and Pat to the White House for a meal even though he was an ex-vice-president. He, on the other hand, later invited Jackie and Rose Kennedy and the children, and had also seen to it that Hubert Humphrey as a former vice-president was on the list to receive White House dinner invitations. At times during this expression of his personal hurt, the mirthless and contrived smile gives way to a more believable show of emotion. His face may relax and for an unguarded moment he looks real, and normally sad.

Nixon gains strength as he goes along. His mood alternates; his delivery becomes surer. The war protesters not only did not help but prolonged the ending of the war in Vietnam by two years. Here was an evaluation reminiscent of Kissinger's two years before when he blamed the American people who protested for "the erosion of central authority" in this country. In each case it is not the perpetrators but the protesters upon whom the blame falls. Nixon's main regret regarding the United States invasion of Cambodia was that "I didn't act stronger sooner."

When Frost asks whether the actual break-ins were not illegal, Nixon retorts with his much-quoted statement, "When the President does it that means that it is not illegal." When asked where one draws the line, whether such authority extends beyond burglary to murder, Nixon retreats, but only partially: "There are degrees, there are nuances which are difficult to explain. . . . each case has to be considered on its merits." If Franklin Roosevelt had thought it was in the interests of the world to assassinate Hitler, what of that, he asks.

He also acquits himself indirectly through others. In the fourth interview Nixon talks about himself through his former vice-president. Spiro Agnew, although he had forty counts against him, was an honest, courageous, decent man. He too was the victim of "a double standard . . . [because he wasn't] one of the liberals' favorite pin-up boys." When asked whom he believed in the conflicting stories given by Peterson and Agnew regarding the charges against Agnew, "It didn't matter," Nixon replies, "I was pragmatic. . . . there wasn't any question . . . that he was frankly going to get it . . . so under the circumstances it became an irrelevant point." Nixon agreed with Agnew that the payoffs he received were "common practice" among governors. "Half the members of the Senate who had served as governors" had accepted kickbacks from contractors, Nixon says Agnew told him. There was no use fighting it. When the payoff case developing against Agnew was laid in Nixon's lap by Attorney General Elliot Richardson who, Nixon couldn't resist adding, had "ambitions" for the vice-presidential job, Nixon steered Agnew toward "the resignation option" only when it became evident that the imminent alternative was a prison term.

At the end Nixon speaks of the sadness of his resignation, waxes philosophic, and reflects on the purpose of life. He has never contemplated suicide, as had been reported, and accounts that he had considered falling on his sword or shooting himself were "just bunk." But "resignation meant life without purpose as far as I was concerned. . . . No one in the world and no one in our history could know how I felt." As he was about to announce his coming resignation, he and Henry Kissinger knelt together in teary prayer in the room where Lincoln had signed the Emancipation Proclamation. Later, says Nixon, "I just by impulse picked up the phone and said, 'Henry, if you don't mind, why don't we just keep that incident to ourselves.'"

He can still tug at heart strings. "If they want me to get down and grovel on the floor, no, never. Because I don't believe I should," he had said in the first interview. At the end he can talk with a look of kindness and benevolence, even at times with the air of tolerance and condescension of a man who gives the impression he thinks he has won. He will always keep on fighting and hopes to continue to be useful. As one listens, one can agree and even admire.

The interviews with David Frost are not the last of Nixon. Reacting after them to the unfavorable press he evoked, Nixon writes another rebuttal of his rebuttal in the *Washington Star,* declaring that the quotes in the summaries reported were blown out of proportion from many hours of recorded interviews. Expanding on his televised remarks on presidential power, he says that a president needs flexibility in interpreting the law "written in other times and for other circumstances." Presidents must have latitude "to go beyond the strict letter of existing law" in times of emergency "for adapting the statutory laws to the laws of necessity and to the laws of reason." The law is not a precision instrument, Nixon writes: "In dealing with a major threat to the public safety, a President who lets himself be paralyzed by the strict letter of the law would violate his oath."

These are not the ramblings of a man out of control, but a defense made with shrewdness and thought. Nixon's line of reasoning cannot be denied and in the abstract would be defended by many. Debater that he always was, it would make an effective presentation for one side of a legal and ethical debate. In fact, as President Carter announces a new series of rules to reform existing CIA procedures, he affirms the same principle and leaves room for the same exception. These new policies will apply, he states, but can be abrogated in times of national emergency. Nixon has always found effective shields behind which to hide what he wants and needs.

In May, our relations with Vietnam take a post-Nixon direction. The United States and Vietnam open talks to establish diplomatic and trade relations between the two countries. In a fresh effort to heal the scars of war, the talks begin without the preconditions that have made such discussions impossible in the past. Each country has something to gain by the outcome: Hanoi, aid and war compensation; the United States, among other things, information on American servicemen still unaccounted for.

A major obstacle facing the discussions, however, is the release of a secret message from then-President Nixon to North Vietnam's Premier Pham Van Dong in connection with the 1973 Paris peace agreements that he was prepared to give Hanoi 3.25 billion dollars in United States aid "without any political conditions." Accused of making this secret deal on aid in order to bring Hanoi to the peace table, Nixon, in a letter to Rep. Lester Wolff, chairman of the Asian and Pacific Affairs Subcommittee of the House International Relations Committee, had written that the proposal was "not at any time presented to them as part of the 'price' to obtain the peace agreement." While Hanoi was now insisting that the United States honor its pledge for postwar reconstructive aid, Washington has contended that the pledge was voided by the resumption of fighting after the Paris peace accord.

Later, Kissinger, in congressional testimony to the same subcommittee, denies that any firm commitment of postwar aid was made to Vietnam or that Nixon had made any secret agreements. Moreover, in view of Hanoi's numerous abuses of the Paris agreement for a cease-fire in 1973, it would be "an absurdity," Kissinger states, for the United States to recognize any conditional obligation. "That would be carrying masochism to the extreme," he says. We did not make them any promises and our promise is void because of what they did.

While Nixon denied that the offer had been made as a bribe, Kissinger now denies that such an offer had been made at all. As he did before in the face of available evidence about relations to Peking and activities in Chile, so does he now about Vietnam. Internally inconsistent and in direct contradiction of data in the hands of the chairman of the committee himself, Kissinger's testimony on the public scene continues to deserve a mixture of incredibility as a cognitive assessment and incredulity as an accompanying emotion. The total reaction is, or appropriately and rationally should be, the two together.

Kissinger retains his magic touch. A favorite of the smart and elite, he continues to charm the intellectual and social communities. His public image is positive, even heroic, and he is treated well, respectfully and fairly, even by the press.

The survival of Kissinger through the history of Watergate is in fact a phenomenon which needs to be explained. Involved in wiretaps, acknowledged architect of much of our foreign policy which collapsed, author of statements in contradiction of evidence, ensnared in indefensible testimony as "inoperative" as much of Nixon's, Kissinger still manages to come out smiling, quipping, poised, and in control. Unlike Nixon, his disturbing dealings remain circumstantial; there was never a "smoking gun." There were no tapes—at least that were known—to make pursuit obligatory. Kissinger is, in basic respects, Nixon without the Watergate.

People identify with Kissinger as they did with Nixon for the ability to perform without being hemmed in by facts or rules. In addition, Kissinger, more than Nixon, has charm and wit, and he was a Harvard professor. Above all, he wards off criticism with a smile, a feature of charisma easy to identify with.

Nevertheless, there are "Kissinger distrusters" as there were "Nixon haters," not labeled as such and not as organized but heard from in palpable numbers. Kissinger receives an ambivalent reception from small but significant segments of the intellectual public. This is most regular and visible in the academic world. A sizable student and faculty protest, for example, accompanies a proposed appointment of Kissinger as a professor at Columbia University.

On July 19, 1977, the same day as Kissinger's testimony in Washington, United States Delegate to the United Nations Donald McHenry clears the way for Vietnam's acceptance by the General Assembly. The United States formally drops its opposition to Vietnam's membership in the United Nations, pledging to work toward "a new era of peace and cooperation" with its former foe.

How things have changed since the days of the old Richard Nixon. Mainly there isn't Nixon around anymore to hurl the epithet "Communist." Goldwater wishes "old Henry" were back and that things were again more as they were. "Kissinger loss" is a widespread psychological syndrome, writes Richard Ullman of the *New York Times*. Another symptom which goes along with this affliction is selective amnesia, Ullman writes, remembering and pointing only to Kissinger's grand diplomatic events and forgetting or ignoring the long list of debacles.

Writers and students of the Kissinger-Nixon years concur in a more critical appraisal. Tad Szulc of the *New York Times* and Stanley Hoffman, professor of government and chairman of the Center for European Studies at Harvard, coalesce in indicting Kissinger's methods and record. While Szulc points out the gulf between private statements and acts of Nixon and Kissinger, Hoffman methodically exposes Kissinger's ethical lacunae and conceptual flaws and the practical errors and limitations which resulted.

On May 24 the Supreme Court rejects the appeals of Ehrlichman, Haldeman, and Mitchell, refusing to review their cover-up convictions. Haldeman and Mitchell will soon be joining Ehrlichman, who is already in a federal prison serving his sentence. A leaked news report indicates that in a tentative vote taken in their closed weekly conference a month before the decision, three Nixon-appointed judges had voted in favor of the review with the other five opposed. Four affirmative votes are required for review. Here was a possible conflict of interest right down to the wire. A fourth Nixon appointee, Justice William Rehnquist, who had worked in the Justice Department under Mitchell, had not participated either in the preliminary deliberations or the final decision.

James Doyle, former press chief of the Watergate special prosecutor's office, in a new book *Not Above the Law*, reveals that members of the prosecuting staff, mainly appointed by Archibald Cox, had become so distrustful of Leon Jaworski, their new White House–appointed boss in 1973, that they considered tailing him on his late-afternoon walks. Suspecting that Jaworski might hope to dispose of the Watergate case "with a quick stroke—guilty pleas and a Presidential resignation," the staff "wondered, worried, and fretted about what he would give to gain that goal," Doyle writes.

Jaworski finds the suspicion "laughable [but] also somewhat saddening. . . . I actually think it was more curiosity than a lack of trust." In 1975, however, long after Jaworski left office, his successor Henry Ruth had reported that Jaworski met with Alexander Haig the day before Nixon's resignation. "Jaworski later told members of his staff . . . that no promises or understandings of any kind had been requested or offered," the report said. But while both Ruth and his predecessor Cox had agreed with Jaworski against the advisability of indicting the president, Jaworski did not follow the course recommended by Ruth as an alternative to seeking an indictment: full-scale cooperation with the House Judiciary Committee's impeachment investigation.

June

Haldeman and Mitchell are ordered by Judge Sirica to enter federal
prison on June 22 to start serving their two-and-a-half- to eight-year
terms. Mitchell will be the first attorney general in American history to
go to jail. Haldeman's lawyer, John Wilson, is caustic about the leak of
the Supreme Court's action four weeks before it was announced. He
feels that the David Frost television program in which Nixon accused
Haldeman of crimes was probably seen by the Supreme Court justices
while the case was awaiting their decision. The Justices could have been
prejudiced, and Wilson hopes for a reconsideration of their decision.
Haldeman enters a minimum-security federal prison camp at Lompoc,
California. Mitchell goes to the minimum-security prison at Maxwell Air
Force Base in Alabama.

Charles Ruff, the last Watergate special prosecutor, states that Nixon
can be prosecuted until 1980 if Haldeman's forthcoming book indicates
that Nixon lied when testifying before a grand jury in 1975. Ford's
pardon would not cover statements that Nixon had made under oath
ten months after he resigned, states Ruff. In a press conference after
Nixon's televised interviews with Frost, Haldeman announces that he
will challenge Nixon's explanation of the cover-up and will "cover everything on the subject, with the gloves off and no holds barred."

Rep. Elizabeth Holtzman of the former House Judiciary Committee
objects to the recent appointment of Leon Jaworski as special counsel
to the House investigation of alleged South Korean influence-buying in
Congress. Feeling that Jaworski failed to complete his job as Watergate
special prosecutor and that "many investigations were allowed to
wither and die on the vine," Holtzman writes, "We still do not know
who ordered the break-in, what the burglars were looking for, and why
no higher-ups were prosecuted."

In closing down the prosecutor's office, Charles Ruff had said that he
was, "for the record, sick of it." If Watergate was a sickness, Ruff had
said, then investigating it too long was also a sickness. Emotional fatigue, says Holtzman, is no excuse for aborting investigations. If the
Watergate prosecutors were tired they should have asked to be replaced by fresh attorneys.

July:

Documents released under the Freedom of Information Act disclose the existence of an eleven-year program in drug experiments. In projects codenamed MK-Ultra, MK-Delta, Artichoke, and Bluebird, experiements were conducted on unwitting subjects to develop a drug which, by producing amnesia, would make former employees of the CIA forget the agency's secrets. Research aimed at "alteration of sex patterns," "disturbance of memory," and "discrediting by aberrant behavior" was conducted by a combination of hypnotism and drugs, from amnesia drops to aphrodisiacs, while other experiments aimed at behavior and mind control were based on behavioral modification techniques through radiation, electroshock, and "harassment" substances. At least one army scientist, Frank R. Olson, who had been given LSD without his knowledge in an after-dinner drink, was known to have committed suicide.

At whorehouses established by the CIA in San Francisco and New York, prostitutes administered LSD and other potent drugs to subjects without their knowledge. Classified documents now made public show that such experiments began in the fifties and may have continued until recently. Programs involving drugs and behavior modification were carried out for years by prominent experts in some of the country's most prestigious universities, medical schools, hospitals, and research foundations.

Ostensibly such experiments were initiated to keep up with alleged Soviet and Chinese techniques for a similar type of mind and thought control. Former CIA alumnus Miles Copeland had written in *The Game of Nations,* "While our citizens may take pride in the solid front of high morality that our nation presents, they can also sleep more easily at night from knowing that behind this front we are in fact capable of matching the Soviets perfidy for perfidy." CIA Director Stansfield Turner admits to a congressional committee that somewhere along the line the projects and the motivation of the CIA changed in character from defensive to offensive. According to a July 21, 1977, article in the *Los Angeles Times* by Norman Kempster, a letter written by a CIA operative (with name deleted) in November 1949 referred to chemical substances of the most ingenious nature as possible ways of committing murder without leaving any visible or detectable trace.

William R. Corson, a respected professional member of the intelligence community whose experience extended from World War II through Vietnam, tries to provide a more sober and informed account of the reasons for the rise and the history of "the American Intelligence Empire" in his book *The Armies of Ignorance*. A dedicated believer in the necessity for a central intelligence service, Corson describes the need for achieving the "ultimate intelligence target: a thorough knowledge of the other great powers' capabilities and intentions, on which the strategic decisions of the United States depend." To accomplish this end under present conditions and in the light of recent events, Corson suggests a number of reforms, generally along the lines recommended by the Church committee of the Senate, such as centralized control and a sharing of intelligence information by the Executive with Congress.

A latest instance of plea bargaining prevents a prison sentence for ex-CIA Director Richard Helms when he pleads no contest to a charge of lying to a Senate subcommittee about the CIA's activities in Chile. Helms himself states that leniency was arrived at in order to spare the country security information which would have involved illegal activity on the parts of the highest officials, up to and including, it is understood, Nixon and Kissinger.

Speaking more freely months later in a television interview with David Frost, Helms breaks a long-accustomed silence and states that the CIA's decision to enlist the Mafia in plotting against President Castro "is one of the greatest regrets of my life." Speaking of various assassination plots, however, he denies "that any poison pellets ever even got to Havana. . . . Assassination is not a way for the American government. It is not a way for the CIA. I was never in favor of it. Murder will out. It will always, eventually, leak around in some fashion that it was done." Scoffing at a suggestion that he had "blackmailed" Nixon into naming him ambassador to Iran after Nixon removed him as director of the CIA in 1973, Helms states, "The whole theory is laughable. I never by word, deed, action, or innuendo threatened President Nixon with anything ever."

August

Time magazine reports that Nixon received one million dollars in cash early in 1973 from Teamsters Union president Frank Fitzsimmons in exchange for barring Jimmy Hoffa from seeking elective office in that union. The courier for Nixon in this transaction was White House aide Charles Colson, the magazine claims. Colson, interviewed by the FBI about the alleged payoff, had denied any knowledge of it. The one million dollars, the magazine says, could have been what Nixon had referred to in the March 21 tape: with regard to the burglars' demands for huge sums of hush money, Nixon says to Dean, "What I mean is you could get a million dollars.... I know where it could be gotten.... There is no problem in that."

Nixon, Haldeman, and Mitchell are ordered by United States District Court Judge John Lewis Smith to pay a total of five dollars in damages to former Kissinger aide Morton Halperin and four members of his family for illegal wiretapping of their home. The Halperins' home telephone had been tapped for twenty-one months, starting when he was a member of Kissinger's National Security Council staff and continuing after Halperin had left his government post and become a critic of administration policy.

This landmark ruling was the first case of a former president's being held liable for damages to a private citizen as a result of official acts taken while in office. Nixon and the other defendants, Smith had found, were liable for their actions and just "like any other citizens" when it came to a lawsuit. It was also reportedly the first case in which damages were awarded to a victim of wiretapping.

September

G. Gordon Liddy, his silence unbroken, leaves the Danbury Federal Penitentiary a free man. His sentence has been reduced by President Carter from twenty to eight years. Upon his release on September 7, Liddy has served fifty-two and a half months, about two years longer than any of the other twenty-four men sentenced for Watergate-related crimes. Refusing to answer the barrage of questions put to him by reporters, Liddy continues quietly to absorb the blame for plotting the break-in. When asked how he feels, he answers with a German phrase, "It doesn't really matter." When asked where he is going, Liddy replies, "East of the sun and west of the moon."

The man of whom Nixon said to Haldeman in a tape "He must be a little nuts" remains unremorseful and unbowed. When questioned by reporters upon his return to Washington as to whether he would burglarize again if asked, he declares, "When the prince approaches the lieutenant, the proper response is 'thy will be done.'" This does not mean, he hastens to explain, that Nixon had authorized the Watergate break-in. But "if any President asked me to work or act in the interests of the United States, I would comply." Unlike Dean, for whom he has nothing but contempt, "I just don't testify against my colleagues," he says. "There are other reasons too ('when I opted for silence five years ago') which I will not disclose." Regarding the long prison term he served: "I have no bitterness toward anyone. Bitterness is a concept that's loaded with self-pity. It's a weakness and a waste." Could he say why he planned the Watergate break-in, or what the burglars were seeking? "I can but I won't. I could but I choose not to," he replies.

In his promised fifth television broadcast, David Frost presents some leftover material from his Nixon interviews. A few questions still of interest are raised—why didn't Nixon burn the tapes?—the eighteen-and-a-half-minute gap—Nixon and China—Nixon and Kissinger—and there are one or two new and unexpected twists as well.

Nixon would have destroyed the tapes, he explains, if he had known that they would become public, or if he had thought that they contained any evidence of criminal misconduct. Three months before the existence of the tapes was disclosed, "I even suggested, and I believe directed" Haldeman to go through them and "destroy those that had no historical value." Haldeman, however, had never carried out "my instruction, if it was an instruction or suggestion." Nixon also felt it was good not to destroy them because they contained much that was contradictory to what Dean and "the other side" was saying. In addition, if he had, it would look as if he had something to hide and cover up. Some reasons contradicted others. As to his own estimate of what his fate might have been without the tapes, Nixon ventures, "Well, as a matter of fact, if the tapes had been destroyed, I believe that it is likely that I would not have had to go through the agony of resignation." He was probably right.

About the eighteen-and-a-half-minute gap: four and a half minutes of it were removed accidentally while Rose Mary Woods was answering the telephone. Neither he nor Rose Woods knew anything else and certainly had nothing to do with the rest of the missing material.

Chou En-lai was impressed with Kissinger as a philosopher because he was a Doctor of Philosophy; Nixon told Chou he was "a Doctor of Brains." Kissinger had flexibility and was an "improvisor": but at the first crisis in 1969, only three months into the new administration, when North Korea shot down an American reconnaissance plane and most of the crewmen were lost—it was over international waters—in studying the options, Kissinger "came down hard" on wanting to take out two or three North Korean airfields. The Chinese and the Russians were testing and would be watching us, he said. It was Nixon who, with the advice of others, thought better of it. One war at a time was enough, he felt; we didn't need two, especially with China and Russia so close. "People who think [Kissinger] was a soft liner and I was a hard liner in foreign policy did not know our opinions."

A curious reference slips in while Nixon is speaking of China: hints of a mysterious plane crash. Nixon is speaking of Lin Piao "who was somewhat discredited you know. . . . He took an airplane flight and they couldn't find the remains. Let's put it that way." "The general conclusion is that there was some deliberateness to that?" prods Frost. Well, the Chinese just told him, Nixon answers, " 'There were some who opposed my first visit to the P.R.C. . . . in 1972. And they got into a plane and it disappeared. And we haven't been able to find it since.' And they just smiled." Might there be a trace of self-revelation? We will remember an incident of a mysterious plane crash here too.

Finally, Nixon comes out with a new explanation of what caused the Watergate—it was Martha Mitchell and her mental condition: "Let me tell you about John and Martha Mitchell—about John's tragedy. . . . It's never been told before. . . . I haven't asked John whether I can tell it —but he's such a decent man. Martha—and everybody loves Martha—

was an emotionally disturbed person. . . . In 1968 during the campaign John had to send her away for about five or six weeks. Later—it was now after the Watergate—here in California she pushed her hand through a window, was going to blow the whistle on everybody. John was being a scapegoat and this and that. We don't need to go into that. . . . It wasn't just booze. Sometimes she could be this way with no drinks and sometimes be perfect with a lot of drinks." Bebe Rebozo asked John, "Why don't you put her away like you did in 1968?" John answered, "Because I love her."

Once John asked Nixon to speak to Martha on the telephone. "Mr. President," Martha then said, "I just want you to know that there are only three men in the world I love. I love John. I love Bebe. And I love you." Finally, Nixon says, "The action was going to fall on John. Dean said Mitchell is the guy. Haldeman and Ehrlichman wanted to put it on Mitchell and all the rest." It is impressive what little concern Nixon has for the sensibilities of others. "I'm convinced if it hadn't been for Martha," Nixon goes on, "and God rest her soul—because she in her heart was a good person—if it hadn't been for Martha there'd been no Watergate. She had a mental and emotional problem which nobody knew about. Because of it John wasn't minding that store. He was practically out of his mind about Martha in the spring of 1972. He was letting Magruder and all these boys, these kids, these nuts, run this thing."

Reacting to Nixon's references to them, Haldeman and Mitchell request leniency and plead to be freed from their prison sentences. Haldeman, stinging under Nixon's callous remarks, charges for the first time that Nixon "was the principal actor" in the crime of obstructing justice in this case. In the harshest words he has used publicly thus far, Haldeman states that Nixon made a "clear confession of guilt" in his latest interview with Frost. Describing the interview as "probably the queerest one of all," Haldeman's motion for leniency notes that Nixon "has proclaimed to the world that he ordered the destruction of tapes which would have incriminated him, but Haldeman omitted to do so. Nixon does not care what he now says since he is wrapped in an immunizing pardon and his pockets are lined with six hundred thousand dollars."

In their motions to Judge Sirica in their first declarations of contrition and repentance, both men express remorse and regret for their roles in the cover-up conspiracy. Although "Haldeman, a Republican criminal, cannot expect the benign and generous treatment from President Carter that Nixon's grateful appointee, ex-President Ford, arranged through an emissary," Haldeman still appeals for treatment "as near as possible" to that accorded Nixon.

Mitchell on the other hand, whose loyalty almost approaches that of Liddy and Ziegler, does not mention Nixon in his court papers but depends on his worsening medical state. In reference to his wife's condition, however, he takes a position opposite to Nixon's: "The Watergate tragedy has had a traumatic and devastating effect" on his family life, his motion reads. "It was the apparent proximate cause of the increasing mental conflicts of defendant's wife. During this same period defendant's wife's physical condition also deteriorated to the point where it resulted in her death in 1976." Watergate affected Martha, not the other way around, is Mitchell's response from prison.

October

On October 5, Judge John Sirica, in his last official act of the Watergate case, reduces the terms of Ehrlichman, Haldeman, and Mitchell, making them eligible for parole after serving one year. Sirica's action, which was in accordance with similar reductions given previously to other Watergate figures, came after he had listened to the pleas of their lawyers and the tape-recorded expressions of remorse from the defendants.

The contrition expressed now by the three men contrasts sharply with their defiant statements of innocence at the Senate Watergate hearings in 1973 and at their Watergate cover-up trial a year later. Says Ehrlichman now, "You are effectively rendering your ethical and moral judgments to your superior when you go to work in the White House. Looking back there were all kinds of red flags. . . . In effect, I abdicated my moral judgment and turned it over to someone else." Mitchell is "truly sorry. My reflections have convinced me my convictions resulted from my actions. No set of circumstances, whatever they might be, would ever again cause me to perform such actions or lead me to commit such deeds." Haldeman, recanting, states, "I have strong feel-ings of responsibility that whatever wrong was done will never be done again by me. I have a feeling I have an obligation to make amends. . . . I have the deepest personal regret for everything I have done. I realize the damage it has done to the nation, and I will carry for the rest of my life the burden of knowing how greatly my acts contributed to this tragedy."

"I guess they will call me Minimum John now," says "Maximum John" Sirica. A month after having reduced these final sentences, ending his career in Washington as an active federal judge, Sirica will now reduce his own activities.

He will work minimal time, choose the cases that interest him, and write a book.

According to an editorial in the *Los Angeles Times,* Sirica's use of "judicial thumbscrews" as pressure to confess or recant, comes under moral criticism. Others, however, wonder how "pure" an approach could have been adhered to while still retaining a chance of proving the case. To Sirica it is clear: "It's a long difficult case, in many respects a sad case. I'm glad to see the end of the tunnel." Summing it up, he feels it all "proved that the system worked like the Founding Fathers hoped it would."

Another book from the Watergate forty takes its place on the best-seller list. Charles Colson follows up the inspiration of his religious experience by writing a book, and a movie of the same title, *Born Again,* is promptly begun. Watergate is again being used not for docu-mentary purposes, not as a study of news or as social commentary, but as a source of entertainment.

Colson himself gives the highest grade to his view and rendition of history. All of his Watergate figures are treated "straight," he feels, unlike the "incredible inaccuracies" of Ehrlichman's book and the tele-vision series based on it. *All the President's Men* was like "peeping through a keyhole: I knew what they did; I was bored by the film." In his own version Colson, in the last analysis, comes out exonerated. While treated harshly enough in early White House scenes that appear in his book, he is still portrayed as something of a victim—of the press, the president, and later of his fellow prisoners. In the end, however, he is forgiven and cleansed and as a born-again Christian is outside judgment.

Colson's conversion serves him well, in life as in his story. His defense is more successful than most. Giving testimony to his present feeling, he serves as his own amiable witness, impervious and impenetrable: "People can accept or reject. I don't spend much time persuading people of the authenticity of my experience. I've never asked anyone to believe me, and I don't care how people vote on Charles Colson, because I'd lose that popularity contest anywhere. But I do sit in detached amusement, watching people argue with me, because it's irrelevant. Whether they believe me or not makes no difference. Whether they accept or reject my message is their decision. The question is whether they hear it."

Robert L. Munger, the executive producer who had amassed a fortune before being born again himself, believes that the Lord guided him toward the Colson project. "I go to Him for creative advice. We're on a winning team," says Munger. There are over seventy million born-again Christians in this country, he points out, and "If only half see the film I'll make money." And he refers to a Gallup poll indicating that 98 percent of all college students believe in God.

January 1978

John Dean will begin a syndicated radio program, "The Right to Know." A series of capsules of news, features, and investigative reports, the new program will broadcast events on the national government scene over a network of thirty-eight stations. The reaction to the announcement is a mixture of interest, skepticism, and curiosity. Why should people believe him, Dean is asked. "The market is really the only test," he responds. "I do have a reputation for telling the truth." Dean appears to have come to terms with these and other questions. He has put this program into perspective, he says, along with many other things in his life. "I believe I've come to terms with what's important and what isn't in my life. If the radio show doesn't go, I know it won't be the end of the world."

Haldeman's book *The Ends of Power,* the second by the big three, appears. The sequence and the motivations which guided the writing produce anything but assurance as to its claim to history. Haldeman himself admits he was set to write an entirely different book when he became inflamed by Nixon's self-justification and references to him and Ehrlichman on the interviews with David Frost. The direction of the writing was changed at once, and this book against Nixon and others emerged. This one, he claims, and asks the reading public to go along with him, is now the truth. One is left to wonder what he would have written without this last-minute change of mind.

Sales are good, although consistency and an advance toward the truth are not considered to be in evidence. Statements of opinion are offered to whet the appetite, but only, in Haldeman's own words, theories, speculations, and surmises from what he knew. No new facts are adduced, no evidence which can settle or put to rest any of the elusive subjects discussed. Among the offerings by one who we can say should know: the Watergate break-in was caused by Nixon. Nixon was involved "from day one or even before." "Richard Nixon himself caused those burglars to break-in." Nixon planted the seed in the mind of Colson who carried out the break-in for him. Haldeman's "own theory" of the motivation was that evidence could be acquired that Lawrence O'Brien, then Democratic party chairman with whom Nixon had had a longtime enmity, was being paid a retainer by Howard Hughes.

Colson was the heavy on the inside team. If the old gang had started to splinter before, by this time they are completely scattered and apart. As each writer in the inner group looks back, he picks favorite others as subjects of his wrath. Colson "encouraged the dark impulses in Nixon's mind," cultivated his obsessions, and acted on them. Nixon's unwillingness to turn against Colson even to this day is seen as a possibility that Colson, even more than Dean, had the goods on him (as others have said about Richard Helms).

The eighteen-and-a-half-minute gap in the tape, the central datum of the final cover-up crime, the mystery which Haldeman had announced he would solve, was caused, according to his "own perception" of the situation, first by Nixon himself who "began to erase all of the Watergate material from the tapes. But Nixon was the least dexterous man I have ever known; clumsy would be too elegant a word. . . . [he] realized it would take him ten years in fits and starts," so he turned the job over to his secretary Rose Mary Woods to finish it. At the first state banquet at the White House after his election, Nixon spilled soup on his vest, after which soup was never served again.

Kissinger is another inside co-sharer-of-the-glory treated mercilessly by Haldeman. The very existence of the fateful taping system is laid directly at his feet. On the question not only of why Nixon did not destroy the tapes but why he set them up in the first place, much of Nixon's motivation for installing the system, says Haldeman, was to counteract "the unpredictable Henry Kissinger." Nixon knew that Kissinger was keeping a log of everything they discussed and wanted a record of his own, especially since Nixon had become aware that Kissinger was "given to second thoughts on vital matters" in public which had previously been discussed in private.

Kissinger's unreliability throughout matched his acknowledged brilliance: "In the White House by day we knew Kissinger as 'the hawk of hawks.' But in the evenings a magical transformation took place. Touching glasses at a party with his liberal friends, the belligerent Kissinger would suddenly become a dove." Diverse sources from different directions converge on this opinion. While privately Kissinger was strongly in favor of the Christmas bombing of North Vietnam in 1972, two months after he had said "Peace is at hand," he was quoted by James Reston in the *New York Times* from "inside information" as undoubtedly having opposed it. After denying to a furious Nixon and Haldeman that he had said this or given any interview to Reston, when confronted later by evidence that he had indeed spoken to Reston about it, he replied, "Yes, but that was only on the telephone."

It was Kissinger's anger at leaks, Haldeman says, again generally confirming accounts by others, that started the FBI's 1969 national security wiretapping policies. One wiretap which was especially important for Watergate history, however, was one that Nixon himself personally ordered. That was on columnist Joseph Kraft who, previously a supporter of Nixon, had turned against him. Leaks were never discovered but "an important precedent for Watergate had been established: the use of private White House personnel for wiretapping."

On the personal level, Kissinger was publicity seeking and self-enhancing all the way. At airports on campaign swings he would deflect the attention of crowds and start shaking hands "as if he were the candidate." Nixon finally had to tell Haldeman to have him stopped. " 'You're just jealous, Herr Haldeman,' " Henry would reply, "but we would only make it through a few more airport ceremonies before he would forget and plunge happily into the crowd again."

In what would be the only substantive revelation in the book, if true, Haldeman announces his theory of the identity of "Deep Throat." Based on the descriptions given by Woodward and Bernstein and what he knew of the goings-on in Washington, both he and Nixon felt that it was Fred Fielding, Nixon's former deputy counsel, who worked under White House Counsel John Dean.

Haldeman incriminates not only individuals but countries as well. The Soviet Union made overtures to the United States to join it in a preemptive nuclear strike against China, against China's then-infant nuclear capability.

After the contents of the book have been absorbed, Haldeman's charges and everything that could be called news in the book is denied and contradicted. With reference to his role and the origin of the break-in, Colson denies Haldeman's entire account: "I took a lie detector test early in the Watergate investigation. It verified I was telling the truth then as I am now." Kissinger, interviewed on the "Today" show, disputes key elements of Haldeman's version of foreign policy events. The Soviet Union did not make an overture to the United States in 1969 to join in a nuclear strike on Chinese nuclear plants: "That is not true. . . . I do not recall any such event and I would not have forgotten it." The Soviet Union brands Haldeman's charges "nonsensical statements which are a lie from beginning to end."

To Haldeman's revelation of the identity of "Deep Throat," Fred Fielding, now a Washington lawyer, declares the charge "sheer fantasy and nonsense. I emphatically deny the story and the accusation." Producing further evidence of his own, Fielding submits a passport and other documents to show he had been out of the country during the days when Woodward and Bernstein referred to a critical meeting at which "Deep Throat" supplied them with key information. John Dean later reveals that his own research led him to a conviction about the identity of "Deep Throat." It is too delicate for him to reveal now, he says, but the suspected person was not Fred Fielding. When Dean called the person he concluded was "Deep Throat," the news was greeted by a long silence at the other end of the phone, and then only mild and weak denial. Although "I could blow him out of the water," says Dean, "my frame of mind is not to."

When asked what he thinks of Haldeman's book, Sam Ervin replies, "Before I would accept his book as credible I would want it corroborated by all the Apostles except Judas. A man that would commit perjury under oath might possibly be tempted to commit it when he is not under oath." Judge Sirica, who is negotiating with a publisher for his own book, states, "Anybody has a right to write a book. . . . It's up to the public to make up their own minds whether to believe it or not." Summarizing, Elizabeth Drew points to more than an ethical question: "This is a man for whom the truth is what serves his momentary purposes. . . . the notable thing about Haldeman is that his moral vacuum coexisted with a simple obtuseness."

April 1978

Ehrlichman leaves the Swift Trail Federal Prison Camp in Safford, Arizona, after having served eighteen months of two conspiracy sentences that could have been as long as eight years.

Jaunty in a blue baseball cap with a happy and affable grin, he poses agreeably for the photographers but dodges all questions with wit and good nature. From the dour and angry look of the past, Ehrlichman's face is probably the most transformed, his manner and attitude the most changed of all the higher-up Watergate figures. The arrogant and negativistic Ehrlichman who faced the public in the earlier stonewalling days is hardly recognizable in the spry and lighthearted figure, tennis racquet under arm, who flies from Phoenix to San Francisco with a retinue of newspaper people following him. Committed now to writing fiction, his second book, also a novel as he considers his first, will come out "around Christmastime."

At a forum at Gonzaga University in Spokane, Washington, about the relationships between presidents and the news media and the public's right to know, four former presidential press secretaries meet to share their experiences and express their views. Kennedy's Pierre Salinger (who worked for Johnson as well), Johnson's George Reedy, Nixon's Ron

Ziegler, and Ford's Ronald Nessen compare notes and philosophies about their jobs. So much interest is evoked—probably in the effect of power on those so close to and caught up in it—that taped excerpts of the program are repeated in the next two months on various public television channels under the title "Some of the President's Men." Salinger and Nessen, as described by one commentator, Harold Rosenberg, appear relaxed and open, and Reedy as professional and condescending. Ziegler strikes this observer as guarded and evasive, recalling a *New York Times* description of Ziegler which, while glib and caricaturish, does capture something of what he conveyed to the American people: "fully prepared to say nothing. If pressed he will say next to nothing. And if backed against the wall, he will say almost nothing."

At this time, however, Ziegler considers himself one of the Watergate victims. Admitting that much of the information he gave out was incorrect, the reason, he says, was that he had been ill-informed. Asked what he had learned from Watergate, Ziegler replies, "I've learned that a press secretary is only as good as what he is told." *New York Times* reporter Seymour Hersh, when asked by the narrator of the program Mike Kirk to assess Ziegler's complicity in Watergate, replies, "He's either a criminal or an all-time classic dupe."

Reedy offers an explanation on behalf of harassed leaders: presidents often mislead the public because "the reality of the man under pressure is different from the reality of others." Pierre Salinger includes himself within the same process of victimization as Ziegler. He too had not been kept sufficiently informed, he reminisces, citing his own point of sensitivity and defensiveness, the ill-fated Bay of Pigs incident in 1961. This aborted military skirmish was no doubt to Salinger what Vietnam and Watergate later became to Ziegler.

May 1978

The big book appears at last. *RN: The Memoirs of Richard Nixon,* arrives at the bookstores, is serialized in newspapers, and is offered by the publishers, they hope, to an eager and waiting public.

There is nothing new. No new fact or attitude emerges from Nixon's solitude or postpresidential period of reflection.

Watergate is faced first, as though boldly and resolutely, but the cover is the same as always. When Nixon first read about the break-in in a morning newspaper in Key Biscayne, Florida, "I dismissed it as some sort of prank." Then came his series of efforts and failures exactly as he has repeated them so often in the past. He is guilty only of carelessness and too much trust, not of wrongdoing in any hard sense. And he is bearing his victimization with quiet strength, with no complaints now against anyone.

Watergate is quickly superseded by his reminiscences over his accomplishments. His accounts of China, détente, his ending the Vietnam War, his strength in the Middle East, and successes in foreign policy establish his place solidly with respect to foresight, hindsight, statesmanship, and motivation.

There is no stock-taking in a comprehensive or long-term sense, no mention of the opposite attitudes of his political lifetime which opposed and blocked the very moves on which he now bases his successes. No retrospective evolutionary development is presented, no need felt to explain any conflict or change. There is no acknowledgment of contradictions, let alone any attempt to explain or synthesize them. Here too Nixon was never wrong, always right. When successive views collided or were incompatible in the long or the short range, he was right both times.

The book sells, but less than expected. Many resent it and even aggressively oppose it. A group marches in front of bookstores in New York carrying a sign with the slogan "Don't Buy a Book from a Crook." Nixon himself acts like a celebrity author, signing special hardcover editions to sell for two hundred fifty dollars.

June 1978

Ehrlichman, interviewed on ABC–TV, states that he believes it will eventually be proven that Nixon "was the perpetrator" of the break-in into the office of Daniel Ellsberg's psychiatrist in California. No facts are added, only his belief that Nixon "set the whole thing in motion" in a search for damaging information on Ellsberg.

It is interesting to see where Ehrlichman separates himself from

Haldeman's main thrust and where each one's individual interests lead him. Ehrlichman's emphasis is on the crime for which he himself was convicted and served time. Haldeman, however, had made the same surmise about Nixon's participation in the Watergate break-in in which he had been more centrally implicated than Ehrlichman. About Nixon's role in this invasion of the Democratic National Committee headquarters, Ehrlichman, in the same interview, says "I don't know."

Another voice is heard on this same issue. Alexander Butterfield, discloser of the tapes, now a business executive in Burlingame, California, reacts to Nixon's statement that he had been surprised by news of the burglary by saying that he believed Nixon knew in advance of plans for the Watergate break-in. Again, however, this is a "belief" from knowing Nixon and White House patterns rather than a presentation of evidential facts. "Under absolutely no circumstances," writes Butterfield in a letter circulated around the nation and confirmed in a telephone interview, "would Mr. Nixon's people on the White House staff or at the Committee to Re-Elect the President undertake any action, much less one of the magnitude of a break-in at the Democratic National Committee headquarters, without the clear and express approval (direction, actually) of the President. I'm amazed at how many Americans don't yet understand the extent to which Richard Nixon was in charge at the White House and monitored and supervised every operation, every activity, every program and every plan. . . . He was never humble . . . and of course along with that 'King Richard—Ruler of the Free World—I'll show those bastards' complex was an unmistakable arrogance. It seemed whoever he spoke to cordially in the Oval Office, staff aides or guest, he orally abused upon that person's departure . . . and usually with vehemence," Butterfield adds.

It is six years after the break-in. The trail of Watergate does not end. It disappears, and then can be seen again. Nixon is making more public appearances, each one reported in the news and watched by the people.

Nixon attends a baseball game in Anaheim, California, between the Angels and Kansas City in the box of the Angels' owner Gene Autry. Shortly afterward he appears again and says he might become a regular at Anaheim Stadium. After the game he visits the Angels' clubhouse, tells Don Baylor not to apologize for his bloop double which beat the Baltimore Orioles 1–0 in fourteen innings. "Take those wins any way you can get 'em," Baylor says the ex-president told him. Nixon will participate in a golf tournament in Indiana, it is announced.

July 1978

On the first of this month, Richard Nixon makes his first address to the public since his resignation. In the small and predominantly Republican town of Hyden, Kentucky, Nixon is honored at a dedication of a 2.6-million-dollar recreational facility named after him. While he parades through the town in a motorcade, tickets for the actual dedication event are carefully controlled and issued only to known Nixon supporters. "He's as smart a man as I've ever seen," says C. Allen Muncy, the judge-executive who was a leader in the arrangements. "He's still sharp as a tack."

To his hosts, Watergate has been blown out of all proportion and means nothing compared to Nixon's foreign and domestic accomplishments. Watergate showed only that Nixon was a human being and that he was interested in protecting his friends. Nixon indicated that he will not run for public office again, Muncy says. Nixon himself is grateful for "a wonderful reception" which "he will not forget in a long time."

The sentiment expressed in Kentucky is not an isolated one. "ABC World News Tonight" announces that Nixon is creeping back into favor. An ABC/Harris poll reports that today in 1978 a surprising 34 percent feel that Nixon "could return to public life." There is of course still the 66 percent who do not consider this a possibility. And the polar positions are strong. A Conrad cartoon pictures a sewer main with a beam of light shining upon it. The cartoon is captioned "Watch This Spot." The sewer main is labeled "The Return of Richard Nixon." Other opinions are more moderate. Rep. John Rhodes of Arizona, the House GOP leader, when asked about Nixon's role in connection with Republican presidential activity, responds, "Any emergence of Richard Nixon as a party advisor would be a risk."

August 1978

Nixon will appear on "The Sam Yorty Show" on television. Among the subjects to be discussed are his views on Proposition 13 and the tax revolt, foreign policy, and the CIA.

Wally George, producer and co-host of "The Sam Yorty Show," plans a nationwide series of "Rallies for Nixon." The idea, says George, is to convince Nixon that he "should take a more active role in public life." The first rally is scheduled for March 1979 to be held in Los Angeles, the second in Dallas in June, and then on to Washington.

November 1978

Nixon visits France and England on a speaking tour. He is received with attention and warmth in France, where he appears on French television. Ninety percent of the French viewers who call in during his three-hour appearance express favorable views or sympathy for him. In a widely publicized and carefully prepared appearance at Oxford University in England, there was a mixed reception. Outside the building in which he spoke, an angry crowd of five hundred students demonstrated, fought with police, threw eggs, and chanted, "Creep! Creep!" "Hurry Up and Die," and "Nixon is dead." Inside the Oxford Union Debating Society, eight hundred members filled every seat and listened to the ex-president with attention and respect. His statements and answers were generally rewarded with warm applause.

1979

On January 19, 1979, John Mitchell leaves a federal prison camp in Montgomery, Alabama, the last of the Watergate defendants to be freed. Punishment and retribution for the crime are now over.

On January 29, Richard Nixon attends a state dinner at the White House honoring Chinese Vice Premier Teng Hsiao-ping. Four and a half years after leaving the White House, he is asked to return "because of his role in opening up the process of normalization" with China.

Each decade or historical era presents its unique form of public complicity in the historical process. In common to them all is the universal and disturbing characteristic of the individual to look the other way. In the thirties and forties the political issue was fascism, in the fifties the paranoid concern with communism, in the sixties the collusion was to the war in Vietnam, and in the seventies institutionalized corruption at the highest levels was the sociopolitical order of the day. Many of us can remember the moving finale to the infamous era of Joseph McCarthy, when Edward R. Murrow told a sober American public, "The fault, my friends, is not in our stars but in ourselves." In every instance, there was a mutuality between the leader and the led.

In our most recent crisis, the people in the end were more moral than immoral. Behind men of courage and principle who read their will, they did exert their weight and finally exact the most extraordinary termination of a presidency in the life of our republic. Perhaps a democracy whose main tenet is freedom by definition lays the stage for both the good and the bad to come into view. In an environment of free choice, both rational and irrational motives can express themselves freely.

We may be at the beginning of a period of evolutionary change. It is surprising how many powerful documentaries have appeared recently, bringing public attention to subjects which burn the conscience. There were two specials on the McCarthy period, then "Roots," and then "Holocaust." In West Germany, twenty million people watched "Holocaust" and were "ready to know." A seven-hour film, *Hitler,* was also widely seen and absorbed. The lesson was a broad and historical one. "I never would make a film about a man named Adolph Hitler," said Hans Syberberg, the director of the film, "but rather about the people who decided to have a Hitler. I want to show that it can happen in a democracy."

Sigmund Freud ended his life studies on a note of cautious pessimism as to which of the two sides of man would ultimately win out. The same was true of a noted successor, Robert Waelder, philosopher, physical scientist, and psychoanalyst, one of the last Renaissance men in psychoanalysis. In a dynamic survey of the history of man, *Progress and Revolution: A Study of the Issues of Our Age,* Waelder noted that the constant oscillation between right and wrong on a global scale could be equated to the struggle between libido and aggression within the individual. The difference, Waelder wrote, is that libido is always waiting for aggression to happen. Every victory of a free society is provisional while every totalitarian victory is irrevocable, perhaps for generations. In spite of this, Waelder notes that even if aggression is a part of man's nature, this "would not prove that man cannot alter it: for man, though rooted in nature, can transcend it to a large degree. As Denis de Rougement put it: 'Man's nature is to pass beyond nature.'"

I have not presumed to answer the question of "how" to make man change in the needed direction. It is enough that I describe as much as I can of the "what" and gingerly try to approach the "whys." If the question of "how" then becomes uppermost to others, I hope they will take it from there. The psychoanalyst can contribute the forces which operate in the unconscious, but for an approach to solutions, a team effort is necessary—with humanists and social scientists, psychiatrists and theologians, and even the physical and biological scientists joining toward a common goal.

Sources and Bibliography

I had no private information about any of the individuals involved in the Watergate phenomenon. If I had, I would not have felt that I could use it. All the data in this book is from public sources. The manner in which what was available was received or distorted, or not received at all, is one of the subjects studied.

The information came from the media. The daily newspaper was primary. The one of most routine use to me was the *Los Angeles Times*. I am indebted to its array of news reporters, editorial writers, columnists, and feature writers. I give special mention to the book reviews of Robert Kirsch, the cartoons of Conrad, and the columns of Art Buchwald, all of which were of central relevance and use to me.

Other newspapers I referred to, but less frequently, were the *New York Times*, the *Washington Post*, the *San Francisco Chronicle*, the *Chicago Daily News*, the *Washington Star*, and the *Monterey Peninsula Herald*.

Time, Newsweek, The New Yorker, The Nation, Life, Washington Monthly, and *Playboy* were sources of material in various contexts.

The television commentators of all three major networks, primarily in the Los Angeles area but in other cities as well, were sources of considerable and steady information.

The following books and articles I found useful:

PRE-WATERGATE MATERIAL ABOUT RICHARD NIXON

Mankiewicz, Frank. *Perfectly Clear: Nixon from Whittier to Watergate.* New York: Quadrangle, 1973.
Nixon, Richard M. *Six Crises.* New York: Doubleday, 1962.

WATERGATE BOOKS

Bernstein, Carl, and Woodward, Bob. *All the President's Men.* New York: Simon and Schuster, 1974.
Colson, Charles. *Born Again.* New York: Bantam, 1976.
Dash, Samuel. *Chief Counsel: Inside the Ervin Committee.* New York: Random House, 1976.
Dean, John. *Blind Ambition.* New York: Simon and Schuster, 1976.
Doyle, James. *Not Above the Law.* New York: William Morrow, 1977.
Ehrlichman, J. D. *The Company.* New York: Simon and Schuster, 1976.
Haldeman, H. R. *The Ends of Power.* New York: New York Times Books, 1978.
Jaworski, Leon. *The Right and the Power.* Houston: Gulf Publishing Co., 1976.
Magruder, Jeb. *An American Life: One Man's Road to Watergate.* New York: Atheneum, 1974.
Nixon, Richard M. *RN: The Memoirs of Richard Nixon.* New York: Grosset and Dunlap, 1978.
Price, Raymond. *With Nixon.* New York: Viking Press, 1977.
Sirica, John J. *To Set the Record Straight.* New York: W. W. Norton, 1979.
Sorensen, Theodore C. *Watchman in the Night: Presidential Accountability after Watergate.* Cambridge, Mass.: MIT Press, 1975.
Thomas, Helen. *Dateline: White House.* New York: Macmillan, 1975.
The Watergate Hearings. New York: Bantam, 1973.

GENERAL SOURCES

Burkhardt, Jacob. *Reflections on History.* Indianapolis: Liberty Fund, 1979.
Copeland, Miles. *Game of Nations.* New York: Simon and Schuster, 1970.
Corson, William R. *The Armies of Ignorance: The Rise of the American Intelligence Empire.* New York: Dial/Wade, 1977.
Fest, Joachim C. *Hitler.* New York: Random House, 1975.
Hoffmann, Stanley. *Primacy or World Order: American Foreign Policy since the Cold War.* New York: McGraw-Hill, 1978.
Ibsen, Henrik. *An Enemy of the People.* New York: Penguin, 1977.
Ionesco, Eugene. *Rhinoceros.* New York: Grove Press, 1960.
Janis, Irving, and Mann, L. *Decision-Making: A Psychological Analysis of Conflict, Choice and Commitment.* New York: The Free Press, 1977.

Marchetti, V., and Marks, J. *The C.I.A. and the Cult of Intelligence.* New York: Knopf, 1974.

Menninger, Karl. *Whatever Became of Sin?* New York: Bantam, 1978.

Milgram, Stanley. *Obedience to Authority.* New York: Harper and Row, 1975.

Miller, Arthur. *Death of a Salesman.* New York: Viking Press, 1949.

Miller, Merle. *Plain Speaking: An Oral Biography of Harry S. Truman.* Berkeley, Calif.: Berkeley Publishing Co., 1974.

Roth, Philip. *Portnoy's Complaint.* New York: Random House, 1969.

Samuels, E., ed. *The Education of Henry Adams.* Boston: Houghton Mifflin, 1973.

Santayana, George. *Selected Critical Writings.* 2 vols. Edited by Norman Henfrey. Cambridge: Cambridge University Press, 1968.

Szulc, Tad. *The Illusion of Peace: A Diplomatic History of the Nixon Years.* New York: Viking Press, 1978.

Walton, Richard J. *Henry Wallace, Harry Truman, and the Cold War.* New York: Viking Press, 1976.

Wise, David. *The Espionage Establishment.* New York: Random House, 1967.

Wise, David. *The Politics of Lying: Government Deception, Secrecy and Power.* New York: Random House, 1973.

Wise, David, and Ross, Thomas B. *The Invisible Government.* New York: Random House, 1964.

PSYCHOANALYTIC SOURCES

Freud, Sigmund. *Civilization and Its Discontents,* standard edition (1930). Edited and translated by James Strachey. New York: W. W. Norton, 1962.

Freud, Sigmund. *The Ego and the Id,* standard edition (1923). Edited by James Strachey, translated by Joan Riviere. New York: W. W. Norton, 1962.

Hartmann, H. "Ego Psychology and the Problem of Adaptation" (1939). In David Rapaport, trans., *Journal of the American Psychoanalytic Association Monograph Series No. 1.* New York: International Universities Press, 1958.

Mahler, M. S. "Pseudoimbecility: A Magic Cap of Invisibility." *Psychoanalytic Quarterly* 11 (1942): 149–64.

McGuire, William, ed. *The Freud/Jung Letters: The Correspondence between Sigmund Freud and C. G. Jung.* Translated by Ralph Mannheim and R. E. C. Hull. Bollingen Series 94. Princeton, N.J.: Princeton University Press, 1974.

Rangell, Leo. "The Decision-Making Process: A Contribution from Psychoanalysis." *Psychoanalytic Study of the Child* 26 (1971): 425–52.

Rangell, Leo. "Lessons from Watergate: A Derivative for Psychoanalysis." *Psychoanalytic Quarterly* 45 (1976): 37–61.

Rangell, Leo. "A Psychoanalytic Perspective Leading Currently to the Syn-
drome of the Compromise of Integrity." *International Journal of Psychoa-
nalysis* 55 (1974): 3–12.
Rangell, Leo. "The Psychology of Poise, with a Special Elaboration on the
Pyschic Significance of the Snout or Perioral Region." *International Jour-
nal of Psychoanalysis* 35 (1954): 313–33.
Waelder, R. *Progress and Revolution: A Study of the Issues of Our Age.* New
York: International Universities Press, 1967.
Waelder, R. "The Principle of Multiple Function: Observations on Overdeter-
mination." *Psychoanalytic Quarterly* 5 (1930): 45–62.

Finally, I wish to cite my patients as sources. I referred to three with
Nixon material. From several other patients, I described mechanisms
which were related although they did not refer specifically to Nixon or
Watergate. All my descriptions of psychological mechanisms and insights came from my aggregate of patients as well as from general
psychoanalytic and psychiatric knowledge. And what most patients did
not say about Nixon or Watergate was also the source of a significant
datum.

Index